ASSUME THE PHYSICIAN

ASSUME THE PHYSICIAN

*a novel medical novel

JOHN F. HUNT, M.D

Visit ReadJohnHunt.com for other books by
John F. Hunt, as well as updates, perspectives, humorous tidbits,
and to witness the birth of the sequels.

"Like" ReadJohnHunt on Facebook
and follow him on Twitter @readjohnhunt for real-time updates.
Assume the Physician is a trademark of John F. Hunt
Cover art by Jim Ross

Assume the Physician / by John F. Hunt, MD
ISBN-13: 978-0-9859332-0-3
ISBN-10: 0985933208

www.readjohnhunt.com

To all who inspire others by not being sheep,
by thinking outside the box,
by swallowing the red pill,
by creating honest value,
and by doing good yourself
instead of forcing others to do so.

This book is to let you know that you are not alone.

The author is grateful to the following:

Dr. Adam Fox—Pediatric allergist in the UK, for his medical slang expertise, for which we shall not hold him responsible.

Dr. Steven Gordon for encouragement and brilliant advice, but don't blame him either.

Mike Davis, RRT, for inventing Punk Rock Medicine.

John Slovensky for offering the red pill to so many in the matrix

Jim Ross for graphic commentary and graphic design

Richard J. Maybury for the Uncle Eric book series that so wonderfully educates teens and adults in honest economic principles

And

The National Institutes of Health, for having nothing whatsoever to do with the funding of this manuscript.

"The art of medicine consists of amusing the patient while nature cures the disease."

-Voltaire

"Against the assault of laughter, nothing can stand."

-Mark Twain

Chapter 1

Protagonists, antagonists, and beta-agonists

"Hey, Eddie, have you studied all your lies yet?" called Dr. Blow, the attending physician tonight at the Sheep's Pen, who was just the most cynical human being in the whole world, and yet always right, which suggested something to me about the current state of the whole world. "We just got another email from the Sheep's Pen administrators that JCAHO may be launching an invasion this week. Hospital admin wants to make sure we do well during the impending Inquisition."

The initials "JCAHO" are pronounced as "Jayco" by most people, and stand for the "Joint Commission for the Accreditation of Healthcare Organizations". I pronounce it "Jackass" 'cuz it's easier and it applies. The employees of JCAHO like to make rules for us all to follow. I know that Dr. Blow isn't particularly fond of JCAHO. I know that Dr. Blow isn't particularly fond of rules.

Although JCAHO has no real authority, doctors are taught to humbly bow down and curtsey at their approach. They are rather like the SS. We are taught to fear them. I was already very familiar with JCAHO because I had worked as an emergency room clerk, as a medical student, and now as a new doctor in the Sheep's Pen. The Sheep's Pen was what Dr.

Blow called the university hospital in which we worked.

I turned my head away from the impacted derriere of my patient who was miserable because he had not had a bowel movement in almost three weeks, which is about as long as I had been a doctor. "Yah, Dr. Blow. Which lies are the administrators encouraging us to regurgitate to JCAHO this time?"

"Looks like all of 'em," he yawned as he read a list from his iPhone. "Standard junk. Plus all doctors will have to know how to initiate a quality improvement working group. And know the maximum allowed material elasticity for a bedsheet, the maximum diameter of a trash can, the minimum allowable carpet fiber density on a floor in the hallway, acceptable temperature range for toilet bowl water, normal expiration dates for milk containers, maximal allowed duration of employee breaks. That kinda stuff. All stuff critical for patient care, you know."

"Sho' is," I replied. My patient was working hard in his effort to help me dig him free. His anus was half open, half closed, and there was a softball-sized mass of unpleasantness that was bobbing in and out of him like the head of a turtle.

Blow was reading more email on his iPhone, then laughed. "Geesh, Eddie. The ACGME wants you to do more documentation. Have you started keeping track of every patient who vomits on you? Cuz they want to know that now. You're going to have to document everything in your little ACGME book."

I learned from Blow's litany of cynical truisms that the ACGME, or the American College of Graduate Medical Education, was the unelected controller of all things related to training doctors. They made rules. I might have mentioned that Blow isn't particularly fond of rules. Blow told me that the ACGME nitpicked physician-training programs throughout the country in order to assure that young doctors would frequently wake up sweaty and panicked from paperwork nightmares. Together, JCAHO and ACGME just might cause the death of the medical profession by drowning, if something else doesn't kill us all off sooner.

Even before I met Blow, I generally didn't have a lot of respect for people who think that their rules are the best rules ever. Nobody had ever given the ACGME *authority* to make rules about how all doctors are to be educated, but nonetheless they *made* rules about how all doctors are to be educated. New doctors, and those that teach them, now find themselves doing enormous amounts of paperwork to document hours worked, vacation time taken, lectures attended, ethics training undertaken, quality improvement programs initiated, and number of times puked on. There was hardly any time left for doctors-in-training to see patients, learn procedures, or acquire diagnostic acumen because they were spending so much of their time documenting how few patients they were seeing and how little time was spent acquiring diagnostic acumen. We doctors-in-training had to work very hard for long hours doing our documentation to prove to the ACGME that we resident doctors-in-training weren't overworked.

I was learning from Blow that the medical system was in trouble. In fact, it was total shit. And my index finger was covered in it because my latex glove had ripped when the turtle playing Hide'n'Seek in my patient's rectum had bitten me. Bits of the gent's impacted package had gotten under my fingernail.

I showed Dr. Blow my fecal-coated finger, pretended to dial a number with it, and asked to borrow his iPhone. He showed me his middle finger in return. I love Dr. Blow.

And I also love Nurse Maid. Jennifer Maid is 26 years old,

5 foot 5 and perfect. She always wears a traditional white nursing outfit, because her mother makes her do so. I hated her once, just for a minute. I hated her because the first time we spoke was when she woke me up in the middle of the night to check to see whether the order I had written for a very unsick patient was truly meant to be for Tylenol '650 milligrams', because I had rebelliously written for '650 pounds'. In my sleepy stupor, I misbehaved badly and told her to screw herself. That didn't go over well with her. She was mad, I felt guilty and stupid, but we got over it, and now instead of *me* telling *her* to screw herself, *she* tells *me* to screw herself, which is fine by me if I do say so myself. I do so love Nurse Maid.

The patients love Nurse Maid too, because she helps them. She can sense a patient's discomfort from all the way across the ward. I guess she smells it, hears it, sees it and feels it. I love her for that. I hate her for it too, because she still wakes me up to deal with those discomforts sometimes. I like making people feel better. It is one of the noblest pursuits and why I worked my ass off to become a doctor. But it is hard to be noble when my ass has been worked off and I am exhausted because what's left of my ass is still working at 3AM.

It is important to mention Doris-Doris. Doris-Doris is the daytime administrative unit coordinator for the hospital ward on which I seem to spend so much of my relaxation time foolishly working. Like Nurse Maid, she is five foot five, but Doris-Doris weighs between two and three times as much. And she is somewhere between two and three times her age too. Doris-Doris's breasts will knock you over if she turns too rapidly near you. I had a patient with breasts that big once. I found a pea under one of them. It was an important tiny green medical clue that my massively obese patient suffered from what cynical doctors refer to as 'Chronic Food Toxicity'. Doris-Doris is absolutely wonderful and knows everything. She knows where the admission forms are. She knows where the lost charts are. She knows how to get the phlebotomist up to the ward in a second. And if you are in her good graces at the moment, she will share her knowledge. If you do her wrong, you might as well be dead, because your life as a young doctor for the next few days will be worse than having stool under your fingernail.

"Dr. Marcus, come here, sweetie," Doris-Doris called to me unsweetly as I finished scrubbing the stool from under my fingernail. "Dr. Marcus, I gotta tell you something. I gotta tell you that you are gonna *piss me off* if you don't get into 78 before they call again. Mr. Jackson got up from the ER over an hour ago. Now get your finger out of your ass and get in there."

"Yes, Doris. Next stop." I would always do whatever Doris-Doris told me, because she was by far the least educated of anyone around and thus the most likely to be wise.

Nurse Maid was in room 78 talking to Mr. Jackson and his wife. While quickly flipping through his chart, I found that Mr. Jackson was 82 years old and had a stomachache. And he was vomiting blood. And his stools were black. Stool. More stool. My heart sank to about three inches under the surface of the accumulating urine in my bladder because he was very likely going to die.

"Hello, Mr. Jackson. My name is Dr. Marcus. I'm the Family Practice ward intern tonight. Sorry to keep you waiting. May I come in?" Blow had made sure that I was polite when I entered a patient's room. On the first day of internship, less than a month ago, he had very nearly dragged me out of a patient's room by my right earlobe after I had walked in without knocking.

Mr. and Mrs. Jackson both smiled, the man's gaze was weak and his face was pale. He was a nice man. A friendly good man. I could see it in his eyes. I could feel his goodness in my own heart. He was going to die. He was too nice to live.

His heart rate was high, probably because he had been losing blood. He was breathing fast too. Not good. Twenty minutes later, I had the surgeons see him. They would kill him for sure. Or maybe, just maybe, they would save his life.

Surgeons come to the ward when they have to, fly through at amazing speed, and return to their nether-regions of the operating theaters where they are most happy, and from whence they hope to never again emerge. All the medical billing rules, medical coding rules, rules for notes and signatures on the chart, and just about any other rule issued by anyone, anytime, anyplace, the surgeons ignore and do so fearlessly. I hated the surgeons, but I knew they were much wiser than internists. I hated internists. Internists would follow all the rules, no matter how useless, and expend countless hours on rule-abiding, especially when it came to records and billing. When the insurance company or Medicare auditors came, the internists had reasonable success, and only had to give back 30% of their income and suffer threats of potential imprisonment for fraud. In contrast, when the surgeons were audited they apologized for never writing a note and breaking all the rules, promised to change their ways, never did, and were given an increase of 30% in payment for their services. I hated that I loved surgeons.

After the surgeons took Mr. Jackson to the operating room, I had a sudden moment of free time. Free time is that most treasured of all things in internship. Rare, thrilling, always uncertain, it was like that first moment of a relationship with that beautiful girl of your dreams. And just as fleeting, inevitably gone, unpredictably without warning, dissipating into the painful repository of pleasant memories the moment that damn puretone sound emanates from the two-by-three inch black unholy box from hell snapped onto your scrub pants.

I hate my beeper. I know Pavlov was right. And I know humans are dogs. I know this because whenever my beeper goes off my heart rate increases and my knee starts bouncing. Hell, when a beeper goes off on some dramatic hospital-based television show like 'ER', 'Scrubs', 'House' or 'General Hospital'—none of which I watch except for 'Scrubs' which is awesome—my body reacts the same way with my knee rate increasing and my heart bouncing. Dr. Blow tells me that it's permanent, and I should apply for disability.

There is a television in the call room that occasionally works. I rarely see a whole show in there. That's because we interns have no sleep latency at all. TV cannot keep an intern awake. The opposite sex in the same bed with you cannot keep an intern awake. An earthquake mixed with a volcano and tsunami cannot keep an intern awake. Head hits pillow and sleep hits head. No delay, no tossing and turning, and no dreams. Other than paperwork nightmares, interns don't dream. I mean no dreams *ever*. This is all because interns are chronically, disastrously underslept. It is better now that there are paternalistic ACGME rules to protect interns from becoming so seriously sleep deprived. The 80-hour maximum workweek for doctors-in-training that has been commanded by ACGME is sort of enforced. But we young doctors pay for that protection by being protected. I don't need protection. I'm no sheep. But being forcibly protected makes people, including doctors, into sheep. I have to fight hard to avoid it.

Let me tell you about call rooms. First of all, sex only rarely occurs in them—at least it isn't like they make it out in television shows. Lights rarely work. Locks generally work in reverse: it is hard to get out of the room when you need to, but any Harry, Dick or Tom can come in and wake you up for the most inane things. The beds are bunk beds, and instead of the mattresses being slept on by sunbathed beauties, they are slept on by unbathed uglies: young physicians dressed in scrubs coated with stool, mucous and blood. The mattresses are the same ones upon which the unscrubbed, rarely-bathed physicians of my grandfather's generation slept, and within which uncounted generations of dust mites have lived their lives, procreated, built civilizations, eaten human skin flakes, and shat out dust mite poop particles to be inhaled by uncounted generations of young physicians as soon as their noses hit the bed.

Dust mite poop. Feces. Fecal particles. Dermatophagoides allergen. This is, to say it impolitely, shit from a bug. And this shit is just the right size to inhale into your lungs. Dust mites are microscopic creatures that walk through mattresses and pillows like we walk through air. Billions live in everyone's mattress, unless you have a waterbed. I asked the hospital administrators for a waterbed, but the hospital bureaucracy — knowing not how to respond — quoted a rule preventing standing water from being present in a hospital. Something to do with avoiding Legionnaires disease. I think they were making it up so they wouldn't accidently let me think I could change anything for the better. Anyhow, no waterbed. So we have dust mites and dust mite poop in our beds. If you are an allergic and asthmatic person (like me), you will suffer and need lots of inhaled medications to overcome the inhaled defecations.

Imagine this. You are an intern allergic to dust mites. You go to your call room and climb in your hot-swapped bed that someone just rolled out of. You immerse your head into your too-warm and a bit damp pillow and take a deep cleansing sigh breath of satisfaction. In that deep sigh breath, unbeknownst to you, you inhale ten thousand dust mite fecal particles into your nose and bronchi and deep down into your lungs. But, you are an intern. You have no sleep latency. So you are asleep immediately. And while you are unconscious the dust mite poop does its work.

Each tiny 3-micron in diameter dust mite poop particle settles in your nose or lungs someplace, and interacts with the cells there to piss off your mucous membranes. They swell, and secrete, and clog, and constrict. Thirty minutes later, when the nurse calls to wake you up to clarify your order for Tylenol, you need an asthma inhaler to help you breathe, your nose feels like you have been punched, you have swollen, dark circles under your eyes from the blood not draining from your lids through your congested nose, and you feel like you have the flu and a hangover at the same time. So you tell the nurse to fuck off and it therefore takes you that much longer to get into her pants. But it was all your fault for daring to try to sleep, foolishly sucking into your airways ten thousand dust mite poop, and stupidly writing an order for too many pounds of Tylenol for your patient. I hate being sick, especially when it's my fault. And it is usually my fault, because I am pretty stupid.

I have an IQ of 182. I don't tell anybody this. And I won't mention it ever again. And you have to swear not to tell anybody either. I am not proud of it, because I didn't earn it. But you need to know this, so you can understand my story and why it isn't completely typical. When I was a kid, some government school counselor told me that my IQ is higher than that of 99.99999% of the people in the world. Two days later I ran away from home. I don't use my high IQ wisely. I think my high IQ just serves to make me particularly smart at being an idiot.

For me, this is neither a new hospital nor a new town. But for most of the other interns, the geography and facility *are* entirely new. New towns mean new viruses that one's body hasn't seen before. A new doctor has to get'em all, working his way through the endemic viruses in his new city. It takes a year or so to run the gamut. It would take longer, except that new interns are always immune-suppressed from exhaustion and dehydration and occasional post-call drunken sprees. And interns get every Dick, Harry and Joe coughing their filthy contagious phlegm into our welcoming faces. All the time. Every damn day. So, interns get sick a lot.

"Are you sick?" Doris–Doris asked me, kindly.

"If I were, would I be here today?" I asked as I took a puff off an asthma inhaler.

Doris-Doris laughed, and her breasts bobbed up and down, generating a small zephyr that lifted from her desk some important sheet of paper, which then slid back and forth in gentle curves as it descended directly and permanently into the trashcan.

"Yes, you would be here," said Doris-Doris, ignoring the paper.

She was right, of course. Sickness is no excuse to stay home. For a doctor, there is no excuse to stay home, ever, unless you are a wimp. There used to be no room for wimps in medicine. Now they have a special room for wimps built in place of what used to be the doctors' lounge, with couches and televisions. The regulations insist that such kinder, gentler treatment for sick doctors be clearly documented in all paperwork submitted to the ACGME. But that's just paperwork. If you blow off work because you are sick, you are a wimp. End of issue. Besides, the real reason for the special wimp room was so that the hospital administrators could blame ACGME for elimination of the doctors' lounge, which the administrators didn't want us to have because having a special place of our own might go to our heads. It was important that doctors not think they were any more useful than, say, the guys who mop the floor in the cafeteria. We are all a big homogenized team of equals working for the greater good, after all.

Mr. Jackson should be coming out of surgery soon. Then a surgeon would give the bad news to the family. Sometimes they did it well. Sometimes not.

"The surgery went very well. We found what was causing your husband's bleeding and resected it. The surgery was performed perfectly by me. I can't imagine it being done better. The surgery went so well that the operating-room staff applauded. There's nothing else we can do and he is going to die."

But our surgeons were better. They didn't blow their own horn. They didn't even tell Mrs. Jackson that her husband was going to die. They just said that the procedure went well and that the oncologist would be in touch with them.

Yes, Mr. Jackson had cancer. Of course it was. Intestinal adenocarcinoma. And at his age it wasn't good. It never is.

Bad diagnoses make me tired. I have to pace myself from the very get go, for I have to survive this year of internship. So I'm going to bed. I'm looking forward to laying my head down on that old pillow and taking a deep cleansing breath before falling asleep.

Chapter 2

Pigs and Goats and Sheep, Oh My...

I woke up with my heart beating fast and my knee bouncing up and down. My beeper was angry and my nose was stuffed up. I felt hung over. I sneezed and coughed twice and reached for the phone in the dark room, knocking my inhaler off the table and under the bed into the 3 inch-deep sewer of accumulated dust and grime that I knew protected the floor from exposure to too much buildup of floor cleaner and wax.

Dialing in the dark is always haphazard. My beeper said to call the 3rd floor medical ward. I made my best guesses as to what numbers to press. I failed.

"Central accessioning," were the words that came through the phone. It was a nasal harsh operator-style voice of someone who didn't want to talk to me, which was fine because I sure didn't want to talk to her either.

I hung up and rolled out of bed to open the door. It was stuck. I kicked it. Light shined in and hurt the backs of my eyes, so I squinted as I dialed the phone for my second, this time successful, attempt.

"Yeah, it's Dr. Marcus. I was paged." I said in my most tired sounding voice, with a hint of self-righteous humility and false concern, in a clear attempt to obtain pity and mercy from the party on the other end.

"Hold on, Dr. Marcus," replied the night shift unit coordinator. Teddy was a nice guy. His long golden locks were like Heather Locklear's but with more lear. He walked ramrod straight, dressed in pleated slacks and spoke with a southern-accented flamer's lisp. Anyone who stood in his presence would be sure he was gay. He was an aspiring, and failing, actor. So was his wife.

A moment later, a welcome voice came over the phone. It was Nurse Maid. "Dr. Marcus, are you sleeping?"

"Not at all." It wasn't a lie because I truly was no longer sleeping. "Should I get you some flowers?" I asked her in our recently acquired code.

"That would be nice," she replied coyly. That was good news... very good news. I started searching around for my toothbrush.

"How are things on the ward?" I asked.

"Shockingly quiet. I'm bored. I have my break coming up. A full hour this time. Want to get some coffee?"

"No. An hour is barely enough as it is."

Nurse Maid replied with a twittering chuckle. "Aren't you sick?"

"So no kissing this time."

"That's no fun." She was speaking *sotto voce* and I could barely hear her now.

"It is for me," I said, foolishly taking a risk that somehow I got away with.

"What room are you in?"

I told her. She hung up. I grabbed my toothbrush and ran out the door to the shared on-call bathroom. The door was locked. Crap. I knocked a little too aggressively.

"Just a damn minute!" came the muffled angry retort. I knew that voice. It was Dick "the Wad" Wadley. His parents had no clue, to this day, what they had done to their son when they had named him. The Wad was an anesthesiology resident and a pain in the ass sometimes. But he was the best intubator in the hospital and a key man to have near you when a patient coded.

"Wad, I need to brush my teeth," I said through the door.

"Yeah, what's new, you stanky intern? Your mouth after sleeping for an hour smells like my ass will after I sit here for the next hour."

"Wad, I got a date. And no time for this," I pleaded.

"Awl right. Hold your balls for a moment." A minute later, the toilet flushed. Wad washed up and came out. He was tall, real tall. And lanky and red headed, with the standard freckles that all red heads seem to have. He smiled a lanky, toothy grin and held up his wet lanky hands. "Don't breathe."

The warning wasn't necessary. I couldn't breathe. The stench was overwhelming. I got laryngospastic and gasped. Wad had eaten Mexican tonight.

"Geesh, Wad. Didn't we ask you never to eat Mexican? Did that gerbil finally die? Don't you believe in matches? Had you been saving that up for a month?" The smell was like the combined excrement of sheep, goats, and pigs, all blended and dumped into the ventilation system, and it was rapidly working its way down the hallway to my call room. I had to act fast. Nothing turned off Nurse Maid more than foul stenches. She didn't seem to mind it when they emanated from a sick patient. But when they emerged from a healthy young man, she flipped off like a light switch.

I searched, fruitlessly, for a bottle of that toxic highly-scented hospital cleaning spray that was usually found everywhere when you don't need it. I rummaged around the lounge area for a book of smoky sulfurous matches, but hardly anyone smoked anymore. It was no use. The whole group of call rooms smelled like Wad's ass. And he was gone, and the blame would be put on me.

Then I saw it. Ah, the wonder. The happiness. Oh, for sure, this would cover up the smell. On the floor in the back corner, under the television shelf, mostly concealed by a pile of discarded scrubs, was the most pleasant sight: a white plastic container of baby powder. Perfumed to perfection, baby powder was the antidote to stench. Sure, inhaling it puts you at risk for some of the worst lung diseases known to man. But so what? It covered up stenk. And, hell, babies had been inhaling this stuff for generations. I ran for it, hoping the container was full, and twisted open the top. I rushed to the bathroom. With a brisk squeeze on the bottle I filled the air with a massive puff of talc. Quickly, I ran up the short hall pounding the sides of the bottle, smoking up the place with the pleasant scent of freshly-clean baby butt, happily replacing the stank of Wad's ass with a pleasantly-scented mist of fine inhalable lung-disease-causing talcum powder. And just in time.

The numbered lock on the main door was being activated. Nurse Maid was about to come in. I ran for the sink and squirted three inches of toothpaste into my mouth in a last ditch effort to not be disgusting. The door opened. Standing there was not Nurse Maid. No. It was Henry. Oh, Henry. Oh, Crap, Oh Henry.

Oh Henry was a night security guard. He was also an artist who painted with acrylic paints on saws. That was his thing. And he was pretty good at it too. Some of his saw paintings used to hang in the ER waiting room. Once, a pissed off brother of a dead guy in the ER saw one of those saw paintings, grabbed it off the wall and spun it around himself, threatening to cut the heads off the doctors who had killed his brother. The brother had died from a car accident. I am pretty sure the ER doctors hadn't been driving.

Oh Henry was a talker. Not a brief talker. Not a respectful talker. Just a talker. All night talker. No way to get away talker. The kind of guy who is pleasant and friendly and always comes into a room when you have no excuse to leave but really don't want to stay to listen to him talk because you have so much work to do. And he was here, now. Nurse Maid came in a moment later.

"Dr. Marcus, you look like you've seen a ghost," said Oh Henry, not sensing my viagravation at his untimely interference with my impending romantic encounter.

I turned and looked at a small mirror on the wall. I was covered with patchy clots of white powder—on my face, on my clothes, and in my hair. There was a gob of toothpaste on the corner of my mouth, which was turned in the upside down grimace that reflexively appears when bitterness is tasted. My toothpaste has baking soda in it. Bitter stuff.

"Oh, geez, don't I?" I started patting the powder from my face and shook out my hair, while licking the corner of my mouth, which made my mouth again reflexively grimace.

Nurse Maid was laughing as she sat down in the chair facing the dark screen of the generally non-functioning television. She, too, knew that our hoped-for rendezvous—so carefully planned, so agonizingly anticipated for more than four minutes now—was not going to materialize. I looked at the back of her head, her dark auburn hair partially covering the perfect skin on her neck. I sighed, inhaling the last bits of floating talcum powder into my dust-mite assaulted, virally-infected, chronically-exhausted congested lungs, and sat down just after Oh Henry settled into the couch next to my girl.

And he talked. And talked. And I listened, politely and in many ways truly interested. An hour later, Nurse Maid left. A tear fell down my face, forming a creek in the white powder. It was another night that didn't work out with Nurse Maid, this time because I was too much of a sheep to kick Oh Henry out. I am not good at hurting feelings. Sooner or later I was going to need to learn to make a stand on important matters. I would learn from Blow.

Blow considered our hospital as most deserved of the name he had given it. The Sheep's Pen. "It's filled to its fences with sheep," he had told me when I had asked for the name's derivation.

"You mean the patients?" I asked, not understanding.

"No, of course not. It's like Animal Farm. The Sheep are the doctors. The Pigs are the health insurance companies and the government, the Rocks are the zillions of inane rules. The Goats are the hospital administrators who fear the Pigs and hungrily rip the grass up by the roots, thus serving to make sure there are no grassroots left for some rebellious sheep to potentially start to use to fight the Pigs. Should I go on?"

"Why not?" I responded, already confused.

"Doctors are Sheep because they move in flocks, turn their heads all the same way when anyone makes a noise, and are easily led by anyone with a hooked stick who claims to be in authority. And they have been led right off the edge of a cliff. A doctor is invariably as smart as can be, but most are stupid as dirt too. They trip on the rocky laws and rules and then the Pigs pick 'em off one by one, threatening and intimidating them to stay in the flock and go where the flock goes and think like the flock thinks. Of course there are Wolves too. They are the lawyers. The Sheep foolishly hire and pay a bunch of Goats to help deal with the Rocks, Pigs and Wolves, but the Goats end up working for the Pigs and constantly nip at and exhaust the Sheep, making it easier for the Pigs to enslave them and the Wolves to eat them. Even the Sheep's own organizations work against them. Take the AMA for example. This is the 'American Medical Association', right? One would think by its name that it's the organization that is supposed to be helping the medical profession help patients. But one would be mistaken. Sure, it lobbies the government a whole ton. It has to, because the government controls most everything in health care now. But the AMA is also the keeper of the handcuffs of the profession. The AMA creates and controls the billing codes we have to use. Then Medicare sets maximum payments for the codes that are then adopted by all health insurance companies to determine how much doctors will get paid. Thus, together, the AMA and Medicare set price controls for the doctors throughout the entire country. There is no better way to destroy productivity and create poverty than by making price controls. Price controls are the ultimate economic handcuff. And they are enabled by the AMA."

Blow paused, and then took in a deep breath. "Did you know that the best subspecialist doctor in the country gets paid to see a patient with a given disease the same amount as the new doctor who just finished residency? Nobody even *wants* to see the new doctor, while the expert is fully booked for six months. But the expert has to bill according to the same stupid price controls that are used for the newbie. The doctors who are well paid are well paid not because they are better doctors, but because either they see a zillion patients per day in an assembly line, or because their leaders know how to best manipulate the billing codes and pay lots of money to lobby Congress to pay their specialty's codes at higher rates than others' codes."

"They do say there is too much money in Washington," I offered meekly.

Blow replied, "Nope, Eddie, there is just too much Washington for sale."

"And our hospital?" I asked.

"Lame. Weak. Wimpy. About the worst. Our administrators are Goats who live in fear and do everything they are told to do by the government and insurance Pig authorities above them that have no honest authority. And they force the docs to obey all the stupid rules too, even though the rules are insane and wrong and defy common sense. JCAHO is coming, JCAHO is coming! Hang two lanterns in the bell tower, run around scared and then panic and spend lots of time dotting T's and crossing eyes, and spend no time with patients. That's our hospital."

"Why don't we fight it?"

"Yo, kid, ain't you listening? Doctors are sheep."

And they are. And, sometimes, so am I.

But I am going to refuse to be sheared. I am going to survive internship without becoming a sheep. That is my mission. I am going to beat the odds. I am going to fight'em. Fight'em until I bleed.

Chapter 3

Blood

I bled.

With great pride, I skipped the obligatory required mandatory training session on 'Diversity Awareness'. I skipped both the primary session and the make up session. The session, and its mandatory nature, had been carefully announced every day for weeks. The Sheep's Pen was trying to make a point to JCAHO that they really followed the rules.

I didn't. I got contacted by an administrator within a week to go to her office. She was one of the goats, one of the enforcers of rules made by people or organizations to whom we shouldn't pay heed. I was going to make a stand.

"Dr. Marcus, it seems that you did not make it to either of the Diversity Awareness training sessions. You do know that it is required, right?"

"Required of whom?" I asked.

"Required of you," I was told.

"Required by whom?" I asked.

"By JCAHO. JCAHO requires it. It's a requirement."

Hospital administrators are scared of JCAHO and would move heaven and earth, murder pets and children, desecrate holy ground, beat themselves over their heads with the jawbone of their ass, and sacrifice their finest sheep on the altar of bureaucracy in an attempt to avoid getting dinged for minor infractions during a JCAHO inspection.

I knew all about JCAHO, so I asked, "Who's JCAHO?"

The administrator coughed. "JCAHO. It's the Joint Commission. THE JOINT COMMISSION for the ACCREDITATION of HEALTHCARE ORGANIZATIONS."

I guess I was supposed to be scared. I stared at her just as if I wasn't scared out of my pants. I said nothing. She said nothing. She was big, powerful, intelligent, and useless. A full minute passed before she spoke again.

"You know, the Joint Commission. They are inspecting us any day now, and we have to be on our toes."

"Why? Are we trying to see over the top of the fence?"

She stared back blankly.

I tried another tactic. "Is JCAHO our boss?"

"No. They are JCAHO."

"Do we work for them?"

"No. Actually we pay them to work for us."

I stared at her with an exaggerated expression that I hoped would convey my exaggerated confusion.

"You are the only doctor that didn't make either session of Diversity Awareness." She shuffled some papers. "I see you also didn't make it to the compulsory essential non-optional module on Teambuilding."

Gosh, I think she was serious. So I stared silently and vacantly in the direction of the space between her ears.

"Do you not understand the importance of these sessions?" she asked me, incredulously.

"What sessions?"

"The training sessions mandated by JCAHO."

"I guess I don't."

"If you don't go to the sessions, JCAHO will take away our accreditation and the hospital will have to close."

I had to process the strange notion that an organization that we pay for and has no authority or power somehow has our administrators thinking that it has authority and power to close our entire university hospital just because I am a delinquent.

I sat for a moment before calmly asking, "What's JCAHO?"

"The Joint Commission!"

"Do they smoke?"

"What?"

"Joints. Does the Commission smoke? Or are they in prison, you know the 'Joint'? Is it a knee joint, or a shoulder joint? What is 'Joint' about the Joint Commission? I bet you don't even know why the word 'Joint' is in their name."

"Dr. Marcus. I sense that you don't take this seriously."

"Your sensors are broken. I do take it seriously."

"It doesn't seem so."

"What doesn't seem so?"

"*You* don't"

"I don't seem so?"

"That's right."

"Good. Then are we done here?"

The large and powerful administrator looked down in frustration at her large knees wrapped in her large black polyester stretchable pants. Or maybe she was looking down in frustration at me. I couldn't tell.

"So I assume you will take the final makeup session?"

"When is it?"

"Next Friday, at lunch."

"No, I can't make it."

"Why not?"

"That's when I eat lunch."

Chapter 4

Stinky Reminders of Life

There was a smell, a horrid smell in the basement. I didn't want it there. Everyday I walked down the hallway in that basement on the way to or from the elevators that connected this stinky underworld with the hospital wards and clinic spaces. And the basement always stunk. Like fish mixed with spoiled milk and diesel fuel. Plus polar bear butt. At least that was my best guess.

I went to the morgue, which was far away but still in the basement, to see who was rotting. There were several people rotting there. But they didn't stink so bad. They were in drawers. They had been nice people. I could tell because they had died.

I did my best to track down the source of the stench. I couldn't find it. I tried to cover it up. I sprayed six cans of Lysol in the hallway one day. The State sent a hazardous materials team to investigate the source of the massive Lysol exposure. The HAZMAT team ignored the stink, and cleaned up the Lysol. I poured two gallons of bleach on the floor. A bunch of rats in a basement laboratory were accidently cured by the chlorine of their researcher-induced diseases, but the stink remained. Finally, I was frustrated, and decided to do something about it. So in my naiveté I went to the administrators, the goats.

We pay the administrators to help us. The administrators are usually too busy to meet with doctors, because they are so busy making paperwork to abide by rules that the doctors don't even want to abide by. I then asked a very simple question, expecting a very simple answer.

"This hospital stinks and I would like to know if you are going to do anything about it."

"Dr. Marcus, I am sure you are under stress. What is the problem." This was a statement, not a question, because she had no interest in the answer. The only true question in her mind was "How do I get this guy out of my office so I can clean out my email inbox?" This particular administrator wasn't large and powerful. She was skinny and weasily, with long grey hair, smiled freely, and enforced rules for a living.

"The hospital stinks. Everyone knows, and nobody does anything," I said.

"What, specifically, don't you like about the hospital?"

"I don't like that it stinks."

"What specifically stinks?"

"The hospital."

"What about the hospital?"

"Let's start at the bottom."

"Okay"

"It stinks."

"The bottom stinks?"

"No. The hospital stinks."

"Dr. Marcus, what are you talking about?"

"I am talking about the hospital stinking and I want someone to do something about it."

"Are you saying the hospital *smells?"*

I groaned. "Obviously."

"Where is the smell coming from?"

I groaned again. "The *hospital*, obviously."

"Dr. Marcus, how do you expect me to help you if you won't communicate?"

"I don't expect you to help me."

"Well, what *do* you expect."

"Nothing."

"Then, Dr. Marcus, are we done here?"

"Not until you help me."

"Help you do what?"

"Figure out what the smell is that is making this hospital stink."

The administrator shuffled through a pile of useless papers on her useless desk in her useless office. She picked up one paper that looked particularly unique in that it was identical to all the others. "Ah, I see. Just last week the HAZMAT team cleaned up a massive chemical spill in the basement. Alkyl dimethyl benzyl ammonium saccharinate. The biggest Lysol spill they have seen. So, I think the problem is solved."

I frowned. I squinted. I squirmed. I flexed my cheek muscles. I strained to not cry. "No. The stink is still there. The Lysol was covering it up and your HAZMAT team took away the Lysol and left the stink."

"What stink?"

I stared at the administrator for more than a minute, without blinking. She stared back at me, but couldn't blink because of her recent Botox injections.

I said, "The stink in the basement."

"How do you know it is in the basement?"

"Because that is where it stinks."

"What is it coming from?"

"How should I know? It isn't my job to find out where it stinks or what is stinking, is it?"

"Well," said the administrator, "what makes you think it is my job?"

"Because it isn't mine, that's why. And any job that isn't mine has to be yours."

"That's not true. For example, I don't change bed pans."

"So?" I replied cautiously.

"So, that's not your job and not my job."

"So?" I replied hesitantly.

"So not every job that is not yours is mine."

"So?" I replied, every bit as cautiously as before, and then with some additional hesitancy for good measure.

"Dr. Marcus, you are frustrating me."

My eyes widened for a moment in frustration. "I frustrate *you? I* frustrate *you?* What are you talking about? Look, I simply am trying to point out that the hospital stinks and that someone needs to do something about it. That's all. Are you going to do something about it?"

"No."

"Thank you. That's all I needed to know. You could have said that before. It would have been so much simpler."

I left the office in satisfied frustration that I had accomplished nothing yet learned so much. First, I learned that the administrator had a recent Botox injection. Second I learned that she didn't know anything about stink. Third, I learned that it was in my hands to solve the problems that made my own life less pleasant than it could be, or that adversely affected my little part of the world. There was no one to support me. No one to back me up. No one the least bit willing to help. No one at all. Not a single person at the hospital would assist me. I called Blow. He would always back me up, support me, and assist me.

"Dr. Blow, the hospital stinks."

The soothing voice of Blow soothed my ears and soothed my heart, even as it soothed the wrinkled furrows in my wrinkled brow. "Yes, Eddie. The hospital stinks. I thought you knew that."

"I do know it. But I want to get it to stop stinking."

Blow sighed. "See you in five."

And in five minutes, Blow was there with me in the cafeteria. He had the look of a man who needed to talk. He didn't need to talk. But he needed to tell me things of import. We sat across from each other at a table, amidst crowding throngs of hospital employees desperately trying to avoid the stink that no one but me seemed to smell, but everyone knew was there.

"Blow, I want to get the hospital to stop stinking."

"Look, Eddie. I know. The whole field of medicine has gone rotten. Are you planning on fixing it single-handed?"

"Christ, Blow, I'm not talking about that. I'm talking about a chemical sensation created by water-soluble volatiles emanating from a putrescent source in the basement of this hospital and accessing the olfactory sensors in the cribriform plate of my upper nose and communicating this chemical knowledge to my conscious brain. I'm talking about a hospital that smells bad."

Blow contemplated for a moment, and then thought a bit. "Eddie, do you remember the smell of your elementary school?"

"No, I don't remember the smell of my elementary school."

"But if you were to smell that smell again, it would remind you of your elementary school."

Where was he going with this? "Yeah," I said. "Sure."

"The same is true for any place that is important, symbolic, in your life. For me, I can walk into any old bar with beer spilled all over the floor, and it will smell just like college to me. All the happy times will come flooding back to me, along with an intense need to take a piss and get laid."

Blow paused for a moment, waiting for me to understand. I didn't.

"So, my question to you is this... What does the hospital smell like to you?"

Ah, so he was seeking repressed memories of symbolic events in my life associated with certain smells. I had to give this some thought. Blow might be onto something. I thought, I thunk, I thank, I considered, I contemplated, but I couldn't get it.

"Let's go to the basement," suggested Blow.

When the elevator door opened to the basement, the smell hit me like a blast of air from a passing truck, and shook me to my axels. Catalyzed by Dr. Blow's simple question, the memories I had been blocking out for so long were back, back in a frenzy of emotion, feelings of failure, loss, boredom, disgust and mostly fear. And they were identifiable memories now. I knew what it was.

Blow looked up at me, evidently satisfied that the seeds he had planted in my conscious brain were now growing like mushrooms among the weeds of my subconscious. "Got it figgered out, Eddie?" He sniffed the air once, nodded, then added, "It smells like moldy cardboard boxes. What is the deal with cardboard, Eddie?"

Cardboard boxes. Not just cardboard boxes, but *wet* cardboard boxes. Musty, damp, soggy, soaking wet cardboard boxes smelled just like a paper mill to my overly-sensitized nose. This cardboard had a putrescent, acrid, bitter, eye-tearing smell to me. But only to me.

"I was 13 years old," I said, "and I was scared. A couple of days earlier, my school guidance counselor had told me something that I was too young to understand and that scared the living hell out of me. Scared me so much that I forgot to do a homework assignment. I didn't want anyone mad at me for forgetting to do the homework. It was something silly like that. But I ran away."

Blow looked at me. We were standing outside the elevator bay in the basement of the hospital, surrounded by hundreds of cardboard boxes that I had not noticed before, although I had sprayed them all with Lysol not long ago.

"Where did you run to?"

"I dumped my books out of my backpack, filled it up with Pringles and soda and a box of cereal, stuffed my pockets with my saved-up dollars, and walked out the door at 5 in the morning. I don't know how far I walked, but I sure did walk. Probably ten hours straight of walking, under highway bridges, along streets. No direction except *thataway.* Out of town, into the city. It was Boston. Nobody seemed to notice me on the street. Nobody cared. I was just off on my own. I missed school that day. I knew my parents were worried sick. My feet got blistered so I sat down for a while and fell asleep. When I awoke it was getting dark. I was lost. The air was misty. It felt like rain was coming. I counted my money. Eighteen dollars. I wanted a McDonalds cheeseburger, but all there was nearby was a doughnut shop that had closed at 4 PM. I found a bridge underpass, some boxes and a blanket and curled up, scared for my life, and feeling miserable for want of a toilet. And that is how it all started."

Blow raised his eyebrows. "How long were you away from home?"

"Five months."

"Holy shit, Eddie! At age thirteen? How did you eat?"

"I stole food. There was a nearby cafeteria. I would buy an apple for twenty-five cents and stuff my pockets with tons of other food and sneak it all out past the cashier. I would run in the back of the doughnut shop and grab boxes of doughnuts when the staff was distracted. After a while, I got bolder. I started breaking into places at night. I got clothes that way, and electronics, batteries, guns. I learned how to steal cars. I had a great mentor. His name was Tony. He wasn't your typical bum. He was a survivor. Of what, I don't know. But he kept me under his wing, taught me how to get by, how to earn a living by stealing from others. He never begged and neither did I. And we lived in cardboard boxes. He was wily."

"Five months," reiterated Blow. He seemed astounded.

"Five months," I replied. Yep, that was a long five months. "Finally, Tony tapped me on the shoulder and said, 'Kid, have you had enough of this yet?' and took me home."

"Just like that?"

"Yep, just like that. But I was never the same again. I had seen the sleazy side of life. My companions were prostitutes and thieves and drug addicts and schizophrenics."

"So, is this why the basement smells bad to you, then?" We walked around the large unlit room. "I think maybe there's a way that the stink can go away now, Eddie."

I replied, "This stink isn't going to go away with five cans of Lysol."

"You've got to embrace it more, Eddie. How many people had a formative adventure like you did, at age thirteen? It's part of the reason you are who you are."

"Yeah, Blow, I know. But I really do block that stuff out of my memory. It wasn't fun at all. It was survival, and I had no qualms about anything. Moral relativism reigned supreme. Machiavelli, I was. A city rat, a road warrior. Whatever it took to survive."

"Eddie, I knew you were special. I didn't know why. Now I know."

I didn't get it. Not then. But the hospital basement mostly stopped stinking that day. I don't have a clue what the weasily skinny gray-haired administrator had done to mostly clean up the stink, but it sure as heck was a heckuva lot better.

Chapter 5

The Barnyard Killer

People were being killed. One doesn't think of serial killers working their evil deeds in a hospital, but it seemed we had one right here in the Sheep's Pen, taking out patient after patient. Sneakily. Unbeknownst to anyone. Nobody seemed to be noticing. Except me. And at first, even I wasn't sure.

As far as I can tell, one Thomas Bowden was the first victim. But there easily could have been more, lost back in the fog of time, before anybody started noticing. Mr. Bowden was a fine man, a hero. He was a soldier injured in battle and had been hospitalized for over a year. He was a patriot, a protector of freedom, and it was particularly wrong that his life was stolen from him by a malicious killer. He came into my intensive care unit, during my third month of exhausting internship, for help. He was murdered.

The next was a woman—Marla Frenchman, recently widowed. She sadly had breast cancer and had just had a mastectomy. Life is too unfair. There was a mild complication from the mastectomy—a wound infection. And she had also acquired a urinary tract infection. Together, these two infections brought her into the intensive care unit in which I was tirelessly working, where she was murdered.

It is common, of course, for people to die in intensive care units. They are pretty sick when they get there, and we do lots of dangerous things to them during their stay. The hope is that they leave by the front door, but they occasionally leave by the back door, with the big toe on their right foot leading the way, decorated with a paper tag tied on with a wire.

At the time, I didn't have any real suspicion after Mrs. Frenchman was killed. Hers was one of many sad deaths in the ICU. But then came more, each with more suspicious circumstances. Three men in a row died in that very same room. Room 7146. I don't recommend that room. If it doesn't have bad luck, it at least must have a ghost or two. I began watching that room 7146 closely. I didn't want anyone else to die in there on my watch. But I guess I watched too closely. No one died in 7146 thereafter, but while I was watching 7146, two people at the other end of the unit were found dead in their beds. And that is when I started to realize that a killer was on the loose. The killer knew I was watching 7146, and was staying away.

Each of these five victims, as well as Mr. Bowden and Mrs. Frenchman, seemed innocent enough people to me, not deserved of malice inherent in the killing of a human being. But that matters not to an arbitrary killer. My theory was that the killer had intentionally moved into the hospital environment and joined the culture of the place, with the full intent from the beginning of using the opportunities available to kill his victims with minimal chance of getting caught. He could have been here for years.

It could be anyone. One of the nurses, one of the administrators, a unit coordinator, a phlebotomist, a physical therapist, a respiratory therapist, even one of the doctors. Even though I was utterly exhausted, tired beyond measure, I had the energy to start eyeing everyone suspiciously. What would *you* do? Everyone was a potential suspect.

One of the nurses caught my eye particularly. Not because she was shockingly good looking, because she wasn't. She wasn't even a she, she was a he. It was a male nurse named Robby.

I understand male nurses. They get to help people and they don't have to be a doctor, therefore getting to keep their testicles. At this point in my indoctrination into the medical system, anyone who has decided NOT to be a doctor gains a pile of respect from me. So I respected male nurses.

The medical profession is increasingly female. Almost all the pediatricians in training these days are female. The other specialties are moving that way as well. It is a good thing. There is no particular need for maleness in medicine. As more females wished for professional careers, it was natural for them to move into medicine. Likewise, as the government and insurance companies took more power away from the doctors, it was natural for male testosterone to start seeking more fertile ground for its power-seeking tendencies. In the recent decades, lots of power has been transferred to the federal government, so the testosterone-infected folk are going to law school instead of medical school, because we all know that lawyers run Washington, and Washington runs the country.

But back to Robby. Robby was one of the best nurses I have ever met, and he was probably a killer. I could tell because I saw it in his eyes. Compassion, skill, experience and understanding all shone forth brilliantly from his dark green eyes, which always had wrinkles of smiles at their corners. He was simply too good a guy; it had to be a carefully manufactured façade. So I kept a particularly close eye on Robby, the killer.

But there were probably several other killers in the hospital too, and they may all be working together, so my vigil remained high. I was not paranoid, not at all. I know not everyone is a killer, at least not all the time, but someone is, at least some of the time, and the only person I knew for sure wasn't a killer was me. And I wasn't really sure about me. So, it could be anyone or everyone, and I decided to not let anyone out of my sight.

I cannot imagine what it would be like to get so little sleep for so long that one becomes paranoid. If I were paranoid, I wouldn't have the energy left to be watching everybody so carefully to try to intercept them before the next kill.

I was watching very carefully when the next kill happened. I couldn't stop it because I hadn't narrowed down the killer confidently to anyone other than Robby or everybody. Robby was away for the week, so he claimed, which left the other likely candidate for the homicidal maniac being everybody. Everybody, that is, except me. And I still wasn't sure about me.

The next person to be murdered by this maniac was Mrs. Agnes Stepham, a lady of some means. Mrs. Stepham was lovely. She had grey hair carefully quaffed and meticulously maintained. She had eyeliner and eye shadow and eye makeup, but none to excess. All tastefully done. She looked at least ten years younger than she actually was. Her wealth came from her cosmetics company, which she had built on her own. Her husband, also a wealthy man, had died very sadly driving in a car accident several years earlier. I don't know why he was so sadly driving in that car.

She had come into the ICU with a high fever and nearly unconscious. But with some antibiotics to treat a urinary tract infection she started perking up and was able to speak. This is when I got to know her.

Mrs. Stepham was a happy person, inside. She had been successful in her career, obviously, and had built up her small empire. But she also pursued other interests. She played piano, and provided funding for charity work abroad. She played bridge and basketball, she watched her figure, but ate anything she wanted (in small portions). She smiled and was dignified, and satisfied with her life. She was one of those people who had no fear of death, because she had lived, produced, created value in the world, stolen nothing, lived honestly, and cared about people.

It was my call night. Every fourth night I stayed overnight at the hospital. It used to be every third night, but the ACGME rulemakers didn't want me to learn medicine or become paranoid so insisted that the hospital put us on call no more often than every fourth night. Being on call every third night in the hospital could truly be pretty hostile to sanity and indeed has a tendency to make people paranoid. But there are some times when it is simply needed. Doctors have to be able to deal with sleeplessness, and there is no way to learn to deal with long hours and hard work other than by working long hours and doing hard work. Look at me. If I had been allowed to be on call every third night, I would have learned better how to deal with exhaustion and responsibility without becoming paranoid. I missed that chance because in their infinite wisdom they made rules.

'They' is the modern term used to describe the anonymous entities that may or may not exist, that we are told make the rules that may or may not exist, said real or unreal rules then being used by the Goats, Wolves, and Pigs to keep the Sheep, Goats, Wolves and Pigs all walking the line that no one could define to a location no one wanted to go.

When I was called to Mrs. Stepham's bedside, I knew immediately that a heinous crime had been committed. She was pale, which is concerning particularly when one has black skin, as did Mrs. Stepham. She was in shock, which by doctors is defined as there being insufficient blood flow to the tissues to be providing for their needs for oxygen and energy. I called for a lactate level to assess how bad the shock was, I gave her a liter of intravenous saline to increase her blood pressure and blood flow. I started a dopamine drip to increase her arterial pressure and increase her cardiac contractility (dopamine is supposed to do that, although I think it was only ever studied in dogs, so who really knows?). I asked for blood tests to see if she was bloody, a urinary catheterization to see if she was uriney, a stool test to see if she was stooly, and an EKG to see if she had enough EKG.

The blood tests told the story. Her white cell count was through the roof. Her platelets were through the floor. Bacterial sepsis. Her urine test showed the source. Bacteria in the urine in older folk can cause real bad problems...and Mrs. Stepham was an older folk. That damn homicidal maniac was at work again. No doubt about it.

Bacterial sepsis, which is when bacteria get in the blood or release toxins into the blood stream, makes patients look horribly sick. Sepsis *means* very sick looking. Shock, changes in mental state, organ failure, death and other unwelcome outcomes commonly result, even if treated rapidly. Mrs. Stepham looked very sick-looking.

This is how bacterial sepsis makes you look so sick-looking: the bacteria release compounds that tell your immune system and blood vessels to do strange things. Bacteria make endotoxin, which causes an enzyme in your body to pump out oodles of a small chemical called nitrosonium, which is similar to a pollutant that comes out of your car exhaust and fills the pleasant sky of Los Angeles. In the body, this nitrosonium causes blood vessels to open too wide. Your body loses control of blood flow. Blood gets stuck out in your tissues, and doesn't come back to your heart very well. Without much blood coming back to the heart, the heart can't pump it out very well. So blood flow slows way down. It's a vicious cycle. I hate those and rarely hear of a non-vicious cycle, or even just a mean cycle. In this mean cycle, the blood in the tissues and organs (like your muscle, liver, brain and other equally useless organs) then gets sapped of its oxygen and other nutrients, and those organs start to get sick, fast.

Without getting enough oxygen or energy supplies, everything in the body stops working normally. Even the blood vessels themselves get sick. The lungs get sick, the heart gets sick. So we start throwing the kitchen sink at the patient, hoping the kitchen sink can fix her. Antibiotics of course are part of the kitchen sink, but they take time to work—time that Mrs. Stepham probably didn't have.

I gave Mrs. Stepham lots more intravenous fluid to tank her up. This gave something for the heart to pump around. That worked great for all of several minutes, which was an amount of time that I had hoped would not be a significant portion of her remaining life. The problem is that the fluid leaks out of the sick blood vessels almost as fast as we can push it in. These sick septic blood vessels, it turns out, are like sieves: full of holes. That salt water I pushed through her veins basically dripped into the muscle, liver, intestinal walls, lungs, abdomen, skin and even the brain. In a few hours of this, Mrs. Stepham was so swollen up that she looked like a black female version of the Pillsbury doughboy. But without the smile.

She couldn't smile now. She had a tube down her throat to help her breathe because her lungs were filling with fluid. Her heart was barely working—it was starved of nutrients, not getting enough oxygen, pumping fast and hard, and was filled with the toxins that were floating around in her blood trying quite effectively to kill her.

I called the pharmacy and asked them to tell me what the most expensive drug in the hospital was. I ordered up a double dose of it. I called the lab to ask them what the most expensive lab test was. I ran the test twice, just to make sure. I called the radiology department to identify the most expensive x-ray test, and had them bring the whole machine up to do it. Twice. I ordered everything *stat,* because I thought it was cool to say the word. 'Stat' used to make hospital staff jump to work. Nowadays it has about as much effect as a car alarm going off in the parking garage. At best it is ignored, at worst somebody throws a fruit at you.

But despite all the 'stat' and all the money and all the effort, I was getting nowhere, and Mrs. Stepham was going somewhere, and fast.

The homicidal maniac was succeeding once again, and there was not a damn thing left I could do about it. Once the maniac got his foot in the door, it was hard to slam it shut.

By morning, I was exhausted. And Mrs. Stepham had left the building. She had been a remarkable woman who I had refused to let die, but die she did anyhow, her soul laughing at my ridiculous notion that I had anything to say in the matter. Heck, I should have known by now that what I say has nothing to do with whether people live or die. I said to the homicidal maniac that he would kill no more. He laughed too, right along with the soul of Mrs. Stepham.

Well, I am still exhausted, and I haven't solved the case of the hospital homicides yet. But I will, says I, I will. I am close, I know it. The first clue came to me tonight. It turns out that all the victims had lived very long lives—into their nineties for the most part. Maybe their age was the thing they had in common that might have attracted the killer to them and allowed the killer to infiltrate into their being. Yep, they had all lived very long lives. All I had to do now was figure out what that shared characteristic might mean to the killer, and I was one step closer. I thought if I could figure it out, I might be able to predict who would be the next victim. I figured that during their last few weeks of life, each had required hundreds of thousands of dollars of uncomfortable and often painful interventions, generally provided at the demand of their loved ones against the doctors' advice, and paid for my Medicare. So, maybe the killer was the Medicare Death Squads.

I posted a notice at the ICU door to be on the lookout for the Death Squads, and be sure to not let them in. It was only up for about six months before the Dean noticed it and tore it down.

Chapter 6

Br'er fox, please don't throw me in the briar patch

It's been said that life is a terminal condition that is sexually transmitted. So, life is like AIDS, I guess. Although it isn't always the homosexuals who get AIDS, most people think it is a disease of homosexuality, even though really it is mostly a disease of promiscuity. Fortunately, AIDS doesn't need to be terminal anymore, for there are good drugs to treat it. Also, fortunately, babies aren't getting it as much, now that we know how to stop them from getting it from their mothers. Well, we do know, as long as the mom helps us to stop it from infecting the babies, and as long as she has access to the meds.

General rules pretty much suck. That being said, however, as a general rule I have never met a gay man or woman I didn't like.

Gay men are not threatening to women. Gay men talk openly about sex, and yet there are no sexual overtones that cause a woman to pretend to be someone she isn't. A woman can just be herself.

Imagine the typical woman. I can't because I am a man, and imagining being a typical woman is pretty much impossible for us men. But I want you to imagine a typical woman. She meets a guy. A good-looking guy, say. She wants to impress the guy because there may be a relationship there. Sex, marriage, kids, stability, security, vacations. Whatever. So she puts her absolute best foot forward. She laughs at his asinine jokes, and makes jokes too. She claims to like to bungee jump, canoe, shoot guns, eat red meat, listen to Tom Petty, watch football, and anything else that makes her attractive in his eyes. Likewise, the man stands tall, talks big, throws big money around, seems interested in her emotions, expresses interest in her activities, and does feminine things with her that make her think he is a rich intelligent jock and yet sensitive. The perfect man. The perfect woman.

The problem is: he isn't. She isn't either. Neither of them is remotely perfect. Furthermore, they aren't even slightly right for each other. They have lied, cheated, faked and perjured themselves into a relationship between two people that don't exist. It is destined to utter failure. Which is what happens. But they have sex a bunch before they go their separate ways, which is probably all that the guy wanted anyway.

So it works for the guy.

But not the girl, who got no marriage, no kids, no stability, so security, no vacation. But she got sex, and I sure hope she enjoyed that at least.

Anyway, the girl doesn't have to worry about any of those things with a gay dude. No marriage, kids, stability, security, vacation or sex. Nothing hangs in the balance. The girl need not fake being anything at all. She can just be herself. Completely herself. When it is said that gay men aren't threatening to women, it isn't sex that is being referred to. It is the woman's very self. Gay men don't cause women to try to be something they aren't. Gay men don't make women threaten their own personality. Gay men aren't threatening.

Well, at least they aren't threatening to women. They can, however, be threatening to men. Not all men, and certainly not me. Anyhow, gay men threaten lots of men. Not because the straight man fears getting his ass kicked. And not because he fears anything else happening to his ass. Not at all. He can keep his cheeks closed and he knows it. No, the straight man fears the gay man because his own sexuality is threatened in a manner that has been difficult to navigate in our culture. In teenage boys, testosterone is pumped out by the truckload. What most people don't know is that testosterone constantly interconverts to estrogen, sometimes at high enough levels to even cause breasts to form in the teenage male who is hyper-loaded with testosterone. If estrogen can grow breasts on a dude, I bet it can influence thinking too. Most every straight male has at least once as a teenager been roused from a dream, some transient homosexual fantasy, that led him to question that characteristic that culture has taught him to most treasure: his manliness. Sometimes the transient feeling is suppressed and goes away and a heterosexual life is led. Sometimes it is suppressed but doesn't go away and a confused life is led until the man unsuppresses it and comes out of the closet after suffering for a long time. Sometimes the transient feeling is encouraged right away, never suppressed and a homosexual life is led until the man realizes that it was just a transient feeling, and comes out of another closet by switching to heterosexuality. But in the usual heterosexual, that transient, remote, but not forgotten fantasy or dream occasionally makes naked the culturally-laid fear that lays within the man. Am I gay? Do I look gay to others? Do people think I am gay? Do people think I am gay and I not know it myself? Do I set off people's GADARs? All these questions and more gay questions pop into their minds. It is very threatening. So non-gays can be threatened by gays.

But occasionally there is a heterosexual man who particularly enjoys the company of gay men, who isn't questioning his sexuality, who doesn't live in fear of what others may or may not think about him. This man doesn't care if someone thinks he is gay, thinks he is rich, thinks he is poor, thinks he is strange or thinks he is a martini. This guy doesn't worry about any such things because he is a complete man. He is the individual who cares only that he satisfy his own expectations, abide by his own morals, create his own value, and be his own self. He is neither a victim of nor product of society, but is a product of his own efforts. He forms relationships with those who mutually choose to do so with him, without fraud, without deceit. He forges no relationships based on false premises. So, women, if you want a non-gay man who is a real man and for whom you don't have to pretend to be something you aren't, look for a man who likes gay men, because he is a man who will be true to himself, and therefore to you.

I am not gay, but I am also not my own man yet, not entirely, so I should still be considered threatening to a woman. I am working on that. But I have one thing going for me that very few people have, which is the awareness that being one's own man, being truly oneself, being unmotivated by the expectations of others, is a virtue for which to strive. I am striving.

"Dammit, Eddie, I told you I needed that paperwork filled out with random bits of false information for ACGME by yesterday. Get it to me!" Blow pulled me out of my philosophically pro-gay reverie. Blow was not angry, but he was pissed off. I could smell it in his eyes.

Blow wasn't angry at me. He was angry at himself for playing the role of a rule-enforcing Goat. In getting me to do paperwork for ACGME, Blow was defying his own core values.

And when you defy core values, you turn into a bowl of jello. Of course you have to have core values to defy. I think many people don't. Blow did.

I looked at my ever-growing and ever-ignored email inbox. I could see numerous nags from administrators informing me about how many computer-based-learning modules I needed to complete on-line (it was now 32) in order to avoid the necessity of their punishing me by sending me more emails about how many computer-based-learning modules I needed to do.

At the top of the list was the squirrel-flu learning module, designed so I could read all about a disease about as dangerous as the common cold, but which had been talked up in the mainstream media, the conspiracy media, and by the government, because it was so readily useful for the purpose of declaring a national emergency and thereby giving the government more power to spend money and buy votes. The government loves a good emergency. So much can be done to the people during an emergency that could never be done normally. If you have enough emergencies, people get used to being screwed. I sometimes think they make up emergencies just for that purpose, but that may be just another one of my microparanoid delusions. Well, except in the case of the squirrel-flu which was clearly an artificial crisis. And maybe the entire Persian Gulf Region. Oh, and Climate Change, by which is meant global warming, except when it is cooling.

"All right, Blow, I will fill out the stupid form with stupid information so that the stupid ACGME can accomplish their stupid goals, which aren't our goals but we'll help them anyhow. Will that make you feel all good inside, Blow?"

I shouldn't have said that. Blow was not only *not* the bad guy, he was THE good guy. In fact, as I was coming to learn, he was really one of the very few consistently good people in the

Sheep's Pen, at least in terms of pretty much *always* being on the patient's side—fighting for the benefit of our patients now and our patients in the future.

But Blow took my comment in stride. He replied, "You are forgiven. I hate this stuff too, and I'm fighting it. It's an uphill battle against an ill wind while surrounded by assholes who believe they are friends yet play defense for the enemy while justifying that they cannot beat the enemy, so we have to join them."

I looked at him askance. He looked askance back at me. If the contorted set of phrases he had just said had been written down, it would not have been worth the effort to read twice to try to interpret it. I was completely confused and asked, "What the hell are you talking about?"

Blow sighed and said, "Look, every residency training program director in the hospital thinks this paperwork we do for ACGME, which we do to document how well we are following all their arbitrary and counterproductive rules about medical training, is utter hogwash. Every one. But these same residency program directors are all sheep. Every one. No one has the nuts to stand up and fight against ACGME. And since they each don't have the nuts, they all do their best to impede the efforts of any one of us who might have the nuts to fight. It is the instinctual tendency of sheep to keep everyone within the flock."

"I didn't know. It's that bad?"

"It is. It's horrible. Tell you what, Eddie. Why don't you come to a meeting of these goat-sheep with me. Just to get a taste for yourself. We'll tell them that you may be interested in running a residency program someday, and want to learn. They will eat that up."

And so began my wonderful experience with disgust and nausea. The meeting of these directors of Graduate Medical

Education at the hospital, and the committee that "supports" them, met a week later. So when the time came, I trudged off the ward with Blow. We sauntered down the hallway and rode the elevator to the pleasantly scented basement. We ambulated along the long hall past the ambulance bays and onward until we got to the underworld beneath the domain of the admin crowd. We took the elevator up to their high-end office areas, and cautiously walked along the halls, noting that each sub-subordinate administrator was endowed with office space so capacious as to make us mere doctors reflexively cringe with victim-mentality before remembering our lowly place in academic society. Blow knew where to go, and went there. I didn't, but did likewise. We took seats in the back corner of a room filled with bright caring doctors who didn't care quite enough to fight against the very-apparent evil of our decaying medical system.

In the room was a long boardroom table, surrounded by chairs—perhaps twenty-five of them. In the chairs sat people who either didn't want to be there or loved to be there. Those who loved to be there in this ACGME meeting were Goats aspiring to be Pigs. Those who didn't want to be there, but were there anyhow, were Sheep being molded into Goat-collaborators. At least that is what Blow told me. I had no reason to disbelieve him. The whole place psychologically smelled like a farm after a large application of turkey-manure.

The meeting began with an attractive and well-spoken chairwoman speaking up and making some announcements about new rules that would be affecting all the medical training programs. Blow whispered to me that this is how every meeting starts, with new rules promulgated by ACGME and a discussion of all the related new additional paperwork that would have to be done in order to accomplish nothing.

Most of the rules on the face of them made sense, until one

began to think. Nobody in the room seemed to think, though, for no one said anything in opposition to the new rules. It seemed they had long ago stopped fighting the evil and stupidity. I kept thinking of Germany in 1934 for some reason. I don't know why.

The attractive woman who ran the meeting said, "We now need to make sure that resident physicians document their hours worked every day, instead of waiting until the end of the week. We are considering implementing a punch card system so they can clock in and clock out."

Blow leaned toward me and said in a soft voice, "No one will even suggest that a punch card might serve to assist in the process of converting medicine from a profession to a job. Everyone at the table will just be quiet. Watch."

And they were. It was as if they had acclimated to a climate of denigration and inanity.

"We are seeking volunteers to mentor new residency training program directors in how to prepare all the documents necessary for the ACGME reviews." Then she added, matter-of-factly as if it were not the least bit contradictory, "We will assign people if there are insufficient volunteers."

Blow whispered to me, perhaps a bit too loudly, "No one is volunteering to have sex with me. Does that mean I am allowed to assign someone?"

The announcements went on for a time, and then I woke up when I heard Blow's name.

"Dr. Blow, we have been informed you want to cancel your residency program. Is that true?"

I was surprised, since I was a resident in Dr. Blow's residency program.

Blow arose. "No." Blow sat down and I felt relieved.

The semi-attractive chairwoman was clearly taken aback.

It took her a full thirty seconds to reply. "Well, we received a message from the head office of the American College of Graduate Medical Education that you asked their permission to suspend your residency program. Did you ask them that?"

Blow stood up. "No". He sat down.

"So you didn't ask ACGME to close your program?"

"No."

"Well, that is strange. Why would we get a message from ACGME then, stating that you asked to close your program?"

Blow arose. "Well, that is strange. I agree. Why should you get a message from ACGME stating that I had asked to close my program?"

"I don't know. It must all be a mistake." She looked at her administrative assistant and said, "We'll reply back denying the request to close the program. That should take care of it."

Blow had stayed on his feet. "Please don't do that."

"Why not?" replied the increasingly confused chairwoman.

"Because I don't want the ACGME trying to butt in on my program anymore, and I want them off my back."

"So you *did* ask ACGME to close your program?"

"No I did not ask ACGME to close my program."

"What did you ask them for?"

"I didn't ask them for anything."

"I don't understand."

"What's new there?" poked Blow, frowning.

"Dr. Blow, you don't need to be disrespectful. Please explain what's going on."

"I didn't *ask* ACGME for anything. I *told* them I was going to no longer work by their inane rules and I *told* them to take me off their mailing list, and I *told* them that I wouldn't be doing their stupid paperwork nor making my residents do their paperwork, and I *told* them to screw off. I also *told* them I was withdrawing from ACGME. To be thoroughly clear, I didn't *ask* them for anything."

"Oh," replied the increasingly unattractive chairwoman, who was losing points every time she opened her mouth. "Dr. Blow, you have to get ACGME's permission to close a program."

"I don't want to close the program."

"But you just said you were withdrawing from ACGME."

"Yes, but I'm still going to teach residents the arts and science of Family Medicine"

"Without ACGME?"

"Yes. Without ACGME."

"Oh." The thought was not entirely foreign to the chairwoman, but so few doctors now got trained without ACGME providing rules regarding their every move, their every experience, their every notion, that most people didn't realize it was possible to learn medicine without them anymore. "Well, you still have to seek their permission to close your ACGME-accredited program."

Blow sighed, "Why should I seek their permission to get out from under them? Are they now the Berlin Wall? Do I have to seek their permission to walk out through their Trendelenburg Gate? Am I not simply allowed to quit? Am I the slave of ACGME now? What happens if I don't ask them for permission but just do it?"

"I don't know. It hasn't happened before. We will ask ACGME."

Blow, who had taken a seat, stood up again. "Yes, please do ask what ACGME will try to do to someone over whom they no longer have power." He paused. Then he said, "When I was telling ACGME to screw off, I filled out a form on their website telling them I didn't need their services anymore. That mighta made 'em mad."

"Yes they did indeed complain," replied the now outright

ugly chairwoman as she pulled a sheet of paper out from a pile of highly important useless papers. "You cannot expect to get away with saying things like, '*I am quitting ACGME because you are power-seeking, collectivist narcissists who impose unilateral rules that make no sense, take the joy out of teaching, and are destroying the profession.*' You cannot say that."

"Clearly I can, because I did."

'But you cannot."

"Why not?"

"Because you can't. It reflects badly on our institution."

"Telling the truth reflects badly?"

"It is *your* version of the truth, Dr. Blow."

"It is *everyone's* truth!" replied Blow, loudly now. "But no one does anything about it. We all are wimps, sheep, useless bags of empty fur who will run off a cliff if another useless wimp bag of fur leads the way. Come on!!!"

There was silence in the room. Then applause. It began gently. One person only. Then it raised to a roar as more and more joined. They stood up and gave Blow a standing ovation. Blow smiled, proud of his accomplishment. These doctors, these teachers of the future leaders of medicine, had finally been roused out of their sleepy thoughtless victimization.

Except this previous paragraph didn't happen. There was no applause. There was no arousal, no awakening. There was only an almost imperceptible, almost silent murmur. That was all. But a murmur is something. It could be a start. Julius Caesar's life was ended soon after some quiet murmurs. But the Roman Republic was still replaced by the Roman Empire and long-term tyranny, so in the end murmurs probably make no difference at all, and we really need to do some yelling.

Blow got kicked out of the meeting. The Family Practice residency program was not closed, nor was it allowed to function without ACGME oversight. Blow was replaced as director of the residency program. He was informed that he wasn't allowed to communicate further with the ACGME in any fashion, and that he would not be allowed to do any more ACGME paperwork. He would not even be allowed to nag the residents to do *their* paperwork anymore. He could only practice medicine, teach and do research. It was a horrible punishment for someone who was inclined only to practice medicine, teach and do research. But Blow planned to accept his lashes without appeal...take one for the team. Or so he said to me in a gentle murmur.

Chapter 7

Moral Hazard

"What's wrong, Dr. Blow?" I asked Dr. Blow, concerned about what might be wrong. He was sitting with his elbows supporting him at a desk, holding his forehead in one hand and a phone pressed against his ear with the other, one eye open with an expression of shock, the other eye closed with an expression of pain.

"God damned insurance company pre-authorization. I've been on hold for twenty-minutes to get this damn insurance company to cover a podiatrist visit in the hospital for Mr. Adams. Unbelievable. Before that, I waited on this damn phone for half an hour for authorization for a prescription for one of my clinic patients. This stuff takes up real chunks of my day and the damn insurance company pays us nothing for the time we spend. And they make it really hard for us to even get through to them on the phone, and they don't give a shit. I'm on permahold here."

"You're a sucker, Blow," I responded a bit too boldly. "Don't do it."

Blow smiled at me and opened both eyes. "Look, Eddie, I've tried these fights before. They don't go far."

"So, bill the insurance company for the time you spent. You're a fully trained attending physician. You should be able to charge out like a lawyer at the senior partner level, say $450 per hour for time on the phone."

"I did that in the past, Eddie. I sent bill after bill to the insurance companies and Medicare for all the time I spent talking to their medical directors and clerks. The hospital billing department refused to do the billing for me, because they are goats and work for the insurance companies half the time. So I had to do it myself. I even stuck my bills on hospital letterhead. Never once did I get paid. Sometimes I didn't hear anything back. But usually they would write me to say that 'It isn't our company's policy to pay doctors except for time spent in direct patient contact'. I don't give a crap about their policy, but that's their horrible excuse."

"Clients don't pay lawyers for only the time they are in the lawyers office, do they?"

"Nope. But unless the hospital stands up behind us, the insurance companies will laugh all the way to our bank, where they will take out all our money and stick it into *their* bank. Believe me, Eddie, the hospital will not support us. When I started writing letters, I got called to the Dean's office so they could tell me I was breaking the law!"

"What law?"

"No law, Eddie. They just say that stuff to make us scared and shut us up."

"So, what are you going to do?"

Blow looked at the phone in his hand and shrugged. "I guess I'm going to be an unpaid employee of the insurance company's cost-containment program."

"No you aren't, Blow. Just say no."

"Then the patients don't get the medical care that they need, Eddie. We have our balls in a vice. Look, I lost that battle, Eddie. You have to take it on. Maybe you can win."

This was the first time Blow had let me down on a point of common sense, a point of ethics, a point of goodness. Even Blow could get beaten now and again. His enemies were taking advantage of his own moral code. Blow wasn't willing to let his current patients suffer because of the fraud and immorality of their insurance companies. It wasn't the patients' fault that their health insurance company sucked, although it was more their fault than our fault. Since our balls all seemed to be in a vice, it was going to be very painful to wriggle out of this situation. It would take a man with particularly small balls to pull them out of that vice. Or particularly big balls that could break that vice. I swore right then that I would never talk to an insurance company unless they were paying me for my time. No pre-authorizations, no pre-approvals for medication prescriptions, nothing. The patients might get mad at me, but it was their insurance company they should be getting mad at, and it was long past time for them to get mad.

I wasn't going to be a sheep.

It was my continuity clinic day, in which I was supposed to see the same patients over and over again throughout the year to help them get and stay healthy, although in reality seeing the same patients repeatedly now rarely happened. I saw mostly new patients who I may well never see again.

The medical education system hardly needs to bother to teach aspiring doctors how to create and maintain a good doctor-patient relationship because, for the most part, patients and doctors in the modern system are increasingly experiencing one-clinic stands. A one-clinic stand, although it can be intense and sweaty, is emotionally irrelevant and can hardly be considered a relationship. You see the patient once, spend lots of time trying to get to know them, try to help them out, record lots of stuff in the electronic medical record, bill the insurance company for the higher fee paid for a 'new patient visit' and never see them again. This system negated the rule to bill at the lower price-controlled rate of a returning patient, while importantly empowering the next doctor to bill the patient at the same higher new-patient rate so as to generate more profits for the hospital system so that the administrators can spend it all on hiring new Vice Presidents of Diversity as well as new Chief Compliance officers in order to stay in compliance with the diverse federal laws that are impossible to follow and are designed to make us all criminals while destroying the last shred of decency in what used to be the medical profession.

Today was a day of newnesses for me. Every one of my patients was new. They were scheduled into the appointment spots for new patients (which were longer in duration) and into the spots for returning patients (which were shorter). It was going to be one of those days when the patients were all frustrated at having to wait so long for me, and even more frustrated when I couldn't spend enough time with them to hear about their great grand-niece's piano recital. It was one of those days that makes me feel lucky I'm not a doctor. Except that I am.

My first patient was new, like all the others.

"Hello, Mrs. Jones," I said, walking in only after knocking conscientiously on the door. "I am Doctor Marcus."

"Pleasure to meet you, Doctor," the lady replied pleasurably.

"What brings you in today, Mrs. Jones?"

"I really liked my old doctor. He was a good man. Always able to spend lots of time with me." She made it sound like he was dead.

"Did your doctor retire?" I asked, hoping that he was not

indeed dead.

She shook her head. “Medicare told me I had to change doctors.”

“Really. Why?”

She shook her head again. “I have been going to the same doctor for many many years. Thirty years, I think. But when I moved to my retirement home, Medicare said I couldn’t go see my doctor anymore.”

“Why was that?” I asked, quite concerned.

“One of the new rules. My new home put me over twenty miles away from his office.”

“Is that a problem? Do you no longer drive?”

“Oh, I drive. I have great vision, and no problems in a car at all.”

“Oh, that’s good.”

“Yes, it is good.”

“Why did they make you change doctors?”

“I told you, Dr. Marcus. My home is over twenty miles away from his office. They won’t let me see him anymore.”

I could only think to say, “Huh?” which wasn’t a highly professional inquisitive methodology to employ to obtain relevant historical information from one’s patient.

“They say that my driving over twenty miles to see him makes my carbon footprint too big. So I had to change doctors. That’s why I am here.” Mrs. Jones was crying.

I excused myself to walk out of the exam room so that I could barf.

When I went back in, Mrs. Jones had regained her composure, although I hadn’t regained mine. I spent forty-five minutes of our twenty-minute follow-up patient-appointment slot going through her medical records, asking her medical history, and doing a physical, at the end of which all she needed was a prescription refill for a medication which three years earlier had been put over-the-counter, but which Medicare only paid for when it was written as a prescription. It was for the world's safest drug on the planet—a non-sedating antihistamine so safe that only God and the President could possibly know why it *ever* required a prescription. Except I knew too, thereby for just a moment joining the esteemed ranks of God and the President. It required a prescription so that pharmaceutical companies could make larger profits with which to make political donations to politicians' superpacs during elections.

This power of prescriptions, and my power to write them, planted a seed in the deep dark moist wormy soily recesses of my mind, and the seed, during the course of my internship year, would germinate and sprout. I hoped it wouldn't be eaten by the goats.

I think I was a satisfactory replacement for Mrs. Jones' doctor, at least for the day. I liked Mrs. Jones, and I hope she liked me. Although I probably would never get to see her again, I suppose there was something good accomplished by saving her the money for gasoline, which wasn't paid for by Medicare. And besides, some huge green savings had been accomplished, and carbon footprints reduced, which would allow Mrs. Jones to environmentally conscientiously drive her car down the road to make her daily visit to her elderly sister, who lived right next door to the office of Mrs. Jones' previous doctor.

You shouldn't suggest that Medicare is stupid because of this. Medicare couldn't have known that her sister lived next door to her doctor, or that they would save no carbon footprints by making her change her doctor. You can't expect Medicare as they make their broad-sweeping rules to know what makes the most sense for every single individual patient, can you? Of course not.

After my first patient of the day, I was only twenty-five minutes behind. So I intended to pick up my pace. But that was a naïve intent. My next patient was a middle aged milquetoast, and as soon as I walked into his room he invited me to his organ recital. I felt very bad for the man. He was a hypochondriac who recited all the problems with his heart, his lungs, his kidneys, his liver, his intestines and every other organ in his body. No short visit this, and there was very little I could do for him, I'm afraid. But the organ recital came to an end, as all recitals do, and I escaped with my life if not my sanity.

I kept getting further and further behind. My next patient had the very difficult disease process known as CHAOS, which was an illicit medical term meaning 'Chronic Hurts All Over Syndrome'. It was usually caused either by depression, abuse, drug addiction, alcoholism, or occasionally by what is called fibromyalgia. I don't know what fibromyalgia is, but it sure sucks. Because I have no understanding of it, I think of it as a disorder of pain interpretation. What might be considered a mild discomfort by the nerves and brain of one person is considered debilitating pain by the nerves and brain of another person. What process causes this, I don't know. But the victims of it take a lot of caring patience, more caring patience than is available in a twenty-minute follow-up appointment slot into which a new patient has been squeezed.

The day went on and on like this, and it wasn't as rewarding as it could have been. I felt guilty about keeping the patients waiting, and I felt guilty about seeming to rush them through the visit. I was rapidly on my way to becoming that asshole physician who has no time for his patients. Shit, it was going to be hard to survive internship without becoming a prick.

My last patient was a kind older gentleman in a well-worn and inexpensive sportscoat that looked like it had been bought on its third go-round through the Salvation Army thrift store.

After getting to know him a bit, I said, "Mr. Bastiat, I think a few blood tests would be beneficial to help us sort out what's going on with you."

"Okay, Dr. Marcus. How much are they going to cost?"

The question threw me for a loop. "I don't know. No idea really. But insurance usually covers it."

"What if I don't have insurance?"

"Oh." I said brilliantly. "Oh. Well, then, I really don't know how much it will cost for the labs. But I do know that the lab expense will cost a ton less than the tax you have to pay for not having health insurance."

"Yeah, I know. Hard to believe that they can now tax us for not doing something they want us to do."

I added to his concern by saying, "I wonder if they're next going to start taxing me for not installing a television in my house that watches me."

Mr. Bastiat nodded. "Or if we don't wear their brown shirts."

"Or if we don't attend the daily Two-Minute-Hate," I added.

It seemed that Mr. Bastiat wanted to get back to his health care before the world of 1984 fully materialized, for he asked, "Do I *have* to have the blood tests?"

"Well, you don't *have* to, but they will help me figure things out. There are other ways we can do things, including simply waiting to see if you get better."

"Well, I need to know how much they cost, before I can decide if I can afford them."

"Yes, you certainly do."

"So, how can I find out how much they cost?"

"I suppose the lab can tell you," I supposed. But I supposed wrongly.

I did feel totally silly not knowing how much my own hospital charged for services so I went out in the hallway and found a passing attending physician and asked him. "How much does it cost to get a metabolic panel run by the lab, and a CBC?" I mentioned a few other blood tests too that might help me sort out Mr. Bastiat's condition.

"Not much, Eddie. The tests don't cost patients very much."

"How much do the patients have to pay?"

"Insurance covers it."

"How about if they don't have insurance."

"Oh, then it will hit 'em pretty hard."

"How hard?"

"No idea. Call the lab..."

So I called the lab.

"No idea," said the lab.

"Are you telling me you have no idea how much you charge for a metabolic panel and a complete blood count?" At this juncture, I wasn't even going to try to find out how much the more complicated tests might cost.

"Sorry. The accountants figure all that."

With some effort, I obtained the phone number of the clinical laboratory's billing department.

"How much do you charge for a complete blood count and a metabolic panel?" I asked.

"Who is being charged?" was the disembodied voice that sounded like a telephone operator from the 1920's.

"One of my patients."

"Well, it depends on which patient."

"Do you mean there are different charges depending on

the patient?"

"It depends on what insurance they have."

"He has no insurance."

"Oh. Umm. I don't really know."

"Can you look it up?"

"Not really. The lab has to send me the billing slip before I can enter it into the computer."

"What billing slip?"

"The one that tells me what to enter into the computer."

"The lab sends that to you?"

"Yes."

"When?"

"After they run the lab test?" the whiney voice seemed to ask.

"Are you asking me?" I asked the whiney voice.

"Ummm. What?"

I had to probe further. "Are you telling me that the lab has to run the lab test before they send you a slip, and that slip will allow the computer to tell you how much to charge for the test?"

She thought for a several moments, or finished picking some dirt from under her toenail, and then said, "Yes. That's right."

"But my patient needs to know how much he is going to be charged for the test."

"We will send him a bill."

"*Before* he decides to have the test. He needs to know how much it is going to cost before he gets it done." I was thinking perhaps she might have been distracted by searching for ticks in a colleague's fur.

"Well, we won't know *before* the test is done. How are we supposed to know *before* the test is done?" She was getting testy. I could tell because her voice was whiney.

"Can't you look the price up on the computer anywhere?"

"No. It doesn't work that way." She decided to be helpful, probably to get me off the phone. "I have to enter in all the insurance information and his demographic data and everything else in. And I have to have the clinical diagnosis code, the CPT code and ICD code. Those codes come from you. You pick those codes after you make a diagnosis. Because we aren't allowed to bill for lab tests if they aren't justified by the diagnosis code."

I was a bit flabbergasted, whatever flabbergasted means. "So, you need more than the lab slip? You need diagnosis codes from me?"

"Well, from whoever the doctor is."

"That's me."

"Yes, then I need the diagnosis code from you."

"What if I need the blood test results in order to make a diagnosis?"

"Well, you use a code that you *think* is the diagnosis, then, I guess. Maybe."

"Oh. So I put a diagnosis in his electronic medical record even though it might not be correct."

"Yes, I guess so. You have to put it in the EMR."

I knew from horrid experience that diagnoses entered erroneously in an EMR tended to become permanent parts of the medical record. Several years ago, when I was working as a clerk, I had accidently clicked the wrong mouse button and a patient suddenly carried for the rest of his electronic life the diagnosis of syphilitic chancre. Poor man was forevermore afflicted with a horrible disease that he didn't have, and couldn't get full health insurance coverage because of his non-existent pre-existing condition.

"Okay, I get it. You have to actually *run* the lab test before you know how much the computer is going to charge the patient for the test."

"That's right," she replied, as if it was obvious, correct, and the way things are supposed to be.

"Can you make an exception, and let me know what it is going to cost, so I can tell my patient *before* he is obligated to pay for it?"

"That's not possible."

"What am I supposed to tell the patient?"

Silence.

Then, after some more dirt was cleared from under her toenail, "That is for you to decide, *doctor.*"

"Thank you for your help." I hung up forcefully, taking my anger out on the poor inanimate phone, and walked down the corridor and back into the exam room in which Mr. Bastiat sat.

"Mr. Bastiat. I just got off the now-broken phone with the laboratory and their billing office. Believe it or not, they cannot tell me how much the tests are going to cost until after they run them."

Mr. Bastiat nodded. "Is that because the tests sometimes are more complicated and more expensive, and then other times are easier to do and cheaper?"

"Sadly, no. It's because their computer billing system is built to function, or rather dysfunction, that way."

"Oh." Mr. Bastiat sat on the exam table, dejected, seemingly beaten by a system he had no chance of overcoming.

"Look, I cannot apologize enough for this, Mr. Bastiat. But let's do this: come back and see me in one week. By then, I will have gotten all the information. There will be no charge for the visit."

But there was a charge. When Mr. Bastiat came back in a week, I didn't charge him anything, but the hospital charged him a 'clinic fee' and a 'facility fee', which I, as just the lowly doctor, had no power to waive. They also charged him twelve dollars for parking. And the lab? It had taken me every bit of that whole week to try to figure out what the costs of his laboratory tests might be. Nobody could be confident, so it was still a guess.

"It looks like the tests will cost about $490. Best guess. That is for all of them, not just the simplest ones." I had priced up everything I needed to help diagnose Mr. Bastiat.

Mr. Bastiat nodded.

"But, we can just do the simplest ones. They're by far the most important, and will get us ninety-five percent of the answers we need. They only cost about $25. If they aren't enough, you can come back and get another blood draw for the other tests."

"Well, that makes sense. Why didn't you recommend that before?"

"Because I didn't think of it. Usually we just order all the tests at once. Get it over with all with one blood draw."

"But that's expensive."

"Sure, but the patients don't usually pay for it themselves."

"Hmm. That doesn't sound very cost-effective."

It wasn't cost-effective. It wasn't at all cost-effective.

"Well, let's just order the cheaper ones. If you need to, you can come back for the rest later."

"Naw. Just do them all now," Mr. Bastiat said, catching me a bit off-guard.

"Okay," I replied, "but that's a lot of money. We can really space them out, safely, too, and we probably won't ever need the more expensive tests."

"I don't want two blood draws. And besides, like you said, insurance will pay for it. So it won't cost me a dime."

"You said you didn't have insurance."

He replied with a wink, "Actually, what I said was '*what* if I didn't have insurance?' But I actually *do* have insurance."

That was a frustrating thing to hear. "So if you didn't have insurance, you would pay $25 for the most necessary tests and wait to see if the others are needed, but because you *do* have insurance, you are going to get all $490 of testing done, even though some of it won't be necessary?"

"That's right. Makes sense, doesn't it? Either choice costs me the same amount. Which is pretty much nothing. So, why not do it the much more expensive and marginally better way?"

"Yeah, why not." His use of the term 'marginally better' attested to some sophistication not previously suspected, but my brain only partially began to click on this.

While my brain tried to click, my hand clicked the mouse around all over the electronic medical record screen, ordering as many tests as I could possibly think of, and checking off diagnosis codes to cover every disease that he might conceivably have.

A dozen pages of laboratory requisition slips began sliding out of the printer next to the computer in the exam room. A dozen pieces of paper that shouldn't be needed in a hospital that uses an electronic medical record, and which contained orders for hundreds of dollars of tests for which Mr. Bastiat would pay nothing, but which would be very expensive for society.

It would be expensive for society because Mr. Bastiat's expensive Cadillac-level diagnostic workup wasn't going to be done for free, even though it cost Mr. Bastiat nothing. It was going to cost real human labor and real supplies of analytic reagents, and electricity, and rent, and finance charges for capital goods. Then there were layers of paid administrators who were paid to make sure the laboratory was in compliance with all the rules and regulations and guidance documents of CLIA and FDA and JCAHO. And all these costs would be charged to his insurance company, and as such contribute to the rising costs of health insurance, which would make health insurance unaffordable for many employers to supply, so they would choose not to supply it, which would lead to the government subsidizing the cost of health insurance by tax code manipulation, which would prompt more employers to buy health insurance, which would lead to more people buying $490 worth of laboratory tests instead of $25, which would prompt health insurance premiums to rise, which would prompt employers to drop the previously subsidized health insurance because it was again too expensive, which would prompt the government to panic and then force everyone to buy health insurance, despite the fact that they can't afford it, and round and round it would go in a ridiculous system of hyperinflation and insanity.

"That's my point, my young doctor," said Mr. Bastiat, who had perfectly read my spinning mind.

Mr. Bastiat, it turned out, was really Professor Bastiat. He was visiting from the University of Chicago where he was a tenured professor of economics.

"Medical hyperinflation comes from moral hazard, kid."

"Moral hazard? What's that?"

"Moral hazard is when the economic costs of one person's decision are borne by someone else. It's incredibly easy to spend someone else's money, and lots of it. In the medical system, this causes prices to spiral up out of control. Moral hazard destroys an economy. The medical economy is an utter mess because of too much moral hazard, which is caused by too *much* health insurance."

And with that insight, this one recognition that there had been so many years of flawed thinking, the reasons for the failures of the medical system all made sense to me. People had it absolutely backwards. It was like Professor Bastiat said. Health insurance was the problem, not the solution.

But I had been taught otherwise by so many teachers. Everyone had tried to teach me that if only everyone had health insurance, the costs would be so much lower. Others preached that it was the unregulated use of high technology that made health care so expensive. I asked Professor Bastiat about that.

"Kid, computers are millions of times more powerful than they used to be, and cost next to nothing now. High technology in every sector of the economy lowers costs drastically. It doesn't increase costs unless some politician tried to be a do-gooder and screwed with the market." He paused for a moment. "Dr. Marcus, how can prices possibly be kept appropriately low when neither the patients, nor the hospital, nor the doctors know how much anything costs?"

"Most people don't care. If they have insurance, it all seems free to everybody, or pretty much."

"Bullshit. Free isn't free. Free costs somebody something. There is no real market of any kind at all in medicine," taught Professor Bastiat. "And no market means no price signals, no supply and demand balance, no ability to optimize the provision of medical care, and no ability to create abundance for all. Costs rise and medical care gets rationed and everyone gets poorer."

"So what do we do?"

"It's for you to fix, not me," the professor said. "I am old. So I'm going to do pretty much nothing. I am going to sit back and watch the five-year plans get made. I am going to watch the subsidies and coercions and mandates and taxes and fines and imprisonments as they try to fix the problem they created in the first place by telling everyone they should be demanding health insurance."

"But people want health insurance."

"No they don't, kid. Everybody hates health insurance. People want health *care.* Health *care* and health *insurance* are pretty much opposites."

"Not in the minds of the politicians."

"Politicians are assholes."

"Hey, aren't you a professor? Are you supposed to talk like that?"

"If more professors talked like me, we might not have a bunch of sheered sheep graduating from colleges in this country."

Professor Bastiat died about three weeks later. It was a car wreck, while he was driving back to Chicago. A bus carrying a contingent of the President's re-election campaign staff was driving very slowly in the Left lane for a long time. Finally, out of frustration, Professor Bastiat tried to pass on the Right, but the bus suddenly changed into the Right lane without looking and ran the professor's car off the freeway.

Professor Bastiat wouldn't have approved of freeways. Freeways aren't free. They cost somebody something. In this case, his life. Moral hazard.

His blood tests had all been normal. Without asking, the lab had run them each twice just to make sure. And charged his insurance company double.

Chapter 8

Well, someone has to do *something!*

Okay, it was getting to me, I admit it. There was just nothing green at the hospital. Sure, there were recycling bins for disposed-of paper, but they were always filled up and therefore unusable. You see, ever since all medical care in the Sheep's Pen was converted to a process conducted by an electronic medical record, there has been an extraordinary increase in the amount of paper waste generated. By hospital policy there of course was no paper waste anymore since the electronic medical record was initiated, so therefore there was no need to pick up any non-existent recycled paper. So they didn't, and it accumulated in recycled cardboard bins to beyond overflowing. Thank God it didn't exist.

Lights were on everywhere. There was no effort to decrease the electricity consumed by lighting. Hot water was constantly being made hot, even when not being used, and thus consuming large amounts of electricity. Plastic bottles and aluminum cans were willy-nilly thrown in the trash container along with the reams of improperly disposed-of paper that didn't exist. Water was flushed down the toilet overly frequently and thereby disappearing into a black hole from which, as students in school were now being taught, this non-renewable resource could never ever ever be recovered, despite evaporation, rain and the whole extremely well-described and understood water cycle. Worst of all was that no one, I mean NO ONE had ever thought to put those signs up in the patients' bathrooms suggesting that they hang their towels on the rack so that the hospital laundry wouldn't be compelled to clean them. I cringe at the thought of how many towels in the hospital were being washed after only one use. I cringe at the realization of how much electricity was being washed down the drain. Or, more importantly, how much laundry detergent phosphate was being washed down with it, so extensively feeding the plankton and algae in rivers and watersheds that the snail-darters were getting suffocated, and then the algae would sink to the bottom, destroying the oxygen in the muds, and create petroleum that future humans would go on to burn, creating footprints all through the carbonosphere. How could I not cringe?

Fortunately, late at night, when any young doctor is at his best, while I was waiting for lab results so I could learn how much the lab tests cost and decide how to treat a newly admitted patient and go to bed, I had time to think about the all important process of greening the hospital. Everyone was greening something somewhere, but not at the hospital. I decided to help.

But I didn't want to do it the way everyone else did it. I wanted to do it better. I thought and I thunk and I thunk and thought, all with my best thinkings at 3 AM. And as I fell asleep drooling on a piece of non-existent paper that I was writing on to order a panlaboratory blood test panel that costs nothing for one of my other patients, it came to me in a flash of exhausted psychotic brilliance.

But there was no way that I would be able to rationally

persuade everyone to do what I thought was the right thing to do, just because I thought it was right. So, I did what all people who know they are right do: I used the power of the system to force my brilliant new ideas on everyone else. I didn't yet have the whole government to work with, but I had the hospital bureaucracy. At least I could force the hospital to do what I knew was right. I could start small. Later, I could go all Napoleon on the whole world. Or all Obama on the world, or all Bush on the world, or all Clinton, Reagan, Carter, Ford, Nixon, Johnson, Kennedy, Eisenhower, Truman, FDR on the world.

I had some friends in Computing Services at the hospital, one of whom made for me a new name, email account and title. I began with an email from this new me:

Mark Edwards, MD, Senior Director and Assistant to the Dean of Environmental Conscientiousness.

I liked it. It had impact. And my alter-ego had no real boss, so I could do what I pleased. It was good. My alter-ego's name was adequately distinct from my real name, Eddie Marcus, so that the computer administrators wouldn't possibly guess.

My first email boldly and proudly proclaimed that I, Mark Edwards, was pleased to have been selected by the Dean's Search Committee on Intramural Externalities to replace the outgoing Director and Assistant to the Dean of Environmental Conscientiousness. I commented on the excellent work of my predecessor (whom I named 'Dr. Alice Ghore'), and noted that the community would be hearing more from me in coming weeks.

I needed to start small so nobody of import would themselves be immediately affected, and therefore notice. Only people who had no power would be affected. That was how to get things done. They would be like blue-collar lobsters (with no political power) in a pot of cool comfortable water, unaware that the flame had been lit on the stovetop.

The next email I present here in full:

> *"To the University Community: The time has come to stop paying simple lip service to the massive environmental issues facing us today, but to actively engage in solving the problems. In an effort to save money and lessen global warming emissions, all fuel tanks on University vehicles will henceforth be fueled with 30% water-based processed petroleum fuel product."*

Hearing of no complaints from this first email, I moved on. The second missive made me smile, if no one else:

> *"In further effort to decrease the carbon footprint of the University, the cardiac exercise stress testing unit will begin scrubbing CO2 from the air in their facility using appropriate renewable technology."*

Silence. So, my third effort to save the planet followed within a few days:

> *"In an effort to promote recycling and limit all waste, henceforth, all trash will be recycled in the supplied green waste bags. If there are no green waste bags in your area, you are responsible for providing them. Lawn and leaf bags, preferably 55-gallon size, preferably manufactured by Hefty, have been approved by the Environmental*

Board at the University for this purpose."

Having heard not a whisper of complaint, disgust, or ridicule about my first three messages, Dr. Mark Edwards initial tests were complete and he decided to get a bit more bold. I wanted to see just how silly and sheepish people would be. My fourth contribution to the environmental recovery of the world was to directly address global warming.

> *"To the University Community: in the ongoing effort to decrease the global warming that is causing arctic ice to melt, which threatens all species that thrive in frigid climates with no source of food, the University will begin a process of using our available technology to combat, directly and obviously, the impending threat. Henceforth, the doors of all refrigerators and freezers are required to be left open two to four inches for a minimum of two hours per day in order to help cool the planet. We recognize that this will only have a small impact, but each step forward counts, and we at the University must be leaders. Others will follow. We will keep careful track of new data that emerge because we don't want to overcool the planet, and we know that we are currently in an interglacial period of an ongoing ice age."*

That should confuse them. And, to my great delight, the very next day there was a policy meeting that resulted in a new piece of paper hung on each ward, advising of the new policy. And refrigerator doors were open everywhere, two to four inches, held in place with a variety of means, such as coke cans and masking tape.

I saw a way to leverage my success. Within a day, I had sent an email into the inbox of every hospital unit administrative coordinator, offering for sale for only $129 each a refrigerator opening wedge, constructed of the highest grade materials, and made in the United States by the participants in the Special Olympics, using only organic ingredients. Special effort was assured to import components using only Fair Trade methods. For extra greenness, the inner material also contained a carbon-absorbing compound. The company offering this product was aptly named, 'Haftado Something NanoGreen Resources, LLC'. This company was aptly owned by yours truly. I would aptly donate all proceeds to a medical mission trip to West Africa that I was aptly planning to take a few months from now with Dr. Blow.

The orders came in immediately. My production facility was so swamped with orders that it took me all night just to process the paperwork. Despite a little bit of argumentative bleating, and some banter about bad science, each hospital ward ordered five or more refrigerator wedges. It was like this for a week before the fervor settled down. My mission trip supply fund was more than $10,000 richer. The problem was I had no product to provide to them.

So, Dr. Mark Edwards had to come to the rescue. The next green initiative email read as follows:

> *"The Office of Environmental Conscientiousness, following our process of Continual Quality Improvement, has formed a working group to evaluate the optimum*

evidence-based methods to improve overall environmental soundness and good stewardship at all levels. During our in-depth research and review of the literature, we have come upon new exciting evidence that helps us understand with complete confidence the complexity and intricacy of our astoundingly unpredictable environment. Although there are many new pieces of information, the following is of most immediate interest: it appears that, because of the adverse effects of chlorofluorocarbon as well as non-CFC refrigerants on the ozone layer, and the higher risk of skin cancer and other disorders, there is now concern about leaving refrigerators open for more than 10 seconds at a time. We are therefore recommending that all hospital units immediately develop protocols for minimizing the opening time of refrigerators to a maximum of 5 seconds. This has been determined to be a major quality improvement initiative, which will serve as a landmark process with attention at the very highest administrative levels of power."

The response was remarkable. One of the Associate Deans sent out a memorandum detailing the importance of abiding by this new, well-considered university program, and the administrator even added some additional flavor by stating that the refrigerator policy was a JCAHO mandate that if not followed would lead to complete cessation of all Medicare funding for the hospital. After that, the administrators seemed to have forgotten that they had ordered the refrigerator *opening* wedges. They had been paid for with university money, not their own, so the expected deliveries not being made led to no questions or concerns at all. It was money in the bank to help poor children in West Africa. But now there was demand for systems to assure that refrigerators were *not* kept open. I had to start hopping to fill this new need.

And the answer was simple. A digital camera could take a picture of the contents of the refrigerator each morning. Then, anyone at the hospital planning to enter the refrigerator that day for as little as a juice container would be required to view the morning's Frig'o'graph—and document that they had done so on a mandatory sign in sheet—prior to opening the door. This would allow for rapid assessment of the location of the desired refrigerated treat or medication, and minimum high-risk door-opening time.

The Associate Dean was grateful when a company that very day proposed a solution that could be used throughout the university that would cost only $1000 per refrigerator. This was taken rapidly to committee; calculations were made including the risk of losing Medicare payments. Marketing was consulted to determine how best to leverage the university's new green thinking by placing information about our organic greenness in the media outlets of the local economy. And the decision was made to initially purchase 200 Frig'o'graph units for rapid delivery.

The business was booming. By the second week, I was getting orders from other hospitals. The web was crawling, spreading the word. I was making a friggin' killing on Frig'o'graphs. That's why I named them Frig'o'graphs. If this kept up, I could build a whole new clinic in one of the poorest countries in the world. In a couple of months, Senior Director and Assistant to the Dean of Environmental Conscientiousness Mark Edwards was planning another email to start wedging open refrigerators again. I was looking forward to receiving that email.

My success in these endeavors helped me learn how so many other people have success promoting ridiculous concepts like magnetic bracelet health-enhancers, ethanol in gasoline, sub-prime mortgages, and mandatory health insurance. The way to get money and respect nowadays is to tell people to do incredibly stupid things while making people think you have the power to do so. I was beginning to understand the world. I was becoming an adult.

Chapter 9

My mommy says I have to take my nap now

I had to admit I was tired. In the last couple of months, I had gone through two cars, two laptop computers, 200 frig'o'graph units to help keep the refrigerator doors closed, and with summer only seven months away, soon I needed to start making a ton of refrigerator wedges to help keep refrigerators open. Fortunately I had hired an immigrant about whose ethnicity, race, sex, nationality, language, and genetic heritage I could not ask but I was sure that either he or she was one-third each of Chinese, Mexican, and Indian. This made for an interesting mix, as my new employee was a ready worker, paid well, untaxed, and happy. I gender-assigned my employee to 'female' to help avoid discrimination lawsuits. She didn't speak English much at all. I had her man the phones. If I were smarter, I would get the university to pay her wages directly. But I am not smarter.

Fortunately, the ACGME quickly provided some new ways to flex my charitable entrepreneurial muscles. They had not released a new mandatory hospital policy in over three days, so everyone knew there was some awful offal in the offing. Something big, ugly, and utterly outrageous. And indeed it did come, and I kid you not, this is real. You can't make this stuff up. The very next day, the ACGME released their new requirement that all medical residency programs develop a policy on education and enforcement of 'strategic napping' to assure that residents received enough sleep-time built into their workday. When Blow first heard about this strategic napping foolishness, his face twisted up in a knot so tight that I thought it would fray into hundreds of shreds, like a sun-burned and rotted manila rope parted by a heavy anchor. Or a sun-dried tomato run over by an oxcart. Or a Botox-injected celebrity face subjected to a gentle breeze. But finally, after his face had settled, the twists in his cheeks and nose dissolved into a small smile of satisfaction. Blow wasn't the head of the residency program anymore. So he could now have fun.

And Blow had fun. Before anyone knew what was happening, Blow quickly moved in to write a strategic napping protocol for residents. In his kind mentoring manner, he allowed me to participate in the drafting of the eloquent document, which was handy because I was pretty exhausted and needed a well-timed nap.

The final product was a work of brilliance, considered and delineated during a major over-binge of scotch and beer, the product of extensive deliberation between two men dedicated to perfecting the perfect. While still recovering the next morning, Blow had the document certified as final, stamped with an official looking stamp, and promulgated among the hospital residents and faculty under his old title of Residency Director, which he had failed to remove from his email signature.

The "Strategic Napping Initiative" was designed not just to reduce, but to eliminate all misadventures that might occur when doctors try to manage ill patients while sleepy, tired, exhausted, stinky, or otherwise impaired. The key elements of the proposal were as follows:

Case:

1. It is well documented that overworked residents get tired and sleepy and their judgment is impaired, and, according to evidence-based methodologies, all doctors require the same amount of sleep and suffer the exact same consequences from lack of sleep. Given their much shorter work hours mandated by the ACGME, residents also now have less training time to learn the instinctive skills for managing patients that come from constant training and repeated experience. Indeed, by the time residents finish their program and graduate, although they may have made less sleep-induced mistakes, they are also less-completely prepared than doctors of the past to function completely independently. This is quite terrifying to the graduating resident as he or she is about to go into the world. Some of the anxiety they feel is directly attributable to being required to abide by nonsensical rules that cause them mental confusion and constipated consternation. This is compounded by the stress of recognition of insufficient education caused by the mandatory reduced duty hours. Stress is tiring and requires sleep to modulate. Strategically performed napping can rectify the herein delineated stress-induced problems.

Plan:

1. Starting immediately, all residents must sign up for strategic napping classes. This can be done through the on-line computer-training module that has yet to be created, or through formal classes that have not been developed. Informal classes must be arranged and documented.

2. Napping must occur for at least 1 hour during every 8-hour awake period.

3. Napping must occur in a private location, in a quiet lockable room.

4. Napping must be witnessed and documented by another individual, preferably of the opposite sex to avoid rumors spreading around of residents being gay. Unless residents are gay, then the witness should be of the same sex to avoid rumors spreading around of residents being straight. The witness can be a paid member of the hospital staff who is on duty, or if off-duty they shall be paid overtime. Non-staff witnesses are encouraged and are to be paid at the part-time overtime rate.

5. Beepers must be disabled prior to napping, and resident duties during the naps will be graciously covered by the Dean of the Medical School. The Dean's beeper number is 666.

6. It is acceptable to not sleep during strategic napping, as long as some form of relaxing exercise is achieved. The nature of that exercise is left to the discretion of the resident and his/her witness.

7. Documentation of the strategic nap session must be maintained, or else Medicare might cease providing funding to the hospital and the hospital will have to close. JCAHO and ACGME each mandate different forms of strategic napping documentation. The Dean has therefore chosen to use both methods. JCAHO requires written documents in database format delineating the extent and duration of the strategic nap. ACGME requires video documentation. Video cameras will be made available for every on-call suite.

8. Although ACGME requires video documentation, it falls under JCAHO to determine acceptability and adequacy of any devices for use in a hospital environment. Ward administrators can purchase JCAHO-approved video cameras that are acceptable to ACGME from "Haftado Something NanoGreen Resources, LLC", the contact information for which shall be maintained in readily findable locations on every ward administrator's computer terminal.

9. For those times when no nap-witnesses are available or willing to remain for the full duration of the resident's mandated nap, the hospital has open tabs with several private local 'strategic nap witness agencies' that are bonded and insured. Because of the newness of this business model, these agencies are found in the yellow pages under the heading: 'Escort Services.'

10. All wards, departments, and administrators are to ensure that all necessary support is provided to the residents for whom this additional set of rules may cause consternation and extra work. Remember, the Administration works for the doctors.

11. Doctors not complying with this new rule can expect substantial punishment as deemed appropriate by the Administration.

12. This is the extent of the new rule. Expect amendments.

I was not so sure how the new strategic napping initiative was going to play out with the physician universe. But Blow reminded me that doctors are sheep. Put it on a letterhead and say it comes from "on high" and the doctors may grunt and disgrunt, moan and bemoan, bleat and debleat, but that is all they will do. Then they will follow the new ruled to a T, and even expand them beyond original intent, in order to avoid the inevitable repercussions of failure to comply that are so broadly threatened and rarely mature.

In this case, however, there was no moaning or bemoaning, because the residents liked the idea. Strategic napping was beautiful. It was required relaxation with the mandatory presence of the opposite sex in private quiet rooms with no beeper on. Blow, already famous, became loved that day. As for me, I needed no credit, nor appreciation, nor honor, nor accolades, nor monetary reward. I just needed Nurse Maid and a strategic mandated non-sleeping napping session with exercise and video documentation.

Chapter 10

Eddie, I told you to take a nap!

As the administration staff on the wards worked feverishly to round up Spanish, Hindi, and Chinese translators so they could order appropriate video cameras from the non-English speaking employee of Haftado Something NanoGreen Resources, LLC, I was fortunate enough to be on call. I got to witness all the efficiency with which the administrative bureaucracy carried out dictums from above, unhesitatingly, unquestioningly. It was an astounding process that reminded me, once again, of certain burgs in 1930's Germany.

First, the morning staff meeting announced the new university policy on strategic napping, and suggested immediate action to avoid ACGME and Medicare sanction. More than one staff member raised the concurrent concern that JCAHO might also sanction the hospital if strategic napping were not immediately implemented. Laminated index cards with the contact information for 'Haftado Something NanoGreen Resources, LLC', were handed out with advice to scotch tape them to the computer terminals on each ward, using biodegradable tape of course. Blanket Purchase Orders were created in order to buy as many appropriate video cameras as was deemed necessary by each department or unit. Cost was no object, as Medicare sanction *must* be avoided.

Within four more hours, the numbers and hourly costs of several local escort services were supplied through email to the unit coordinators and department administrative staff. There were a few chuckles, several guffaws, and a couple of headshakes, but nothing more than that.

A new policy was established, confirmed and entered into the historical lore of the hospital. It wouldn't be overturned now without a congressional investigation proving high crimes and misdemeanors, which would never be undertaken because most of the politicians had themselves committed high crimes and misdemeanors and didn't want anybody to think that there was an easy system to hold them accountable.

The video cameras were not yet even available because of the high call volume experienced by Haftado Something NanoGreen Resources, LLC. So, I volunteered to be the very first resident to experience the burdensome obligations of the new strategic napping initiative.

Fortunately, Nurse Maid was off duty, so she came in to witness my nap and got paid overtime for it. Dick Wad, the bowel-angry redhead anesthesiologist who had been complicit in befouling my numerous previous attempts at bedding Nurse Maid was nowhere to be smelled, thanks be to the grace of God. The call room was private, lockable (at least from the outside) and all other components of the new policy were available. In an incredibly rare act of voluntarism, one of the administrative administrators—a greasy little man with thick round glasses and a shriveled goatee—offered to perform the mandated written documentation for JCAHO. I declined his kind offer and encouraged him to keep offering his services to other residents who would no doubt be grateful to have him assist.

Nurse Maid came into the call room to find my teeth brushed, talcum powder floating around like new winter snowflakes filling the air with pleasant and inexpensive perfumery, and me, myself, dressed as God had planned for me myself to be, by His grace.

"My gracious," said Nurse Maid, astounded by just how much God had graciously bestowed upon me with the help of this little Blue Pill obtained from a Canadian online pharmacy. Damn online pharmacy. Never use your real email address for if you accidentally do, you will subsequently get inundated with innumerable daily emails offering to sell you numerous penis-enlarging therapies of dubious safety and equivocal efficacy.

But the darn pills from Canada, manufactured in India and imported through Nigeria, worked to my benefit, and I suppose to the benefit of Nurse Maid, who carefully documented the duration and the extent of all components involved in the strategic nap, including the extensive portion of said nap that was dedicated to achieving exercises of my choice.

At one point, Nurse Maid—exhausted from her extensive documentation—offered a suggestion for the developers of the strategic napping protocol. "I know that the exercise chosen is at the discretion of the resident, but don't you think it might be a more sustainable initiative if you recommended that occasionally the exercises be selected by the witness?"

I replied, "I will certainly recommend your wise suggestion to the program developer, who I believe is Dr. Blow."

She was satisfied with my response, which allowed her to continue guilt-free, abiding by my temporary control of the chosen exercises of the strategic nap during which I did not sleep a wink.

After my mandated and exhaustingly bureaucratic hour had been thankfully completed, I turned my beeper back on and called the page operator to advise her to send the appropriate page calls to me instead of the Dean. The page operator breathed an intense sigh of relief, for reasons I don't begin to understand.

But the next day, I received a threatening call from the Dean's office. I referred the call to Blow. Less than an hour later I received an apology for the misunderstanding from the Dean himself, and even appreciation for all the voluntary effort I was putting toward the strategic napping initiative. I was told to expect a written commendation for being the first participant, for apparently I had performed nobly and well, with fortitude and integrity.

I rather thought so myself.

Chapter 11

Punk Rock Medicine

It was a strange concept, of uncertain meaning, but I liked the idea right off the bat.

Punk Rock Medicine, or PRM in common medical parlance, was the brain child of a young respiratory therapist who had wanted to be a doctor for many years, but despised bureaucracy, systems, rigidity, insurance companies, control, in-the-box thinking, idiocy, and morons—all the centerpieces of the modern medical system. The young man didn't have a chance. If he became a doctor, he would self-implode in an explosion of expletive excretion. Perhaps only I stood between him and his goal of utter personal destruction. That and the painful process one has to go through to get into medical school.

"Pal," which is what I called him, "Pal, you will make a great doctor, of that I have no doubt. But being a doctor isn't the only way to help people, you know. You help people as a respiratory therapist. You create value in the world by helping people breathe, and I hear that breathing is almost as important as sex."

"I know, I know," said Pal. "But I want to be a doctor. I

wanna be a doctor. I wanna be a doctor."

It was pitiful. I was tortured, horrified, disgusted. That had been me six years ago. In some ways, I had aged twenty years in the past six years, but then I had regressed twenty-five years in the past one year. I was like a mature wizened cynical teenage toddler. But, I could help Pal out.

I hired him to work for me directly. Now, I was an intern and of course couldn't hire anyone, nor pay anyone, because I got paid remarkably poorly. Young doctors make shockingly little money for people who have attended school, and performed well at it for twenty years. So, by 'hiring Pal' I mean I took him under my wing. He was too worthwhile to allow to get sucked into the goat rodeo shoveling sheep shit around the Sheep's Pen.

First, Pal needed to see how a guy who thinks like him gets by in the medical field. It turns out I think like him, or he like me, in many ways. Second, Pal needed to see that doctors aren't special heroes, but just regular folk.

So I hooked him up with Dr. Blow, who thinks like me, and thinks like Pal, without thinking like either of us, and sure as hell isn't a regular folk.

Now Pal knew Blow, just a little, from some intersecting times in the Intensive Care Unit. But Blow didn't really know Pal yet. Pal could range from highly respectful to outright irreverent depending on with whom he happened to be talking. He had an amazing ability to sense assholes. He called his asshole sensor his 'AADAR' and it was pretty much smack on the money. When his AADAR got set off, he quickly shifted the gears on his 10-speed racing bike of a brain into full 10th gear irreverency. But if his AADAR didn't go off, he was in the first gear of full respectfulness. With new people, he was in first gear (full respectfulness) until his AADAR beeped. Or until he had started liking the new person, in which case he would start shifting up and down through the gears, increasing and decreasing his irreverency based on time of day, phases of the moon, and most importantly, on the inanity of whatever conversation was currently ongoing.

Blow was definitely no asshole and didn't cause the AADAR to beep or alarm, and Pal's respectfulness was in first gear for their initial time together. But Pal soon had Blow pegged pretty well, and by the time that Blow was next on service as the ward attending, Pal had lubed up his gears and was planning on shifting through them.

"We have a visitor for a couple of weeks," Blow said to the flock of ego-boosters, consisting of medical students and interns who followed him around the Sheep's Pen on rounds like ducklings follow their mother duck. "Pal, can you introduce yourself?"

"Sure," said Pal. "My name is Donald. But my mama calls me Jemima. You can call me Daffy."

Pal sounded like Forrest Gump.

"What do you do, Daffy?" asked Blow, wondering where Pal was going to go with this.

"I used to run a coffee shop, but now I run a coffee shop. Plus I like taking care of patients, so I do that too, while drinking coffee." Pal took a sip of his coffee.

"You're a respiratory therapist, aren't you?" Blow knew full well that he was.

"In my spare time I am. But I'm thinking about going to medical school, and Dr. Marcus thought it would be a good idea to hang with all'y'all for a while."

Blow decided it was time to start toying with Pal, the way Pal was toying with him. "Pal, I know you were raised in the Bible belt. Can you lead off rounds today with a prayer?"

"I would be honored," said Pal with some extra southern in his accent. "Dear Lawd, I just want to thank you for this hospital, this mighty fortress of healin' and worship. I just want to thank you for the nourishment that is provided to us by the cafeteria food. I just want to thank you Lawd for giving us this time of fellowship, residencyship, and internship together. Bless these rounds as we round around the ward today. Bless Dr. Blow for rounding the rounds with this team, and bless we egoboosters as we consume nectar of the gods to stay awake, and bless the nectar of the gods that I sell in my coffee shop that doesn't exist. Lawd, make the Walls strong and thick and send the Sieves to burn in the almighty heat of the fires of hell laid out by you in your infinite wisdom and glory. Amen."

"Amen," was repeated in gentle appreciation from around the team of white-coated folk.

"What is a Sieve?" asked one of the med students.

Blow replied, "A Sieve is an ER doctor that admits to the ward every patient that comes into the ER, in order to cover his ass and take no risks. A Sieve can rarely be comfortable sending a patient home. A Wall is an ER doctor that never lets any patients through the ER and into the wards. When you're on call, you will appreciate the Walls and despise the Sieves."

As expected, it turned out that Pal was really good at the practice of medicine. Within a day he was helping the medical students figure out the EMR, he was helping the interns choose strategic nap witnesses, and he was helping the nurses recognize how attractive he was. The nurses liked him because he wasn't a doctor. In the occasional downtimes and at night on call, the students and interns liked to hang out with him. He was about their age, but he had years of real-world hospital experience under his belt. He had less education but more smarts. Less student debt, and more wisdom. And when not on call, Pal introduced the interns and medical students, and the nurses, to the best bars where it turns out he made more money than by being an RT. He hustled pool.

After a couple of weeks of clinical rounds with Blow, he had a better handle on what it would be like to be a medical student, an intern, and a rounding attending, and decided instead to continue being a respiratory therapist while earning his Ph.D. in Physiology, invent things, and get rich.

A good respiratory therapist is central to the maintenance of an intern's sanity. There is nothing, absolutely nothing, that a respiratory therapist hasn't nebulized or tried to nebulize. Nebulization is the way we make medicines suitable for inhalation. A nebulizer incorporates a small air compressor used to turn liquids into tiny inhalable particles, just the same size as dust mite feces and talcum powder, perfectly shaped to settle into your lungs. Asthmatics are treated with nebulized medicines.

I needed caffeine. The RT room would have a nice inhaled espresso for me if I called in advance. Pal was there, killing time, thinking up new ideas for unusual machines to attach to mechanically ventilated patients. Measure this, measure that, whatever, it doesn't matter, because patients who were that sick still died, or lived. Nothing anyone had ever measured, nothing anyone had ever tried to do, made any damn difference. Yet. But Pal was trying to change that.

But right now, he was trying to change a piece of plastic on a respiratory nebulizer machine that was going to give me the caffeine fix I so ardently required. It seems that Pal had left a few critical pieces of my coffee apparatus at the bar last night, where he was using them to make inhalable tequila. A bit of saline and a squirt of lime mixed with a teaspoon of tequila, inhale ad lib. Your lungs are a straight shot to your brain of course, with the blood from there completely bypassing your liver. Nebulized alcohol is the way to go. High potency tequila shots, at a fraction of the cost. A fifth would last five times as long. One teaspoon of inhaled tequila was as strong as a swallowed full shot, but ten times faster in its assault on your brain. That it assaults your lungs on the way by is only a minor issue. It ain't like smoking crack at least. It ain't a hot oxidized toxic poisonous compound filled with contaminants and carcinogens. Nah. Tequila is just a cool toxic poisonous compound filled with worm guts.

Pal was working on an optimized delivery method for inhaled booze, designing liquid concoctions that would be tolerated by the lungs, and may even make the lungs healthier. He had the notion that he could make a killing on it. The Food and Drug Administration wouldn't care, so there was a chance for him. It wasn't a food or drug, after all, it was booze. It wasn't the Food and Drug and Booze Administration. There was no law against inhaling booze. Not yet. No doubt they would make a law to prevent it. Remember, 'they' are the people who make rules. When 'we' make rules, we are 'they'.

Pal was struggling, rushing to get the bits of plastic aligned in the correct way to assure that my caffeine inhalation fix was safe and potent. There was a leak in the plastic tubing and the whole room smelled like a Starbucks while bits of suspended high-pressure-extracted espresso coffee droplets circulated into the ventilation ducts and out into the nearby ICU nursing station.

Nurse Maid was working in the ICU tonight. The last thing I needed was for her to OD on inhaled caffeine. She was hard enough to handle sober. I rushed out to the nursing station to perform a biochemical warfare biosafety inspection, assuring the nurses that they were in no danger, and most importantly assuring myself that I would be in no danger later when Nurse Maid would have come off her caffeine OD that thankfully wasn't going to happen.

When I returned, Pal was twisted underneath a medical machine of such excessive complexity that it must have been invented by the devil herself. The green scrub pants covered most of Pal's butt, the remaining sunlit portion of which smiled up at me in a most disquieting manner. I wanted my caffeine, badly.

"Hey, Vent Jockey, I want my coffee, badly," I said, indicating that I wanted my coffee badly.

"I think I got it figgered out," said Pal in a voice muffled by the screwdriver held between his teeth. "The honswaggle was switched with the freens, and so the pressure popoff was blowing out."

I had no desire, motivation, energy, or interest in trying to translate what he said because it was so terribly important.

"Can I get my fix now, Phlegm fetcher?" I asked, hopefully, needing, wanting, craving that extra boost of decoffeenated caffeine that would serve to keep me awake when everyone with self-respect, dignity, honor and sanity would be asleep. I stepped closer to the half-naked cheeks, which were really half-covered because I am a glass-half-full kinda guy. Pal squeezed his head around a corner of the blue metal plastic machine and reached his hand up toward me, holding within it a clear vial of all natural organic inhalable wakeup juice. I would have to stretch to reach for it, over the all-natural organic pink shining male buttocks. It was worth it. I can't believe I just said that.

After eight minutes of pure liquid purified caffeine, grown in the pure gardens of Colombia and exported directly to be imported directly into my lungs, I felt like a new man. Just before my inhalational invigoration, I had felt like an old man. Now I was ready to take on the night's duties. "Thanks, Snot sucker," I said to Pal, as I patted him on one of his pink cheeks. "You're a good friend."

My first duty was to take signout from the housestaff that had been covering the patients during the day. The housestaff consisted of first- through third-year residents who were tasked with primary caretaking of the patients. It used to be that patients were each individually assigned to one of the residents, and the residents were then always in charge of their care for the duration of their hospitalization, of course always under the indirect supervision of the attending physicians. In that way the residents of those days took full ownership of the patients. But now, because of the ACGME rules, the residents only took ownership of the patients for the hours that they were on duty, signing over full responsibility to the doctors on-call for the night. This was one of the many components of the conversion of medicine from a profession into the equivalent of a toll collector on a highway. Punch out at the end of the day, sign off on responsibility, go watch American Idol and the Kardashians as they Take New York, and come back the next day to address the problems of the next day. Not the patients, the problems.

It was not uncommon for the residents to refer to their patients by room number: "729 hasn't had a BM in three days." The dehumanization was a secondary impact of the deprofessionalization. The deprofessionalization was part of the Core Competencies curriculum that were, in the minds of the ACGME, central to medical education, and were therefore demanded by the ACGME, the organization previously referred to as the self-empowered authority over all medical teaching in the nation. The Core Competencies were stolen from nursing school curricula, were never in any way tested in medical residencies before being mandated for doctors, and were the most unprofessional set of rules that any professional would encounter in their profession. The most relevant Core Competency was called 'Professionalism'.

Each of the residents now gets evaluated frequently based on the six Core Competencies as dictated by ACGME. My favorite attending—Dr. Blow of course—was the best evaluator. On my first formal report, he wrote about me under the Professionalism Core Competency section the following:

"Dr. Marcus strives every day to be more professionalism. He considers being professionalism to be the most important component of medical training."

Another Core Competency is called "Systems-Based Practice". Here I truly did deserve kudos, because who else of my junior status had contributed as extensively as I had to the medical system of the hospital? Frig'o'graphs, strategic napping assistants, policies to assure that money flows out of the dysfunctional American medical system and into the hands of orphaned children in Africa. I got straight A's from Blow in "Systems-Based Practice" even though he had no idea what Systems-Based Practice meant. Neither did I. Neither did the administrators who enforced Systems-Based Practice at the hospital on behalf of the ACGME administrators, who also didn't know what the term meant.

Blow loved evaluating my abilities as a doctor based on the mandatory ACGME delineated 'Professionalismistic Quality Improvement Characteristics'. According to this system, I was a helluva good doctor.

In any event, I took sign-out from the housestaff as quickly as possible, because Kim Kardashian was going to be doing nothing on television soon, and therefore the people signing out their patients to me felt strongly motivated to do so quickly so they could rush home and watch Kim Kardashian do her nothing of importance as she Took New York. I kept thinking about the movie *Idiocracy* and how incredibly prophetic it was. Pretty soon, dumbed-down doctors would be rushing home to turn on the next episode of the new reality show *"Ow, My Bawls!"* so as to see all the new ways one can smash one's balls.

After sign out, I got a call from Blow. Wouldn't you know. It would be fun. Any call from Blow was an opportunity to learn.

Chapter 12

What an Ass I Am

"You can handle this, Eddie," Blow told me, which is when I knew I had no chance of handling it. "He probably has chrome-induced ischemia with resulting incarceritis." That means chest pain that occurs out of the blue after a criminal is arrested, handcuffed and taken to jail. But that isn't what this criminal had. I had never had a patient like this. Blow dumped this one on me in order to make me a national celebrity. I already was a national celebrity in my mind, so to be one for real had real meaning to me. I was grateful to Blow. I loved Blow.

My patient, Tom, had been shot in the right shoulder. The bullet had gone through flesh not bone, although it had torn a little muscle tissue out through the skin in an injury that looked like a tablespoon of tomato bisque. It was an injury that would need treatment with a bit of salt water, a gauze pad, some antibiotics and two rows of nine stitches.

I was a Family Practice intern, not on a surgical rotation currently, so why was Blow getting me involved in a minor surgical case now, you ask? Because Tom was special, that's why. Now, every patient is special, but Tom was extra special.

The surgeons had consulted Family Practice because they had some non-surgical questions about this special patient. In this case, Tom's brother had once had a rash when he was given a drug like Ancef, which is a great cephalosporin-class antibiotic for anyone who has been shot, and the surgeons thought it was appropriate to ask me if there was any reason to be concerned, since they wanted to give Tom Ancef and were worried about an allergic reaction. You see, surgeons don't like treating rashes, and they prefer to think about anatomy, not biology. They don't generally take care of siblings of patients. They don't enjoy paying much attention to the hearts or lungs except to make sure those organs are healthy enough to tolerate surgery. To a surgeon, the heart is primarily a pump to get Ancef to a wound. Many surgeons will turf anything remotely non-surgical to whomever's beeper number first comes to mind. It turned out the beeper code for the covering Family Practice Attending (Dr. Blow) was the only number that wasn't intentionally smudged to the point of illegibility in the dry erase markers used on the whiteboard to keep track of who is on call for consultation to the Emergency Department. So when the surgical resident looked to find someone who could help Tom, he found Blow, who found me.

Okay, the surgeons had a sensible question, I had to admit. Allergies to antibiotics can kill occasionally, and rarely—very rarely—these allergies may run in a family. Despite everything I have ever said, never said, or thought in the previous paragraphs, I have to admit that almost all surgeons are thoroughly thoughtful doctors, and intensely competent. One of the characteristics most important for a good doctor is the awareness of what one does *not* know, and a willingness to seek help, even when it puts your ego at risk to do so.

Everyone knows that most surgeons have enormous

doses of overselfconfidence. Hyperego. But heck, they 1) deserve to, and 2) have to. They *have* to because nowadays they have to cut through a patient's skin without making scars, avoid nerves, avoid pain, avoid mistakes, avoid avoidable injury, and in so doing assuredly resolve whatever disease the patients has, because if they don't do all of those things, they risk lawsuits from the patients, and they risk being blamed for the original disease that they worked so hard to cure, and that they had trained for eleventy years to maximize their chance of curing, and they risk having to hear about the patient getting to spend their lawsuit winnings sailing a yacht to Vegas. All while the surgeon, who had tried very conscientiously to cure the patient, gets to work a hundred hours per week trying to cure disease in others, while preventing lawsuits from other uneducated over-demanding cave-dwelling reality-show watchers.

So a surgeon needs to have an ego larger than the full grown-progeny of Montana and Texas. Ego is necessary to defend oneself against internal or external critiques. The ego has a shocking ability to defend against such critiques, and it has no ability or desire to discriminate between appropriate constructive criticism and inappropriate obnoxious criticism. An example of inappropriate obnoxious criticism can be found in most any article written by most any movie or food critic.

The ego *will defend* you against any criticism, anytime, anyplace. It is always loyal to you even when its actions are destroying you. Everyone has an ego. The size and power of the ego is designed to balance the self-esteem with the size and importance of the potential critiques

The male surgeon is the prototype for the high-self-esteem individual. The high self-esteem individual often leads an unexamined life, in the words of Socrates. Their ego utterly ignores small critiques, blowing them off entirely. No need to contend with them, because those critiques are no threat. This is what the nurses perceive as obnoxious, cocky, smug, arrogant, conceited, swaggering—this lack of any ability to give any credence whatsoever to any small suggestions for improvement. But the surgeon's ego isn't designed to deal with small critiques, because the potential critiques on surgeons aren't small. They are enormous. Major morbidity type of critiques. Death-of-patient type critiques. Think about that. A surgeon spends twelve years of school before college, four years in college, four years in medical school, and five to seven years in residency and fellowship to prepare to operate on you. That is, let me see, about twenty-six years of school. All that work and a huge chunk of one's life is dedicated to being prepared to NOT do it wrong. Yet wrong happens. Can you imagine how small a mistake it takes for a patient to die in surgery? Can you imagine what it would be like to spend your whole life preparing to do something and then doing it wrong? Can you imagine doing it so wrong that it kills a patient? Can you imagine how you would feel about your life if you, just once, *sucked,* after all that preparation? The surgical ego has to be strong enough to deal with that, because otherwise the surgeon would suffer complete utter collapse when the inevitable mistake does happen. The surgeon's ego is what it is, because it has to be.

So, I love it when a surgeon knows what they don't know and admits to it. That means that they are willing to listen to their own self-critiques. And that means that, at least for that moment, the surgeon isn't obnoxious, cocky, smug, arrogant, conceited or swaggering. He is just wise. I loved the surgeons.

I hated the surgeons for consulting me for a brother's past rash that wasn't even there anymore. Damn egotistical obnoxious cocky smug conceited arrogant bastards thinking that my time was less valuable than theirs.

So I had to interview Tom's brother about his rash. Tom's brother's name was Jerry, of course. To abide by federal privacy policies, first I had to get permission from Tom to allow me to ask his brother health questions related to Tom. Then I had to ask Jerry permission to ask about his rash. It had occurred years ago, after Jerry had been prescribed ampicillin—an antibiotic chemically related to Ancef. He had been given the ampicillin for strep throat and had developed a rash a week later, about the same time that he was diagnosed with Mononucleosis. 490 dollars of tests later, or no money spent on tests at all, would provide to me the same conclusion: the reaction was a classic combination of ampicillin with infectious Mono. This was not an allergic rash, just an immunologic rash. There was no concern here about a fatal anaphylactic reaction. The surgeons should be able to treat the bullet-induced aeration of Tom's shoulder with the Ancef.

Tom had been shot by a police officer when he tried to avoid arrest for a crime, an horrific crime of which he had been accused, quite literally with a smoking gun in his hand. The crime was murder. He had reportedly shot a man three times in the chest. Dead. Tom's brother Jerry had tried to prevent him from shooting the man, but had failed. What followed next was a major scuffle. Jerry had punched Tom and took the gun. Tom punched Jerry and tried to get to the gun. Jerry dragged Tom to the ground. They had thrashed around, wrestling in fraternal enmity, locked in each other's grasp so firmly that the police officers that arrived shortly thereafter were unable to pull them apart. Tom had reached the gun and one of the police officers decided to shoot him.

Tom's victim—a man whose death is relevant to my story, but whose life is not, lay dead on the ground not far away.

Tom's fingerprints were on the murder weapon. The police interviewed Jerry and learned the story. Tom was guilty as guilty could be. Yet he wouldn't spend a day in jail. In fact, he couldn't be kept in jail.

The police officer guarding Tom's Emergency Department room door pulled me aside. He said, "Doctor." Police officers and firemen were always highly respectful of doctors. This is rather the opposite of government-employed social workers who think doctors are stupid. "Doctor, we are way over our heads here. We need you to keep a murderer off the streets for a bit while we sort things out. The surgeons are going to be done fixing his shoulder soon, and then they'll discharge him to us. We cannot lock him up, even though he is an accused murderer, and obviously guilty as hell. Is there anyway you can admit your patient to the hospital until we have time to figure out what to do?"

I understood the dilemma. The police were completely up the creek on this one. I figured this one might rock the legal world on its head, and yep, it sure would make me the national celebrity that I already was. There didn't seem to be a lot of choice as to what needed to be done. I had to lie to someone.

I lied to Tom, as well as his brother Jerry, who was sitting next to Tom on the side of the bed. Tears were in the eyes of both the brothers.

"I think it is best if I admit you to the hospital for a while. It *is* a gunshot wound after all, and it may get infected. I think intravenous antibiotics for a couple of days would be wise."

Actually, the wound probably didn't need more than one dose of Ancef, but that was beside the point. Patients don't expect their doctors to lie and therefore are willing believers. Doctors don't lie much, so don't worry. But this was a special case. Tom was a special patient.

I talked to the surgeons, who were grateful beyond measure for my willingness to take on what would be no doubt an administrative and media storm as I admitted a murderer to the hospital. The insurance company would no doubt reject the effort to get the admission authorized, because quite truly Tom had no requirement of being hospitalized. I would have to stretch the severity of his injury substantially to obtain insurance company approval. But since I didn't talk to insurance companies, the clipboard-carrying compliance officer nurse person—who was employed by the hospital to help the insurance companies capture criminal doctors trying to admit their patients to the hospital when they should have been getting sicker at home—would assuredly have trouble justifying to the insurance company the need to stay in hospital. But even she had common sense and might, just might help in the endeavor. For this was an unusual situation.

Tom and his brother, tears still in their eyes, nodded acquiescence to the need for admission.

"Maybe," said Jerry, "this will give us time to sort things out as brothers. Time before jail."

In my calming manner as a calming physician, I foolishly said without any hesitation, "I hear there will be no jailtime."

Tom's eyes—the eyes of an impassioned murderer—opened wide, revealing hope where moments before there had been only despair. "You think?"

"Yes, I think. But it will be a mess, an absolute mess. Look, I'm your doctor now, and I want to help you. After you get upstairs, I'd like to talk with you for a while. Talk with you both, if you don't mind." I said this last as I looked at Jerry, who also had some hope in his eyes for the first time.

I spent the next three hours researching on line the issues that were so obvious to everybody, but apparently had never before been addressed in the legal world. It was pointless to call any of my lawyer friends because they wouldn't have a clue on this one, and I used to feel guilty about having lawyer friends. The sad truth is that many of my friends are lawyers. Now I don't feel guilty about liking them. I think they are better than the doctors, because the doctors have let the system become horrible, without doing anything. At least the lawyers chose law school as opposed to participating in the health system's collapse, as the doctors were doing, including me. So I was no less proud of being a friend to lawyers than I was of being a friend to myself. I would have to address that cognitive dissonance after I dealt with this current criminal law emergency.

After I did my thorough professional three-hour google research on a legal matter about which I knew nothing and had no training, I became what is probably the world's expert on the matter at hand. But there were ethical consequences, so I needed to commune with my ethical advisors. I called Nurse Maid, because I was due for a supervised nap.

"Jennifer," I said, using her name because I know women like to hear their names when they have been made love to, and because I knew her name, "Jennifer, what do you think is the *right* thing to do about this? Tom killed a man but can't go to jail. What can be done?"

Nurse Maid looked at me and kissed my forehead. "Why did he kill the man?"

"He killed the man to defend his brother, Jerry, from the emotional abuse that the man was continuously abusing him with abusively. The man that Tom killed kept taunting Jerry. Jerry never responded, but the man kept digging at him. Every time Jerry came near this guy, the man would hurl insults and invectives. It made Jerry feel horrible, and it built up over many years. Tom heard these insults too, but they were never directed at him, only Jerry. Jerry was losing self-esteem. He was getting depressed, anxious, insisting on staying in bed all day, not exercising, not eating at all. He wasn't bathing. You know, all the signs of a severe depressional collapse. Tom could take the insults, but not the loss of his brother's self-esteem. One day Tom just couldn't stand it anymore. Tom told the man that if he ever came by again, he would kill him. When the man did come harass his brother again, Tom kept his promise and killed him."

"I would think that the man deserved it, almost."

"Maybe, but it wasn't up to Tom to determine that. Tom killed a man. End of that issue. Established fact. The man he killed was armed only with meanness, and wasn't directing his angst at Tom, but just to Jerry."

"It's sort of an assault," replied Nurse Maid. "Sort of. Heck, if that man was emotionally abusing your brother, wouldn't you consider him to be *assaulting* your brother?"

"Maybe. But if my brother was an adult, as Jerry certainly is, I would consider that my brother should handle it himself."

"Tom loved his brother so much that he was willing to kill a man, and go to jail for it, to protect him? That sounds like a loving brother."

I slapped my forehead. It occurred to me, finally. "Yep, and that is the spin we need for the media. This situation is so screwed up that all we need to do is to make Tom look like a hero who loved his brother. We throw in a few other spins about self-defense too, and we could make this happen."

"Self-defense?" queried Nurse Maid. "That won't be spin at all."

"No, it won't be." I rolled to get out of bed, but Nurse Maid was in my way. Blast it.

"Eddie, your mandatory supervised nap-time isn't over yet. Do you want me to report you?"

I didn't. I had gotten in too much trouble with the administration lately. I didn't want another report that might prompt them to insist I go to another diversity-in-napping training session. Plus, these naps weren't so bad.

When my mandatory strategic napping session had been successfully concluded, I emerged and jaunted forth to the ward, on which my exciting new patient should be receiving his unnecessary doses of Ancef. Before I had a chance to get to the room, I heard a scuffle at the far end of the ward. I looked to see about 66 news-reporters and 6 cameras coming like a mass of hornets down the hallway toward the nursing station.

I quickened my pace and ducked into the hospital room to see Tom there, with his brother as always beside him, supporting him, holding his hand.

"Gentlemen, I don't have time to tell you my plan. The reporters are here. I'm going to do my best to settle this issue fast. Do you trust me?"

Tom and Jerry, still morose and harried, both nodded solemnly.

I popped out to the ward, where the Unit Coordinator was trying to corral the demanding swarm of satanic rodent-insects into a far-too-small conference room. I had to act quickly before the cave-dwellers from the adminosphere and lawyers from the hospital showed up on the scene to screw everything up and take all the celebrity attention away from me. I needed that important attention to 1) sell my book that I would never write, and 2) be elected to public office for which I had no intention or desire to ever run.

"Liars and Ingenuousmen of the Press," I began speaking into the hubbub and noise, barely audible. But there was a rapid silence just after I spoke, for I was wearing a long white coat and a stethoscope around my neck. The stethoscope around my neck was known as flea collar—usually the mark of an internist, who were commonly called “fleas” by other doctors for their tendency to be the last things to jump off a dying body, generally to another dying body. Anyway, my flea collar and white coat were badges of medical authority and the swarm of locusts in front of me were mostly young, enthusiastic little media turds who were obviously easily swayed by my carefully manicured appearance of professionalismness.

“Ladies and gentlemen of the press,” I repeated. “I am Dr. Eddie Marcus, and I am in charge of the patient about whom you are seeking information. Why don’t you ask me questions in an orderly manner, and we can take care of this business.”

The locusts embarked on an immediate vocal swarm, each shouting as loud as they could to get their question to the front of the line to be answered by this most important doctor standing in front of them. I didn’t particularly like the questions that I heard initially, so I made my own up.

Holding my hands up to calm the multitude, I said, “The first question I heard is, “Do you think the killing was justified? From what I have heard, the killing was not only justified, but necessary to prevent injury to his brother and to himself. The victim of the killing was himself effectively killing both Tom and Jerry, that is obvious to anyone knowledgeable.”

Another series of questions were shouted at me, even louder this time. I didn’t care for any of these questions either.

“Yes, that is correct,” I answered to everyone and no one in particular, making no reference to the question that I was in no way attempting to answer. All eyes were on me, and all eyes were confused. “No, that is not accurate,” I added for emphasis. Then I nodded, and then shook my head and said, “There is some truth to that possibility.” Nobody had a clue, which was the natural state of reporters, so they were feeling pretty much at home.

Sadly, it got somewhat boring after I had spent all this time informing them of nothing at all. So I said, "Of course I cannot answer any medical questions about my patients. What did you think? That because you are reporters you have some right to get private information handed to you on a platter? Well, I will not share patient information. Except that the man that was killed had leveled a constant assault on Jerry. That assault caused Jerry to get so depressed that he was unable to eat or get out of bed, and Tom was compelled to protect himself from this assault. Tom acted out of love for his brother, and in his own self-defense. Self-defense."

As a result of this argument, I got my ten minutes of fame and was interviewed all over the country for almost a week, because the media liked the self-defense argument that I had formulated, even though it was lousy. The police loved it. The cliché district attorney—eager to get re-elected—loved it. The talk shows loved it, boy did they love it. Everyone loved it. Because it could barely, just barely, be believable. And that could allow Tom to not go to prison, which otherwise he assuredly would have for killing a man in cold blood. You see, it was impossible to put Tom in prison for the crime he committed and that his brother had fought to prevent. Impossible. Tom was guilty as can be. But Jerry was utterly entirely innocent. There was no legal justification to incarcerate Jerry. You can't put an innocent man in jail in this country. At least not yet. So they needed an excuse, any excuse, to let Tom go. And I gave it to them.

You see, Tom and Jerry were conjoined twins. Siamese twins, inseparable, attached at the thorax and sharing one very loving, oversized, heart.

Chapter 13

Overdosing on Drug Reps

As a celebrity, I now get invited to all the big medical get-togethers in town. Of course *everyone* gets invited to all the big medical get-togethers in town, because they are put on by the pharmaceutical reps, who are trying to sell you drugs. Why the drug reps are selling drugs to doctors is beyond me. They should be inviting the patients to big free dinners and selling *them* the drugs, but they know better because the patients don't pay for the medication themselves very often in this country, and seem to have voluntarily given up any authority to choose medications based on value, cost or anything else. So, the drug reps perhaps should be inviting insurance companies and government bureaucrats to big dinners, because it is the insurance companies and government bureaucrats that make most of the choices that sink or swim a pharmaceutical rep's sales numbers. Recently, the drug dinners for doctors have been cut back a lot. We are told it is because the pharmaceutical companies are becoming more concerned about ethics. But I think it is because the drug companies now are buying yachts, whores, and golf carts for the bureaucrats and insurance company decision-makers instead of for the doctors like they used to. But that's just my thought.

There were still the occasional pharma dinners though. There were still efforts to turn the doctors into drug-prescribing profit centers for big pharma. The beautiful blond pantsuited pharma rep that you weren't supposed to be able to keep your eyes off of, who intentionally exuded subtle sexuality and perfectly coordinated flirtatiousness, would invite the doctors to a dinner, next Wednesday, at the best restaurant in the city, at which there would be a brief presentation by an expert from out of town. The doctors used to bring their spouses to these events and would come in droves, but now the spouses weren't allowed to come—as a result of some semi-law, I think. And now the doctors mostly didn't come either. So the pharma reps turned to their newest manipulation. They turned to the thought-leaders.

What the heck is a *thought-leader,* you may ask thoughtfully. The term 'thought-leader' was developed by someone somewhere sometime (surprisingly substantially after 1984). However, for ease of explanation, let's assume it was created or adopted by a high-level marketing muck-a-muck in *very* big pharma who wanted to manipulate the entire medical profession by one giant boondoggle into prescribing more of their most profitable medications. Along comes evidence-based medicine and with it 'the thought-leader'.

A thought-leader is a doctor with political impact on the prescribing practices of their fellow physicians by person-to-person communications and by writing journal articles that get read (as opposed to journal articles that just fill an academic's curriculum vitae). But most importantly, a thought-leader is a doctor who has impact on the writing of the evidence-based medical guidelines for the management of a given disease, a disease of importance to the sales of the profitable on-patent medications being purveyed by the large pharma companies.

Large pharmaceutical companies are marketing companies. Internal Research and Development has shrunk to being a small portion of their efforts. Large pharma now farms out their research, and does so by acquiring new drugs from small companies that haven't yet become mired in bureaucracy. Don't let large pharma fake you out by saying how important they are to modern medical research. They are useful only because they buy small companies that *are* important to that research. However, they are important to modern medicine because they are the Madison Avenue of health care. Large pharma companies are intensely effective marketing organizations, and in a modern way, snake oil salesmen. No, they don't sell stuff that doesn't work, like the snake-oil salesman of the early 1900's that our Food and Drug Administration was created in part to stop. No, I said *modern* snake oil salesman, the kind that our Food and Drug Administration was created to encourage. The modern snake oil salesman sells you stuff that works, but it really doesn't work any better than the much much much cheaper stuff that is no longer profitable to sell because it is off patent and generics have come in to bring prices down. Neither FDA nor Large Pharma are terribly excited about the poor people getting stuff that only the rich used to be able to afford, so they work tirelessly together, in a sort of psychotic love-hate relationship, to stop such from happening.

And indeed, what has been created for our benefit is a medical economy that is a confabulation of rules, regulations and fraud. Sometimes the companies create diseases that didn't even exist before in order to sell drugs to people who weren't sick until they were told they were sick. Other times it is less egregiously fraudulent, but fraudulent nonetheless. Let's take the case of a prototypical new pharma blockbuster drug. It could be any of the big blockbusters. A new asthma inhaler, a new cholesterol lowering drug, a new anti-depressant, a new drug for attention deficit disorder. It doesn't matter. Let's call this drug 'Esgetbeteral'. In any event, Esgetbeteral is a drug that treats whatever disease you want it to. Let's say asthma. Esgetbeteral is manufactured and sold by LPC, Inc. (Large Pharma Corporation, Incorporated), and is in actuality essentially the same drug as Getbeteral, which was a long-standing highly successful and worthwhile treatment for asthma. But Getbeteral came off patent and the resulting generic competition caused revenues for LPC to fall, as the drug had to be sold for so much less money in order to compete with the generics. Lots more patients received this good drug inexpensively. Patients were happy, but LPC wasn't making as much money as they wanted. Now, in the good ol' days, LPC would invent a new drug for the next disease that was needing to be treated or cured. They would patent it and earn an excellent and honest return for an excellent and honest helpful new drug that made people healthier. But this is not the good ol' days. We now live in the days of rampant and expected fraud. So here is what happens now:

LPC, intellectually bankrupt and bureaucratically mired, but rolling in dough from their previous earned success with Getbeteral, has their R and D department perform a tiny little chemical tweak to Getbeteral, and calls this "new" drug Esgetbeteral and patents it. It doesn't work any better than Getbeteral, but that is okay, because they can make it *look* like it works better. How? By performing studies just the right way, and leveraging the evil collectivist mentality of evidence-based medicine, that's how. The large pharma company carefully designs the study, and enrolls enough patients to make doctors—who have now all been brainwashed to think that evidence-based medicine is predicate to the gospels of Matthew, Mark, Luke, John, and the Law of Yahveh himself—believe that the study must report the truth. Then large pharma performs lots and lots of tests on the patients in a huge study as they compare the Esgetbeteral to Getbeteral. By statistical Las Vegas/Atlantic City/Native American Casino/Mississippi River boat chance alone, a couple of these tests (known as "outcome variables" to make them sound more official), show that Esgetbeteral performed better than Getbeteral did. Now, here is the trick. It takes only a shockingly small study to prove that there is a "statistically significant" better outcome for one drug than another when the better drug is importantly better, really better in a way that matters. However, when a company knows that a new drug may only be, at most, *very slightly* better, then they know it will need a large study to be able to show that tiny little improvement to be statistically significant. And statistically significant, regardless of whether it has any clinical significance at all, is what the young doctors have been brainwashed to think is important, and what the older academic doctors have brainwashed themselves to think. The net effect is that the less useful a new drug is, the larger the clinical studies will have to be to prove its 'worth'. Yet the larger the clinical study performed, the more powerful the new drug will be in the minds of the doctors brainwashed by groupthink, even when the new drug is no more effective at all.

So the new drug, although no more effective than the old drug, is thought by the medical masses to be 'proven in large clinical studies to be more effective' and is prescribed as a result of that. Of course a massive marketing campaign to the doctors and patients encourages these prescriptions. The new drug is on patent, and therefore it is much more expensive than the now generically competing old stuff, but the new stuff has momentum, and the patients aren't paying the difference in price anyway, so they don't care. Most of us have tax-incentivized health insurance to pay for medications, which makes most of us not care about caring. The patient wants the best, since it costs no more, even if it really isn't the best. The large pharma companies buy a few more yachts for the medical directors of the insurance companies and a few more whores for the bureaucrats while concurrently appealing to their ethics by convincing them that large studies show that the new drug is better than the old drug and they better not keep the newest and best from being available to their clients and voters. Bureaucrats and insurance companies cave to the pressure and bribery, and Bingo, we have the next blockbuster drug.

Esgetbeteral is no better than Getbeteral, but Large Pharma Company sells it like crazy, insurance companies raise their premiums to cover the expense, making health insurance then get more expensive. As a result, less people or companies can afford health insurance, thus increasing the number of the uninsured, so the government makes a law that forces mandatory health insurance, which doesn't make it more affordable but does increase the number of laws we unwittingly break everyday. I have Professor Bastiat from Chicago to thank for my understanding of all this. Remember him? I do. I remember the lessons I learn from patients. In contrast, I rarely remember a damn thing that I read in a medical journal.

So, what is that "thought-leader?" As I mentioned, thought-leaders are the people who write the treatment guidelines. The guidelines purport to be better at managing a patient than the doctor who is actually in the examining room with the patient. The guidelines assume that the patient in the exam room, that room so far away in time and geography from the room in which the guidelines were written, is just like every other patient on the planet, or at least a clone of the average patient enrolled in the large pharma companies' clinical studies on which the evidence-based guidelines are based. The guidelines never see the patient, yet assume authority to profess what has become essentially mandatory treatment regimens, the only regimens approved for payment by the insurance companies or government, and the only regimens which will pass JCAHO's quality improvement mandates. And passing JCAHO's quality improvement mandates is the only thing hospital administrators care about, because if they don't pass, the administrators might get spanked by nobody and nothing bad will happen.

The thought-leader that LPC, Inc. brought from out of town on this given Wednesday was going to give us a nice talk on the substantial benefits of Esgetbeteral in the management of our asthma patients.

I walked into the fine and locally-famous French restaurant Wednesday evening, post-call, exhausted, still in scrubs, with my hair tussled and my armpits evanescent. The feeling of post-call grime and stickiness is not just superficial, but goes deep into one's being. All I wanted was to fall asleep in a tub and let the shower on the wall shoot water at my body for two hours. But I had promised Tracy, gorgeous blond pharma rep Tracy with the tight black pants-suit (which is how I differentiated her from gorgeous blond pharma rep Elise with the tight black pants-suit), that I would come, and I didn't want to stand her up or hurt her feelings. This was an important night for her. I am sure her feelings would be hurt if I failed to show. Sure of it. And I think I mentioned, I don't like hurting anyone's feelings. Tracy needed doctors to come, not many, but some. Enough. Too few doctors would make the thought-leader from out of town feel like his time had been wasted and that was bad. Because, here is the secret: This whole evening wasn't about Tracy's thought-leader having an opportunity to convince us doctor-sheep to prescribe her company's new drug. No. The whole evening was about Large Pharma Company, Inc. getting more opportunity to influence the thought-leader to incorporate Esgetbeteral into the next set of asthma guidelines. That was the whole purpose, the point of the evening. The thought-leader—who was getting paid two-thousand dollars for his time and expertise—didn't know this fact. The doctors eating in the restaurant while listening to the thought-leader talk that night didn't know it. Of course I didn't know all this stuff at the time, myself. Even Tracy with the tight black pants-suit didn't know it. But you can bet two-thousand dollars to a doughnut that the marketing execs at LPC, Inc. knew exactly what the purpose was.

Because that thought-leader would be showing a bunch of doctors a bunch of powerpoint slides made by LPC, Inc. that preached the glories of Esgetbeteral. And then tomorrow, he would do it again in the next city, and then next month he would show them again somewhere else. He would be showing these slides over and over again, and putting his own reputation behind his words. Over time he would believe them more and more, indeed, he would *have to believe them,* in order to protect his own ego. And it would work, because he was only one of dozens of such thought-leaders lecturing to the sheep doctors of the country, and someday soon, those thought-leaders would all get together and write new guidelines that would dictate how all doctors everywhere must prescribe for their patients.

And, in an amazing scene of utter hypocrisy, the large

pharma companies themselves all got together, led by LPC, Inc. to self-regulate these evenings of drunken well-fed pharma marketing, so that the government wouldn't regulate them. And how did these oh-so-concerned ethically magnanimous large pharma companies choose to regulate themselves? By doing exactly what the government had threatened to do. That is to insist that the thought-leaders only present slides that are approved within the FDA regulatory oversight—only the material from the pharmaceutical package insert could be presented, and a few other large evidence-based clinical studies. No anecdotes, no reporting of personal experience was allowed within the framework of the evening's events, for fear that anecdotal, experience-based, patient-based medicine would contaminate the 'real' science of evidence-based medicine, and cause young naïve doctors to inappropriately prescribe medication that the experts at FDA and LPC had determined was suboptimal. The large pharma companies stood tall on their ethical platform to fight such horrific malfeasance, and so agreed in mutual self-regulation that only evidence-based medicine be presented in these marketing orgies. Which is, of course, precisely what they wanted in order to maximize their profits, because evidence-based medicine allowed for—and had come to mandate—the elimination of all common sense or individualization of health care, and said elimination meant they could sell more expensive drugs. There was no room for common sense or individualization of patient care in a medical system run by politicians, so common sense had to be expunged. And it had been.

"Hi Tracy," said I.

"Hi Eddie!" she responded with apparent glee and concurrent coyness, winking at me slightly. Tracy, like all the other pant-suits, could absolutely positively *not* be considered a dumb blond. She was smart, attractive, quick-witted, knowledgeable, well-trained, and highly professional. Not professional in the way that ACGME wants us young doctors to learn to be professionalismistic, but in terms of "geared for success". Tracy was top-flight. She knew my name immediately, although we had barely met. She was trying to impress me, because she didn't know that her real job was to make the thought-leader expert from out of town feel all warm and fuzzy.

She guided me over to the thought-leader, a Pakistani-Brit from London, who now taught and performed research at a major medical teaching center in New York. He had a fine accent that was a joy to hear, and a demeanor of wisdom and experience hard to match. He had large floppy lips and a bulging jaw that made him look like a fish. His name was known, but not outside of his subspecialty. He had been on the writing committee of the most recent set of asthma guidelines, so he was top-tier in the pharma list of big-wigs to influence...ummm, I mean to *leverage* for the sake of their excellent teaching ability so that the doctors of America could learn best practices.

"Dr. Marcus, I would like you to meet Dr. Nowittaleem. Dr. Nowittaleem, Dr. Marcus is one of the interns in Family Practice, but has made quite a name for himself already."

Dr. Nowittaleem looked at me out of the side of his face for a moment and said, "Ahhh yes. The Siamese Murdering Twins. Your patients, huh?"

I nodded. "Yes. It was an honor."

"Well, you sure did remove the judicial system from a pickle with that one. And just an intern, at that. How did you keep the senior doctors out of the headlights of the press?"

I laughed inside as I considered how little Dr. Blow would be willing to stand in the headlights of an oncoming reporter.

"It was easy. The senior doctors wanted nothing to do with it. I took the brunt, therefore."

"And you are now famous."

"And I'm famous. For a little while."

"So, Dr. Marcus, what are your plans?"

"I'm trying to figure out my plans now. First choice is to quit medicine while the getting is good, but I'm up to my eyeballs in debt, so I need to find a way to pay it. Second choice is to quit medicine, but I can't because I have too much debt. I'm leaning toward my third choice, which is quitting medicine, so that I can get a real job and pay off my debt. My other choices aren't as appealing because they don't allow me to pay off my debt."

Dr. Nowittaleem, although attuned to the ongoings ongoing in the world, was not attuned to the goings on in a mind as thoroughly befuddling as I thought my own mind was, and so he smiled with a genteel nod and turned away to the next doctor to whom Tracy in the tight black pant-suit was introducing him.

There were only a small handful of doctors who had accepted the invitation to come to the dinner. I recognized a couple of surgical interns, who couldn't care less about an asthma drug, but were single and wanted to schmooze Tracy. There were others in the room, and I soon discovered that they were nurses and unit coordinators. Tracy had obviously stacked the room with people to prevent the out-of-state expert with the cool accent from feeling his time was being wasted lecturing to an empty room. We all chatted for a while, I moving from person to person to get to know each in turn.

I drank some wine, on an empty stomach. I drank some more wine while dehydrated from my overnight call. I drank even more wine while being thoroughly sleep-deprived. With my instinctual depravity, I should have been aware that such wine drinking in my post-call state might lead me to say things that Tracy might not appreciate later.

During this time of my social imbibing, I felt increasingly light. When we all were requested to sit at the tables—lined up so that we could all see the slides projecting on an old white screen at one end of the room—I nestled in between two nurses I had not previously met. I didn't feel the need to nestle in between the two surgical interns, although they didn't feel snubbed by this because they seemed to have not even seen me, standing as I was in the same room as Tracy.

"Beth, what do you do?" I asked, sneaking a quick sniff of my corrupt armpit while pretending to wipe my nose on my sleeve. In retrospect, neither of those moves is likely to be appealing to a young nurse.

Beth had short dirty-blond hair, pale cheeks, was slightly chubby with a few well-placed freckles and a nice smile with one moderately crooked tooth in the front that was hardly visible unless one looked at her. She was perhaps 21 years old, probably straight out of nursing school.

She replied, "I am a nurse on 4 West. Trauma Surgical Unit."

"Wow," I replied, genuinely interested, although not intrigued. "How is that?"

"It's good. Fun. Scary sometimes. But I have lots that I can learn, and that's nice."

"What did you learn today?" I asked, fearing the answer. I was suspecting a recitation about the new methods of documenting nursing competencies, or a delineation of the process by which she helped the hospital maintain its "Magnet" status to attract more nurses to work here. Or perhaps she had learned a new set of pharmacy rules that replaced the old set of new pharmacy rules, all designed to make the rapid provision of medications to the patients safer and more impossible to accomplish. This sort of utterly painful garbanzo beans was what I usually, almost invariably, heard from a newly-minted nurse about her day, and they were usually proud of themselves, and appropriately too, because the nurses had hard hard jobs, and had no authority whatsoever to fight against stupid rules made by the hospital. The doctors did have the authority, but didn't know that they had it, and so didn't use it. The nurses didn't have the authority to fight the rules, but as they got higher up in the nursing ladder, learned they did have authority to enforce rules that others made. So they did. The young nurses were awesome wonderful angels in a difficult situation. The older nurses who had managed to avoid rising up the nurse-managerial tree were godsends, the teachers of young doctors, the saviors of sanity and careers and of patients' lives threatened by dangerous interns. But then there were the enforcer-nurses: they could be identified easily because they all carried clipboards. Any senior nurse that carried a clipboard was to be avoided at all cost.

But Beth was not in any pre-conceived camp. I am glad I'm not judgmental, prejudicial, or opinionated, because had I been, my world would have been rocked by this young nurse who was clearly outside the boxes that I and everyone else had stuck her in. For instead of reciting useless make-work as her day's occupation, she instead, to the delight of my ever-increasing internal happiness, said this, which I will translate on the fly for your edification:

"Well, first I had a fight with the knuckledraggers [orthopedic surgeons], who were insisting that my patient get a bone scan from unclear medicine [nuclear medicine—part of radiology], even though he was medically unstable. The shadow chasers [radiologists] had found a pleural effusion [fluid collection in the chest] in my patient that was huge. The stupid intern, oops, no offense, missed the effusion when she listened to my patient with her guessascope [stethoscope] this morning, even though I told her that the breath sounds were poor. That bitch sure is one 45C [possessing one chromosome short of the normal 46 human chromosomes and thus likely mentally disabled]. The slashers [surgeons] were all busy and didn't have time to drain it, so I had to insist. That didn't go over well. Meanwhile, my patient was crashing [trying to die] and his kidneys were shutting down. I had to get permission to stick him in a one-point restraint [catheter in his bladder] so I could track urine output, and I couldn't get in touch with the slashers of course, so I ended up having to get a wayward member of the stream team [urologists] to give me the go ahead on something that should be just allowed in any sane system. Thank God that the Dick Squad [urology team] had been rounding in my unit just then. Then the guy obviously needs to be tubed [intubated for mechanical ventilation], and I still can't get in touch with the damn slashers, so I had to page the gas-passer on call [anesthesiology resident] who along with the vent jockey [respiratory therapist] managed to keep my patient alive. The patient had been all sauced up on happy juice [narcotic pain relievers] so he was pretty much a chocolate hostage [constipated]. That isn't any good for healing, so I finally got the 45C surgical intern to go bobbing for apples [digitally disimpact [stick finger in rectum[bum] and dig out hard poop ball]]. He pretty much exploded after that [evacuated his entire colon] in a massive Code Brown [big nasty stool that stinks up an entire ward]. But that solved most of my patient's problems right then—it took the pressure off his kidneys so his pee started flowing, which helped drain the effusion, which helped him breathe so that his snorkel [endotracheal breathing tube] could be pulled. I almost had to transfer him to the ECU [Eternal Care Unit—in other words, death]. Damn cutters [surgeons] don't care about anything except operating."

I looked at Beth with my eyebrows raised. Rarely had I heard such a fluent effluation of medical slang flowing from even an experienced *doctor*. *Never* had I hear it from such a spring-chicken nurse. I asked, "When did you graduate from nursing school?"

"About six months ago, why?"

"Ever think of becoming a doctor?"

"What? Are you kidding? Why the hell would I want to do that?"

And with that statement, Beth landed herself a place on my all-star roster of non-sheep. I was a one-woman man romantically, but Beth was someone I would pay attention to professionally as I did my best to keep my tiny little corner of the hospital humming.

I had an epiphany.

"I need to introduce you to Jennifer Maid. You and she might have interesting conversations. Beware, she might try to recruit you to work with her."

"I know Jennifer already. She's great. But there's no way I'm going to a medicine ward to ward off the short-order chefs [pathologists in the mortuary] from their rightful tasks all day, and to help out with Slow Codes to China [efforts to resuscitate patients so old that the doctors walk to the code instead of run]."

"I understand that. I sure don't want to drag you down. So, what's your plan?"

"I may go to pediatrics. The kids are worth every second of my time. Besides, peds is refreshing. I think I'm at risk for getting a little snide and cynical if I keep working on adult wards."

"You think?"

I turned with a smile to the other side, where the other attractive nurse of the evening sat quietly eating her salad. She played with the chicken, but didn't eat it.

"Are you a vegetarian?" I asked, planning on being rude if she was.

She was. So I got to be. I threw in my standard laugh-getter, which was obnoxious as hell and funny as hell, at least to me. "If God had intended for us to be vegetarians, he wouldn't have made animals out of meat." I laughed loudly inside my own brain at my own inside humor.

"I eat fish," she said hopefully.

"Do you fish?"

"Actually, I don't. But I *eat* fish. Do you fish?"

"Why, yes, I do."

I sipped at my wine, described as 'robust with an austere bouquet, complex hints of layered opulence, and a complete unctuous finish'. Now, I am not a self-professed wine connoisseur, so I had no idea what that bullshit meant. To me, the wine tasted like I had just chewed Viagra.

It was a pleasant evening overall, ensconced between two attractive nurses eating a nice meal, sitting across the table from Tracy in the black pants-suit, and ignoring the propaganda emanating from the mouth of the thought-leader, words that bounced around the room, back into his fish-lipped mouth and down his throat as he eagerly swallowed everything he was saying: hook, line, and sinker.

Chapter 14

Yahtzee!

I had won the game! Never, not in all these months of internship, not in all those years of medical school, *never* had I won the game. But now, now I finally had. The pleasure would not last long, but it was sweet.

When on inpatient service, the average intern manages about eight to ten patients at a time. Many more patients than ten and the intern will suffer serious hard-drive failure, total system crash and the blue screen of death all concurrently. And the patients don't do so well either, as they suffer serious heart failure, systemic crashing, and the blue skin of death all concurrently.

Patients require the most work at three points during their hospital stay: first is their admission. This is when all the history is taken, a full physical is performed, a tentative diagnosis established, and a plan of therapy made. It is also when the doctor's orders are provided to the nurses and ancillary health care providers. The second point when there is work involved is when your patient tries to die during the hospitalization, which is fortunately not a standard occurrence. The third significant effort point is at discharge, when all sorts of unnecessary paperwork must be performed. It is at discharge when the intern has to write new prescriptions for all the medications that the patient has always been taking, and for which he already has prescriptions filling his bedside table drawer. It is at discharge that the Quality Assurance documents have to all be fraudulently crafted to look like people actually do the mandatory quality assurance which has nothing whatsoever remotely to do with delivering better healthcare. It is at discharge that the intern needs to dictate the patient's history and hospital course into the electronic medical record, which is easy if the patient has been there three days, and can be a nightmare if the patient was in hospital for two months. Oh, yeah, we actually try to *see* the patient on the day of discharge—if we have time when we are done performing all the bureaucratic counterproductive rigmarole—so that we can teach them how to keep themselves out of the hospital next time, not that we really know how or that they will ever listen to us.

But, all my work was done and I had won the game. It was 5 PM on Friday afternoon—a time when usually I would be sitting in the resident lounge signing my patients over to the night call team—but I had no patients to sign over. I had discharged them all! Wow. I therefore did not have to come to the hospital tomorrow. Wow again. Saturday free, Yahtzee. It was an awesome thought, particularly because I also had Sunday off as my pre-scheduled mandatory ACGME-mandated mandate that everyone get one day off per week. So I really had the whole weekend off.

I called Nurse Maid. Was there a chance? Was there any chance at all that she would be free from clinical duties for the weekend also? It couldn't happen. No young doctor should be entitled to such fortune as this.

"Jennifer, it's Eddie," I stated into the hospital phone, the excitement of hope building in my tone. "I won the game. I'm off for the weekend. Are you by any chance free? For the whole weekend?" Silence, and then I heard what I wanted to hear. "Yah? Where do you want to go? Yah? Okay. Let's go then. Pack your bag. I'll call you in a bit."

Problem was that I didn't have the money to fly us both to the Bahamas. Crap. But I was a doctor and was supposed to have the money, even though I got paid about four bucks per hour after twenty years of education, and had a bazillion dollars in student loans from the government with which to do battle, loans that were thankfully guaranteed by the federal government, because there was no way in hell I could ever repay all those loans, and I didn't want the federal government to lose out on getting back the money they had loaned me, so I was really happy that the federal government would come in and pay the federal government when I couldn't pay the loan myself, which I had no intention of ever being able to do, even though I was pretty rich, actually, on paper, because the hospital now owed me nearly a bazillion dollars for frig'o'graphs and strategic mandatory nap-observing consultancy. But that money was all going to get donated, so I was planning on being forever broke, living off my intern pay, my petty, ridiculous intern pay, and I didn't have money to go to the Bahamas with Nurse Maid.

But Blow did. Not to go with Nurse Maid, but to loan me. I told him my plight, and he opened up a credit line for me for two thousand dollars, right there and then. Two thousand dollars all for me. That was like an ounce of gold.

An ounce of gold a hundred years earlier had only been worth thirty-five dollars. I remembered reading that somewhere. "What makes gold so expensive, now?" I asked of Blow, not really expecting a response. My expectations and reality rarely align.

"Eddie, gold isn't any more expensive than it has ever been. In the Roman Republic, an ounce of gold could buy you a top-of-the-line toga and a designer pair of sandals. Now an ounce of gold will buy you a top-of-the-line suit and a pair of designer shoes. Gold pretty much always, over time, maintains its value. It's the dollar that has collapsed in value over the last century."

I hadn't given that much thought before. I guess it is like Einstein and relativity. It depends on your perspective. On the one hand, you could say the dollar is getting less valuable compared to gold. On the other hand you can say that gold is getting more valuable compared to the dollar.

"It depends on which you trust. Do you trust gold to be real and solid? Or do you trust a green piece of paper that the government prints willy nilly whenever they want to send themselves on trips to the Bahamas?"

"Umm, I can't spend gold."

"It's not so easy right now, but give a few more years and there is little chance of the dollar being able to buy you anything at all, because it will be like toilet paper."

"Surely it's not that bad."

I got the fully expected response from Blow. "Don't call me Shirley." But then he added, "It's that bad. Completely and utterly that bad. Why do you think I'm willing to loan you two thousand bucks now, when I know the hospital isn't ever going to pay you a salary equal to what you are worth, and I know you'll never be able to pay me back before paper money becomes worthless? Why? Because I think you are worth more to me in the future than two thousand dollars will be."

I was touched. Genuinely touched. I said so.

To which he responded, gruffly, "Only because two thousand dollars won't buy me a cup of coffee in the future, because it will be worth toilet paper."

Well, at least I was worth more than toilet paper.

I googled and yahooed and searched on Travelo-Expedia-Kayak-Cheap'o'air until I found that gem, that one diamond in the sand—the round trip to Bahamas deal including resort accommodations for two. With money to spare. Leaving in three hours. Pack our bags and go!

When we landed in Nassau, it was midnight. By the time we were in bed, it was 2 AM. By the time we got *out* of bed, it was noon. Emerging from our hotel, we felt in our bones that we were alive. It could only be described as a perfect, beautiful gorgeous day. There was a gentle breeze coming along the beach, bringing to our souls the essence of salt air mixed with the perfume of Caribbean flowers. The world was right again. No more slush, no more bleakness. As so many had before me, with equal fortitude and conviction, I decided that I would never leave this place. Well, I *would* never leave if Blow had loaned me two million pieces of recently-printed green paper instead of two thousand.

We held hands and walked barefoot in the sand, on that soft squishy partly-packed part of the beach where the sea climbs up the gentle slope and then washes back out as the rolling and bouncing grains of sand gleefully chase the water back into the ocean. We looked for shells, and found them. Special ones. Intact, or broken, it mattered not. With purple bits, and shining bright fluorescent pink and green. Black. Bleached white. Recently evacuated, still the home to a hermit, or long abandoned. My pockets were stuffed with them.

Jennifer looked brilliant. She danced as she walked, spinning in the wind, sending the water around her feet into eddies. When she bent over to pick up a shell, she sent a feeling through my body that was inexplicable to me.

Rightness. She was right. She was honest, caring, true, smart, and living.

She tipped her head to the side slightly as she looked at me, one eye partly closed to defend from the sun. She saw something in my face that I hadn't known was there. "What is it, Eddie?"

I shrugged. "What is what?"

She shrugged back and apparently dismissed it. I knew though. I knew what she had seen. What she had seen on my face on that beach that day was love.

So this is what love felt like. Wow.

Wow.

I stopped. I stood still. My spirit was still. It was a new experience. Before now, love was a word, a phantom, a probable fiction, a fanciful self-deluded notion that served the purpose of those who made their income pandering to those who spent their income seeking the non-existent unprovable lie called love. It was no longer a lie. Now it was a truth, *the* truth. Wow. This truth couldn't lie to me. This would last forever.

I hadn't been in love before, so I had no reason to doubt the permanence. I hadn't fallen out of love before, so I had no recognition that such was possible. I hadn't experienced anything beyond mild infatuation and not so mild severe lust, so I didn't know what it meant to go so much farther than that, and to have so much of oneself on the line.

But it was happening. I gazed intently at Nurse Maid. "Jennifer, I think I love you," I said, in my effort to be direct and forthright and honest and to let the love of my life know my true feelings. That Jennifer was now fifty yards further down the beach, upwind and completely out of earshot, in no way hindered my honesty and forthrightness, nor the earnestness of my declaration.

I ran through ankle-depth water ebbing and flowing on this very gently sloping patch of beach, running to catch up to Jennifer, who was meandering slowly in the wet sinking sand, unaware of anything in life except the surf, the sand, the shells, the sun and the breeze. Perfect lines of perfect legs perfectly placed in a perfect setting. I caught up to her and grasped her hand and she gasped briefly, caught by surprise. I swung her around and we danced, water splashing in all directions as we spun and twirled to the prominent sonorous bass that was the primary audible component of the music emanating from the beach bar of a nearby resort. Jennifer was laughing, her eyes bright and cheerful, brimming with glee. It was a happy day. The next day was likewise.

But the Sheep's Pen was still there. Despite my highest hopes, no giant bulldozer had come to knock the place to dust. The Sheep's Pen still had much to teach me.

I had to go back.

Chapter 15

QWERTYitis

Dr. Superiori and Nurse Hypercare were standing in two-dimensional grandeur, larger-than-life, more brightly colored than any non-superhuman medical provider, graphically enhanced, perfectly contoured, intensely expressionful. They were eight feet tall, and had recently been positioned where everyone in the cafeteria would be impacted by their powerful aura. They were the cardboard promoters of the new electronic medical record—the EMR—that the hospital was spending huge amounts of money to force upon us, in place of the older new electronic medical record that was thrust upon us two years earlier at great expense, which in turn had replaced the previous new electronic medical record of three years before that. But this new EMR was subsidized by federal government stimulus money, and therefore just had to be bought.

Blow and I had bumped into each other on GI Rounds in the cafeteria as we each had sought our morning breakfast and our morning caffeine. My automated, self-grinding, nebulizer-enhanced caffeine inhalation machine was back in the shop for repairs, so oral ingestion was my only choice.

Blow and I walked past Dr. Superiori and Nurse Hypercare. Then, suddenly, Blow stopped in his tracks. He took three steps directly backward and stood gazing up at the chiseled face and stern but confident eyes of the administrators' image of the perfect doctor. The graphical environment in which this perfect specimen of cardboard medical maleness was placed was an operating room, with a large glass window separating the surgical theater from the scrub room and the corridors outside. His long white doctor coat was unbuttoned and blowing out behind from the strong wind that so commonly courses through the corridors of the surgical suite to cool the hardworking people who would of course not wear their white coat in that area of the facility.

Blow was reading the text that served as the description of Dr. Superiori's credentials, text printed in a font that was chosen—after five months of marketing research—to be most likely to convince the hospital staff of the modern and exciting advantages of the newest new electronic medical record. Blow was mumbling the words that he read, "Superpowers: hyperefficient dictating. Powertyping. Able to access surgical notes anywhere on the planet. Utilizing the new Electronic Medical Record."

Blow shook his head. He turned to the larger-than-life image of Nurse Hypercare. "Superpower: Clinical care and compassion skyrocket at her command." Nurse Hypercare was the glorified image of one of our real nurses, with a digitally enhanced bust thrust out aggressively into the unsuspecting passersby, and her chin placed prominently so as to assure us of her complete and utter confidence in the powers of the new electronic medical record.

Flash Pharmicus was the next superhero, standing large right around the corner. Superpower: Able to scan prescriptions in the blink of an eye. The wind was again blowing, this time through his pharmacy, as the full body image of the perfectionized pharmacist was presented with his chest likewise thrust out, and in hypermotion: a man dancing with arms outstretched while looking like he was about to throw his cell phone at you.

Blow shook his head. "This one is going to be bad, Eddie. This is gonna be the worst."

Now that I was a doctor, I could understand Blow's concern. I was standing there, staring at these cartoon-human hybrids of medical professionals who actually worked in our hospital, presenting to us all their superpowers that had been so thoughtfully determined to be exciting and convincing and encouraging and uplifting to the masses of medical serfs, and I was totally and utterly embarrassed. I gazed around the cafeteria, seeing the families of our patients at tables, eating their okay food under the gaze of the EMR superheroes, and I hoped, so much hoped, that they wouldn't notice them, or me. Of all the marketing crap that had been foisted by the deans and other administrators upon the hospital over the years that I had been around as an employee, medical student, and now doctor, this one took the cake, perhaps because as a doctor, I should be particularly *proud* of where I worked, rather than intensely embarrassed.

Before I teach you about medical records, let me tell you about academic medical center marketing methods. As an academic medical center, we should be focused on teaching, research, and the difficult clinical work at which community hospitals and community doctors aren't as proficient. Over the years, the proficiency has altered. For example, if you need heart bypass surgery, you really do want to go to a community hospital, because the cardiac surgeon there will have performed three such surgeries per day for years, and be excellent and highly skilled, whereas at an academic center, the surgical caseload of bypass surgeries will be lower, with lots of nibbling less-experienced cardiac surgery residents and fellows hoping for their occasional piece of the action—that action being cutting your heart. Cardiac bypass surgery is no longer cutting edge. It is a community hospital procedure. But it used to be a cutting edge university hospital procedure. Years ago, the university hospitals had done their jobs and, when ready, passed it on to the community hospitals.

In contrast to the strengths of the community hospital, the academic university hospitals were designed to do the cutting edge work, the research supporting it and creating it, and the teaching necessary to bring the best cutting edge advances out to the community hospitals as soon as possible. These are the strengths of an academic medical center.

However, that is no longer the way the system doesn't work. The way the system doesn't work nowadays is that we in the academic medical center get paid primarily by the government's price-controlled system, under the control of Medicare and Medicaid, which sets prices using some indecipherable system that involves lobbying. It is a big lie, cheat and steal, and then our administrators actually *invite* insurance companies to come in and lie with us, cheat at us and steal to us just as much as Medicare does. Even though the academic centers have all of the highly advanced technologies and exquisite knowledge and experience of their professors of medicine and surgery, the net effect of our insane system is that the academic centers can't charge any more than the community hospital can charge for their doctor who is practicing guideline-based medicine, relying on those narcissistic medical guidelines written by doctors from the academic medical centers who have never seen his patient.

The Administrators' response to the financial woes of our

academic hospital is always to try to build on our weaknesses. Because we teach and perform research, we in academia do not see as many patients in a day as the community providers do. Our biggest weakness is that we don't provide efficient and rapid clinical care for the masses of people presenting with common ailments. Doctors who choose an academic life aren't interested in seeing fifty patients per day and producing dollars in the hospital bank accounts, but rather they want to teach, write papers, conduct research and advance the field. So what do the administrators do, always? They mandate that the academic doctors see fifty patients per day so as to put more dollars in the hospital bank account. They then offer to help the doctors by placing ridiculous advertisements on the sides of buses and on the radio to market our hospital in the community so as to generate more visits from patients presenting with common ailments, in an effort to try to take business from the community hospital. Our administrators try to overcome our weakness while taking on the strengths of the local hospitals. It is like Einstein choosing to do battle in the ring with the top three all time victors of the World Wrestling Federation, as opposed to taking them on in chess. Well that is the nature of administrators. These goats have power, because we sheep gave it to them, and they use their power to sheer the sheep further and drive the whole flock over the cliff to drown in the raging seas.

There is no surer path to failure than to spend all one's energies trying to overcome weaknesses in an organization. There is no surer path to success than by building on one's native strengths.

So, the marketing efforts that I hear on the radio: they nauseate me. I will paraphrase them slightly here, so that I don't malign my own university. 'The Sheep's Pen: Perfection

Transcending Measure.' 'The Sheep's Pen. Using evidence based medicine to provide ultimate medical care. Defying Measure.' 'The doctors of the Sheep's Pen: Quality Surpassing Any Measure.' These phrases were plastered all over town and promoted warmly and sensitively on the radio in an intensely loud whispering voice. I always hoped that the administrators someday would see that the phrase "Defying Measure" was completely in contradiction to the dictums of the measurement-intensive process employed by evidence-based medicine, as well as the measurement-intensive quality assurance programs that they were professing made us so good. By now, you know what I think about evidence-based medicine and quality assurance programs.

The administrators were spending lots and lots of money on these advertising campaigns so that they could bring in more money in order to pay for more advertising. More patients were coming to the Sheep's Pen outpatient clinics, and more patients were being admitted to the hospital. The attending doctors were all seeing more and more patients (the residents weren't allowed to) and doing less and less writing and teaching and research and less examination and adoption of potential new valuable technologies. They were getting more and more disgruntled as they were being pushed, month-by-week, year-by-day, and the net effect is that the Sheep's Pen was bit-by-yard becoming a shitty version of a community hospital. Administrators aren't known for their 20:20 vision, although they sure can spend a lot of money and time writing 'vision statements'.

Allow me to teach you about medical records. I have credibility to teach you because I had worked for a long time in this hospital as an Emergency Room clerk before medical school, when it had entirely paper records. That was before the electronic transition began in earnest, prompted by regulations, subsidies and the threats of fine and jail time so as to encourage voluntary compliance with the politician's view of social-environmental responsibility. I had experienced all the various electronic medical records transitions in the Sheep's Pen, because I had also been a medical student right here at this hospital during these times, and you need to know, it is the medical students who are the guinea pigs upon whom electronic medical records are first tested. Actually, 'tested' is not the correct word. 'Tested' implies that 'they', who ever they are, will make changes to the system as the result of the feedback provided. That is a false implication. Actually, the medical students are better described as indentured servants, serfs, slaves, victims that can take the pain of the inane computer hassles away from the residents and the attending doctors. Over time, '*they*' became smarter, and this time they were making the attendings sign, oversee and supervise every detail stuck in the medical record in order to protect the medical students from the pain of indentured servitude.

Here is the trick about the electronic medical records: they are designed for the purpose of capturing more data to make the job of billing Medicare, Medicaid, and insurance companies easier and more lucrative. Optimized insurance billing is their primary objective, their *raison d'etre,* their true purpose. We are told that the EMR is designed to prevent medical errors, to speed up access to medical information, to share medical information so as to avoid redundant lab tests, and to keep a more thorough and complete medical history. In fact, and as an aside, the EMRs do accomplish those purposes, but at an additional very expensive cost that of course the government experts forcing them down our throats didn't consider.

"Hello, Mr. Jackson," Dr. Messina announced, as he entered

the outpatient examination room without knocking. Dr. Messina was the resident in internal medicine that had his continuity clinic on Mondays. Today was Monday.

Dr. Messina reached out to shake the cold, mildly anxious milky hand of Mr. Jackson, and then turned to a computer on the wall across from him. Mr. Jackson stared at the doctor's back as Dr. Messina expertly walked the keyboard and mouse through the maze of computer screens that to the newest generation of physicians provided all the information one needed to know about a patient.

After an interminable three minutes of silence, Dr. Messina asked Mr. Jackson, "Is this right?" He asked this question without the slightest change in position, his head still focused on the computer screen as if the screen possessed the ears to which his voice was aimed.

Mr. Jackson's mindset was somewhere between confused and bemused. Slowly, ever so slowly, there was the almost unrecognizable rise also of a feeling of, what was it, oh yes: disgust. Disgust so tiny as to be imperceptible, but growing, perhaps.

"Is what right, Doctor?" Mr. Jackson politely queried.

"Do you still take colchicine?" the doctor added without turning around, his voice containing just a faint hit of controlled frustration.

"Yes, Doctor, I still take colchicine from time to time," replied Mr. Jackson to the recently trimmed hairline on the back of the doctor's neck.

Dr. Messina's hairline moved upward and downward slightly as he nodded his face at the computer screen absentmindedly. He then clicked the mouse through a few more boxes on the maze of data collection screens, evidencing more frustration by a sudden decline of his shoulders, before saying to the computer screen, "There is no way to record in the EMR 'from time to time'. So how often would you say you take the colchicine?"

Mr. Jackson was a rebel. He said, "Every Monday, Wednesday and Friday, except the second week of each month, when I take them on Tuesday and Thursday. Except on leap year."

But Dr. Messina was lost in his digital world, and missed the entire farcical medication schedule. He said simply, "Huh?"

An audible sigh that went unnoticed preceded Mr. Jackson's next words. "I take the colchicine when needed. Why don't you just check off the box that says '*prn*'." The initials '*prn*' was medical shorthand for 'as needed', and a patient's use of the term should have indicated to any doctor that the patient was medically trained. But Dr. Messina just nodded the back of his head at Mr. Jackson, and with satisfaction clicked his mouse into the correct box to indicate that Mr. Jackson took his colchicine *prn*.

The next several minutes continued in relative silence with a few intercessions of questions directed by the doctor toward the patient, or rather the computer screen, with seeming disinterest.

"So, you are here today because you have a sore ankle. Is that right?" asked the back of the head. Upon affirmative response, the hand restraining the mouse clicked on another box and another faint trace of satisfaction ensued.

"For how long?" Click, sweep, click, sweep, click.

"Is it worse at night?" Click.

"What do you do to make it better?" Click, followed by ignoring while saying "hmmm" and nodding the back of the head.

It went on like this for some time. Finally, the doctor was satisfied that he had clicked all the necessary boxes that would create the conditions necessary for the EMR to allow him to move on to the next phase of the medical diagnostic process, the physical exam. The back of the head turned away from Mr. Jackson, accidently revealing the doctor's face for just a moment, a brief moment cut short by the face moving directly into Mr. Jackson's ankle. Mr. Jackson now gazed downward at the top of a head just beginning to show evidence of a family history of early male pattern balding.

"Does it hurt here?" said the balding pate as the hand so accustomed to intricate control of a computer mouse prodded clumsily and inconsiderately at Mr. Jackson's swollen and tender joint.

"Yes," responded Mr. Jackson to the slightly thinning hair. "It hurts there, but mostly when I stand on it."

"What makes it hurt worse?"

"When I stand on it."

"Does it hurt worse when you stand on it?"

Silence.

A barely concealed sigh emerged from some orifice below the top of the head looking at Mr. Jackson's ankle. Apparently in an effort to explain his question, Dr. Messina asked, "Does it hurt worse when you put weight on it?"

"Yes."

The mouse hand wiggled the ankle around, pushed up and pushed down on it and wiggled it some more. It pulled on a few toes. Then the head turned around and Mr. Jackson looked up at the neat hairline on the back of the neck as the doctor went back to attending to the doctor-computer relationship he had conscientiously developed with his screen and his mouse. He clicked and swept and clicked and swept. Mr. Jackson's vision was fine and he could see that Dr. Messina was checking off various boxes under a computer screen titled 'physical findings'. There had been essentially no physical exam performed, but the doctor was checking off a surprising number of boxes under a column headed with the word 'normal'. The doctor knew what Mr. Jackson didn't, namely that the EMR would not allow billing at the higher visit rate unless there were lots of boxes checked within the physical exam section of the EMR. Mr. Jackson sighed again, at this point not caring.

Dr. Messina clicked and swept and then typed a series of words, clicked and swept a few more times. A printer next to a sink once used to wash hands in the olden days started humming and four pieces of paper were spit out. Dr. Messina's non-mouse hand reached over to the printer without looking and in an amazing feat of practiced contortion, handed the still hot paper to Mr. Jackson without the remainder of the doctor's body turning away from the screen.

Mr. Jackson couldn't see the doctor's eyes move to the top of the computer monitor where the name of the patient was noted in the top left corner of each screen. "Mr. Jackson," the doctor said, now confident in the name, "I think your gout is acting up. These instructions will tell you how to manage it. I also gave you two prescriptions. I think if you follow the instructions, you will find your gout will be better. You will need to stop eating red meat and don't drink any alcohol. If you have any questions, don't hesitate to call for an appointment and come back in."

With that, the doctor clicked a couple of more buttons on the computer, receiving in return a happy beep that indicated that the computerized documentation was completed satisfactorily and thus allowing the EMR session to be closed and insurance billed, and then he turned away from the screen and walked out the door, feeling fully satisfied that he had expertly completed his full EMR documentation without a single error.

Mr. Jackson walked out a few moments later, never to come back, leaving the papers unread in the unused sink.

So, you see, the electronic medical record has a major cost not anticipated by the administrators and government officials forcing them down our throats. It disconnects the doctor from the patient in an egregious and unforgivable way. It is, however, what is and what will be, because we have been told so by the people who rule the sheep.

Chapter 16

Emergency Education

I sat at the small desk near the nurses' station on the pediatric ward. The desk was littered with the paper medical records that didn't exist, bedside charts that weren't at the bedside, a laser printer that seemed to constantly be belching out additional contraband paperwork, and a phone that rang all the time but couldn't be heard. I was reading through the recorded scrawls of the attending physicians, who now had to write specific words in the charts everyday, because if they didn't, Medicare and the insurance companies would use such oversights as excuses not to pay.

Over and over again, the attendings had written, "Patient seen, examined, agree with impression and plan as recorded by Dr. So-and-So." Had they not written this phrase everyday in the chart, the hospital would not be allowed to charge for that day. There had been a transient effort by the doctors to use a pre-printed stamp that said those words, but that was quickly outlawed by somebody somewhere who made rules. The outlawed stamps could have been outlawed by Medicare, by JCAHO, by the Compliance Dean, or by a clipboard carrying enforcer nurse, but no one knew, and when Blow had asked who was responsible, he was blown off. But it had indeed been outlawed, so we all were assured, and that is all that was supposed to matter to us.

There were yellow sticky flags throughout the contraband paper chart. These yellow flags were designed to catch the eye of the physicians to correct aberrant entries in the chart that had been caught by the aforementioned clipboard-carrying nurses who served as the hospital's compliance-enhancing thought-police. Many flags were chastisements for the use of abbreviations no longer considered acceptable in the Newspeak lexicon ruled over by these thought-police.

The thought-police compliance-enforcement clipboard-carrying nurses were not my best friends, as I might have mentioned before. You can think of them like parking enforcement officers who stand by a parking meter waiting for it to click over into 'violation' so they can whip off a ticket just as you approach your car. These nurses were nice people, I am sure, but they had burned out from seeing patients, and now were paid by the hospital to enforce arbitrary rules invented by the insurance companies and the government for the purpose of providing excuses for said blood-sucking organizations to not pay for medical services rendered. Instead of telling said organizations to fuck off and pay what they are contracted to pay, the administrators of our hospital help the insurance companies to enforce the rules that they actually shouldn't want enforced. Then, because administrative costs to deal with insurance company mandates kept getting higher at the hospitals, the costs of health care went up, and then insurance companies had to charge higher rates for the insurance and then write more arbitrary rules to try to help limit how much they had to pay to the hospitals. So the hospitals had to hire more people to help enforce the rules that they should instead have been fighting against. An incalculable amount of wasted human effort was occurring everyday.

It was one o'clock in the morning as I aimlessly flipped to the next yellow flag. "Non-allowed abbreviation" was the pre-printed statement on the sticky yellow flag, which had a built-in arrow pointing to the hand-scrawled letters: "LOFD", written in my own hand a few days earlier. I had written this in response to a comment from a hospital volunteer that a patient was unconscious. I had run to the room to see my 9-year-old patient out of bed doing jumping jacks with his 4-year-old visiting brother. Dutifully, I had noted the volunteer's observation and added LOFD, 'Looks Okay From Door.' This statement means a lot more than you might think. It doesn't mean that the doctor (me) is blowing off the concern of the volunteer, or blowing off the patient and his potential needs. It doesn't mean that I was being lazy. Rather 'LOFD' is shorthand for a description of a patient that looked *so* good that there wasn't even a need for closer analysis at that time. It conveys a full paragraph of meaning in four letters. Four now unacceptable letters.

I didn't care a whit for following their rules, so I pulled the yellow stickies all out of the non-existent paper medical record and threw them in the receptacle for non-created recyclable imaginary paper trash.

Blow was home sleeping. Nurse Maid was home sleeping. Doris-Doris was home sleeping. Beth, the cynical young nurse was home sleeping. Pal, the respiratory therapist was home sleeping. The parents of the children on the ward were home sleeping. The patients were sleeping. The night-shift unit coordinator—the aspiring actor with the long flowing locks, pleated pants, $500 shoes, and a practiced, southern-accented lisp—who was not gay, had his head resting on his desk, and perhaps was sleeping too. It was a quiet, peaceful evening. I stood up from my desk to head for my call room. It had all the feeling of one of those nights in which I could sleep for four full hours or more.

My beeper went off right then. It was the Emergency room of course. So much for my night's sleep.

"Are you the intern on call for Family Practice?" asked the ER resident.

"Nope," I replied sleepily, "I'm the intern on call for Family Practice."

Silence for a moment. Then the humorless ER resident continued. "I have a patient to admit to you. Asthmatic 4-year old. Fifth hospitalization this year for asthma. We have given him four nebs of Esgetbeteral and a shot of 'roids, but he isn't clearing. Needs to stay for a few days."

I asked, "Chest x-ray?"

"Didn't do one. He has several typical asthma-looking films from his previous visits."

"I'll be right down."

I had done a long report on asthma when I was in college. Somehow the disorder had maintained my interest ever after, so I paid more attention to what I heard, and what I read. And I thought about asthma too. And I talked with the allergists, and listened to the pulmonologists, and paid attention to the respiratory therapists so that I could learn how to best diagnose and manage asthma. And I went to the pharmaceutical drug dinners at which data were presented about asthma so I could learn what the thought-leaders were going to be manipulated into incorporating into the next set of asthma management guidelines.

The four-year old boy sitting awake on the bed in the ER was black, just like me. His mother was black. His sister was black. His auntie was black, and the auntie's son was black too. I never understood how so many people in one family could all be from the same race. Such coincidences continue to astound me.

"Hello D'Andrew," I said as I walked into the room, knocking gently on the doorframe as I did. D'Andrew looked up at me with an obviously skeptical and suspicious frown. He had an IV in his forearm, placed by an ER nurse no doubt, because the young doctors were now incapable of placing IVs because there were so many hired ancillary staff paid to place IVs that the new young doctors never had an opportunity to learn or practice. The mildly painful IV placement had made the child skeptical and suspicious. Sometimes IVs were necessary, and sometimes they were just placed because it was required by a protocol in a guideline document written by experts who had never seen the patient. I wondered which situation this IV was in.

I stayed by the door, far from D'Andrew, and said in a gentle voice, "Hi. My name is Dr. Marcus. I am here to take care of you and help you feel better."

I retreated outside the door for just a moment to reach for a round rolling stool and slid it slowly inside the room and sat on it, still remaining far away from D'Andrew. I caught the eyes of his mother, sitting on the bed, obviously worried. I smiled faintly and nodded to acknowledge her concern.

D'Andrew's chest was moving far faster than it should have been. His nostrils flared slightly. And as we talked, he would cough a harsh and useless cough. I smiled at him. He provided a half-hearted smile in return, but then returned to staring at his toes. D'Andrew wasn't wiggling around the bed, wasn't jumping up and down or playing as a four year old should be, as exciting and stimulating to a small child as an Emergency Room environment is. No, his body had told him to not move much at all, so as to conserve oxygen.

The ER resident stepped in for a moment and said, "His

oxygen sats are 95%. Not bad at all," and turned immediately to leave. So the child's blood oxygen was okay. Often an asthmatic child with his blood saturating this well with oxygen would be sent home, not admitted. But this child shouldn't go home. He was working too hard to breathe, even though the numbers on the oxygen saturation monitor were okay. It is common in lung diseases to be faked out by numbers on a screen.

A child's fear zone is focused mostly on his head. A wise doctor will stay as far away as possible from the fear zone. D'Andrew's little smile had given me confidence that he wouldn't panic upon my approach. I stayed small and moved slowly over to D'Andrew. He didn't seem to mind. I touched his foot, the part of the body farthest away from his fear zone. He didn't flinch. I twisted my stethoscope into my ears and listened to his knee. No flinching. Next, I listened to his stomach. Then I moved the scope a bit closer to the center of his zone of fear and was able to listen to his lungs for as long as I needed to. Something wasn't right. Asthma causes wheezing most everywhere in the lungs, of a variety of pitches and tones, rather like an orchestra tuning before a concert. D'Andrew was wheezing, certainly, but it sounded more like a kazoo—a wheeze of just one pitch, echoing throughout the chest each time he breathed either in or out, just a little louder on the right than the left.

"Has D'Andrew choked on anything lately?" I asked his mother.

His mother frowned for a minute and said, "I don't think so." Then, to her son, "D'Andrew, did you choke on anything in your mouth?"

D'Andrew didn't really know what that question even meant, but shook his head 'no' because he guessed maybe that 'no' was the answer his mom wanted.

"Has he had a cold?" A cold was by far the most common trigger of asthma attacks.

"No."

"How long has he been breathing this way?"

"He started getting sick at the babysitters, Saturday night. We were at our Country Club's charity fundraiser."

I asked several more questions, and then listened to D'Andrew's heart, felt his pulses, and gently palpated his neck. I said to his mother, "I'm going to ask the ER doctors to arrange for a couple of x-rays of his chest before we admit him to the hospital, is that okay?"

Mom nodded.

I was able to sit on the rolling bed now, right next to D'Andrew. I smiled and put my arm around him. "Hey pal. You're going to be fine. You know what'll make you feel better? A little oxygen. We can give you some real easily. You get to pretend to be a fireman and wear oxygen, just like the firemen do. I'll show you."

I found nasal oxygen tubing in a drawer, hooked it up to the wall and ever so slowly put it behind D'Andrew's ears and gently placed it in his nose. I turned the valve on to put about a liter per minute through his nose. Quickly, his oxygen saturations increased to 100% and his breathing became calmer. 95%, as he had been before, is normal, but he had been working really hard to keep his sats that high. He could breathe a little easier now. Although oxygen can be dangerous for some people with lung disease, it isn't for people who just recently got sick.

I stepped out of the room. "Hey Jack," which was the ER resident's name, although I would have called him Jack even had his name been Ben. "Can you flash a couple of films on him, including expiratory films. I think he might have aspirated a goomba. Homophonous wheeze on the right."

Jack nodded, professionally. To a doctor, missing a diagnosis could be embarrassing and lead to defensiveness. But a good doctor, even when missing a diagnosis, isn't embarrassed, as long as *someone* figures it out in time. It is good to have multiple people helping out and giving things thought. It appeared that Jack was a good doctor for he didn't seem embarrassed. Furthermore, he had known the child should be admitted to the hospital, even though the oxygen saturations would suggest otherwise. Good doctor.

An hour and a half later, I got paged by the ER because they had finally gotten the x-ray taken. That's about right in our current system. Why take 10 minutes to do something when you can take 90? As far as I can see, there is no particular *need* for it to take 90 minutes. It is like *everything* in medical care these days—slowed down because the same people who think everybody should be forced to have health insurance for their own good also think they are smart enough to create all sorts of medical economic rules and controls to 'optimize' health care delivery, behaving exactly the same as Stalinist 5-year planners, and with equal effectiveness—and in so doing chop off Adam Smith's invisible and humble hand.

The people who like to make rules are anything but humble. They know they are smarter than everyone. They know that *their* priorities are what everyone *should* want, and they feel responsible to make sure that everyone is *forced* to accept their brilliant priorities. And they feel wicked good about it, because they also are completely certain that they are doing good. Sadly, the inevitable result of such narcissism is complete misallocation of resources, imbalance of supply and demand, and 90-minute waits when it should be ten minutes.

D'Andrew's 90-minute-long chest x-rays showed a large

area in the right lung to be cloudy, and another large area to be overly clear. The expiratory films showed that D'Andrew could exhale much better from his left lung than his right lung.

"Hey Jack, I think the kiddo has a foreign body in his right mainstem bronchus." I showed him the x-ray findings. "Would you mind consulting ENT or surgery before I admit him?"

"D'Andrew," I said to D'Andrew and his mother at the same time, "I am going to ask some other doctors to come help you feel better too. We are all here to help you." I turned to his mom. "This may be just asthma, but it may be something else. It looks like there is something clogging up one of the airways to the lower right lung. It might just be mucous, but it is suspicious to me that it might be something he choked on. I am asking some other doctors to see if they want to look in his airway with a special thin camera to see if there is anything down there. While we wait, we will keep treating him for asthma. Does that sound okay?"

She nodded and said, "Thank you, Doctor."

"Sorry to keep you up all night. You must be tired."

"I am. But we're used to it. He's worth it. Sorry to keep *you* up all night."

I replied, "He's worth it."

Parents are such wonderful people.

Sometimes.

Beep. Beep. Beep.

It was the ER calling again. Whoever was paging me didn't know I was already in the ER. I nodded to D'Andrew's mom, patted the little guy on his head, smiled, and stepped out.

They needed me to see a child who had a cold and the mom insisted that she be admitted to the hospital. The little girl was nine years old, and her parents were divorced, or separated, or just sleeping around. It took little time to realize that the child would be fine, didn't need to be in the hospital, and that mom was pissed at the father because it was his weekend to take the child, but he was in jail, and she had planned to take a trip with her boyfriend of the month and needed her child to be in the hospital so that she could get drunk and screw.

"I am telling you doctor, she has pneumonia. I cannot tell you how many times she has been sent home from the ER and then gets pneumonia and almost dies."

I looked at her clear chest x-ray. I saw her oxygen saturations were 99%. I saw her breathing very easily and slowly. I put my hand on her head—no fever. I listened with my stethoscope and heard only the sweet sounds of normal airflow. Nothing to suggest pneumonia at all. That doesn't mean that pneumonia isn't present, but it sure makes it unlikely.

"Ma'am, what makes you think she has pneumonia?"

"Because I am her mother, and I know it. You doctors are all alike. You never listen."

Now, good moms often, if not always, know more than doctors, I am the first to admit. But bad moms suck and don't know shit. Bad moms care more for themselves than they do for their child. Bad moms are selfish, self-centered, self-focused, and behave like bad teenagers. It is the doctor's job to figure out who is the good mom, and listen intently to her, and who is the bad mom, and try to manipulate her out of causing harm to her child. Fortunately, when a mom acts like a teenager, it is pretty obvious. This was a bad mom, and my job was clear. I took mom out of the room, smiling at the little girl and winking, to indicate that all was okay, then closed the door.

"Thank God you brought her to the emergency room. This may be a case of asymptomatic pneumonia!" I said with exaggerated emotion and a heaving chest indicating my fear and sincerity.

The mother nodded her head knowingly. "I thought so. I told the other doctors. Idiots."

"It is very hard to diagnose it. But if it is, she may need some intensive therapy. Probably starting tonight. Insurance hardly ever covers it, and it is very expensive."

The mother started shuffling her feet.

"Last I checked, it was about $20,000 just to get it started. You have Medicaid, right?"

"Yes."

"That's too bad. Medicaid never covers this therapy."

"What is the therapy?"

"Lung resection, whole lung lavage, interventional bronchoscopy, endodermal lysis, excretory analysis and deviant perturbation. After those procedures are done, we have to fibrillate the parenchyma, keringle her dradel, and then provide intermittent petulation."

The mother provided another knowing nod. "That is what they tried for my mother. It didn't help her."

"It usually only works on young people, like your daughter."

"Is there any option?"

"Yes. There is a chance that she doesn't actually have asymptomatic pneumonia. If she's in the hospital, we are obligated to treat. But if you take her home, you can observe her there and see what happens next. Invariably, if it really is asymptomatic pneumonia, she will get worse. Then bring her back. If she gets better at all, then you can be confident that she doesn't have it. You can save a lot of money that way."

She nodded, clearly relieved. "Okay, so I should take her home?"

"And save lots of money. Remember to come right back in

if she is getting worse in the next couple of days."

"Okay, that's what we will do. Thank you doctor." The mom would take her daughter home now and tell her friends just how dangerously sick her daughter might be and how most of the doctors missed the diagnosis, and by so doing gain lots of attention.

"No, problem. Just doing my job." Beep, beep, beep. "Excuse me, I need to answer this."

"Dr. Marcus, are you the FP on call tonight?" asked the secretary in the emergency room of a small community hospital outside of town. It was 4:30 AM, so if I wasn't the on call doc, I sure would be pissed off at the page operator.

"Yes, what can I do for you?"

"Hold for Dr. Turf, please."

I held for Dr. Turf. I didn't like Dr. Turf. I had never met the man nor ever talked to him, but his name sucked.

"Dr. Marcus?" the voice of Dr. Turf was that of a woman, indicating the likelihood that Dr. Turf was a woman.

"Yes, it is I," said I.

"I have a patient I need to turf to you," Dr. Turf didn't say. Instead, she said, "I have a patient that I think belongs in your hospital. He is a 17 year old with something wrong with him, but I don't know what it is. He is disoriented and slurring his words, behaves like he is drunk, is belching, and has horrific flatus."

Yes, this was someone I wanted to invite into my hospital, that's for sure.

She continued, "His blood alcohol is zero, he denies using any drugs, his urine tox screen is negative."

I interrupted, "Did you get a head CT?" A hidden head injury with bleeding around the brain could mimic drunkenness.

"Yes, normal."

"Any fever?" Meningitis or encephalitis could be an explanation.

"None."

"Did you tap him?" By this I meant a spinal tap, looking for afebrile meningitis.

"Not yet."

"When did this start?"

"The parents noted it when he came home after a party."

"What the heck did the kid ingest or smoke?"

"I don't know. He denies using any drugs at all." And then she repeated, "and the tox screen was totally negative."

I thought back, way way back, to my months living in the cardboard boxes. The runaways around me used all sorts of weird drugs. There was something, something in my mind.

"Bad flatus?"

"Yes, he describes them as 'beer shits', excuse the lingo."

It clicked as soon as I heard the 'beer shit' phrase. My mind clarified and pulled the memories together.

"Ask him if he was trying to get high on nutmeg."

"Nutmeg?"

"Yes nutmeg." Nutmeg causes the worst stupidest useless high when it is ingested by the stupidest useless teenagers trying to get high by being stupid.

A few minutes later, Dr. Turf picked the phone back up. "Bingo," she said. "Nutmeg. The kid ate a whole bottle of the stuff."

"Cool. He'll certainly pay for that. I don't know that there's anything you can do for him, or that you need to do for him. Maybe give him a liter of fluid and some Tylenol and tell him not to be an idiot."

"Done. Thanks tons, Dr. Marcus."

The next week, I got called to the Dean's office to be congratulated for an excellent phone diagnosis of nutmeg toxicity that avoided an unnecessary patient transfer. Dr. Turf had sent an email to the Dean praising me. I liked Dr. Turf.

No one commented about my recognition of the gumball stuck in the lung of D'Andrew, which I thought was a real save. Fortunately, no one questioned my seriously made-up diagnosis of asymptomatic pneumonia. I fear had anyone heard about that, I would have had to go to remedial sensitivity training, which I would then have to skip because it would interfere with my diversity awareness quality improvement teambuilding training session, which I would in turn blow off in favor of lunch.

Chapter 17

It's the Real Thing

So, it turns out that some people, not all mind you, but some, like to stick things up their butt. I don't understand this myself, but after working for many years in an emergency room as an administrator, and then as a student and now as a doctor, I have been forced to conclude that it is indeed true that some individuals like to stick things up their butt.

Everyone knows that tale of the actor and the gerbil. But let me tell you a true tale that is probably now well known by doctors throughout America, no doubt augmented and changed as the inevitable urban legendization occurred.

Once there was a young intern, not terribly different than me. A little wiser than most interns, young Dr. Dan was a favorite of the nurses and a hero of mine, during my time before medical school when I was an emergency room administrator. He was a surgical intern, which means that he spent three months of his first year as a doctor working 26-hour ER shifts, alternating every other day. Obviously this was before the beginning of the ACGME's war against common sense, one campaign of which involved making various work-hour rules to limit the ability of young doctors to become exceptional.

Dr. Dan took signout from Dr. Barbara. Barbara was the other surgical intern currently rotating through three months in the ER. Together, alternating day-by-day, the two of these docs, straight out of medical school, would provide what is known as minor surgical coverage. Every patient that came into the ER during these three months that was assigned by the triage nurse as a surgical case would be managed initially, primarily, solely, and entirely by either Dan or Barbara. Mostly what they saw were UBIs. Unexplained Beer Injuries. Most of these were readily manageable and occurred in patients with high Tattoo to Tooth Ratios (TTRs). Sometimes there were worse cases though. They could ask for help from higher ups—residents—if it was more than they were ready for, such as head injuries from high-side donorcycle accidents, shotgun wounds to the chest, and self-inflicted bow and arrow wounds to the occipital lobe of the brain. Attending physicians were not available in the ER in those days, ever. During those years, calling an attending was clear evidence of 1) weakness, 2) lack of preparedness, 3) lack of ability to take on challenges, 4) lack of a chance to be an extraordinary doctor. In sharp contrast, nowadays calling an attending is 1) a sign of good judgment as it reflects the young doctor's awareness of the insufficient knowledge he has gained during his severely time-restricted work week, 2) a mandatory component of the ACGME-mandated supervision paradigm, 3) a recognition of ACGME-critical *systems based practice* in which the patient's needs are considered in the context of the broader issues of medical regulation, insurance company finances and social welfare, 4) a necessity given that the attendings cannot comfortably allow interns and residents to have full authority over the patients because the interns and residents weren't allowed an opportunity to take full responsibility for them.

This was Dr. Dan's 26-hour shift that would soon no longer be allowed by the soon-to-be-created creativity-limiting rules that no one would ever know who made. It was 2 AM, and he counted the 16 hours left before he would be signing back out to Barbara at 6 PM. Each was a good surgical intern. Each wanted to make sure all their cases were cleaned up, stitched up, unbent, resected, or embalmed prior to the daily changeover.

Dan and Barbara had quickly become favorites of the firemen and policemen of the city, most of whom I knew from my position working in the ER. Dan had stitched up a few fireman, and set the broken limbs of a couple of cops. Barbara had managed all the second degree burns when a burning building collapsed and fell on two firemen (both rescued, but needing Dr. Barbara's excellent ministrations). Firemen and policemen love the Emergency Room docs. Just like an infantryman in war loves his corpsman.

I saw the man limp in the door, wearing pajamas, stooped over, at an angle, clearly in great pain with every step. I was young, just out of college, but I was the chief administrator signing patients into the ER that night. I popped out of my large protective desk structure, which was rather like a fortress, three sides of chest-high desktop, with the fourth side a wall with a whiteboard filled with the names of all the people I might need to nag to get something done overnight in the hospital. The limping man looked like he needed a wheelchair, so after I popped out of my administrative fortress, I grabbed a folded wheelchair, deftly flipping it open and then sliding it right in front of the man, offering him the seat and an opportunity to be treated, for a moment, as a king.

He declined.

He said that sitting would kill him.

So, I ushered him to the triage nurse while I asked him just enough questions to get the health care process started: his name, his age, and what his complaint was. I knew he was hurting. It wasn't time for insurance cards, filling out complex forms, or asking questions that he would be asked again by the triage nurse, and then again by the doctor. I wasn't going to bother this hurting man with required HIPAA forms to sign and other medically useless, nay counterproductive legalistic piles of shit. Compare this to the last time *you* went to the ER. Now you have to give the ER administrators your insurance card before they will even waste their valuable time asking for your name, which they must have before you fill out the three pages of redundant information, followed by the HIPAA consent form. We will discuss HIPAA someday, but not in this book. It will make you nauseated. Not nauseous. To be *nauseous* means that you make other people want to vomit. HIPAA is nauseous. So is JCAHO, and so is ACGME. They are all nauseous.

This patient's name was John Thomas, and he wasn't nauseated, but his bum was sore, and what I learned made him nauseous and I wanted to vomit.

"How long has your bum been hurting?" asked the triage nurse. Sheila was the most experienced nurse that the ER had who wasn't yet carrying a clipboard, and therefore tended to work the triage desk, which required far more knowledge, wisdom, and common sense than other positions in the ER. Sheila was also absolutely stunningly cute, and always wore the white nursing outfit—skirt and hat, as opposed to the scrubs and doo-rag of the modern nurse. She was, sadly for me and happily for her, married to one of the city firemen, a handsome and friendly guy himself. She was older than me and way out of my league anyway. Years later I would meet Jennifer, who was also out of my league, but was a nearly spitting image of Sheila, being as she was Sheila's younger sister.

"About five hours," replied Mr. John Thomas, a man I had learned was just shy of fifty years old.

"Has this ever happened before?" Sheila asked.

"No. Well nothing like this. I have never had this kind of severe pain before, that's for sure." He groaned as he leaned over further on the desk.

"Have you been having diarrhea?"

"No."

"Constipation?"

"Not really."

"Fevers?"

"No." Another groan.

"Blood in your stool?"

"No."

"Did you swallow anything that wasn't supposed to be swallowed?"

"Do you mean, like, poison?"

"Well that too, but I meant, like, a coin, a rubber ball, or anything else other than food."

"Oh, no, nothin' like that." Groan.

"Are you sure you don't want to sit?"

"No, definitely no!"

"How about lying down."

"Okay."

Sheila guided Mr. Thomas across the ER, down a short hall to the minor surgical room, and helped him onto a medical bed on wheels. He lay down on his side, groaning and shivering.

Sheila called the surgical intern, Dr. Dan, to come take a look.

Which Dr. Dan did.

Dr. Dan walked into the room a bit bleary-eyed from his 20-minute nap. Falling asleep was very easy for an intern, as I have previously mentioned, but waking up is often a near impossibility. Dr. Dan was not fully awake, his hair was sticking up like the stuff at the top of a pineapple, his white coat was on inside out, and his scrub pants lacing was loose, causing his pants to fall down constantly. He fiddled to adjust that problem, pulling his pants up quickly. "Good evening Mr. Thomas. I am Dr. Dan. What is the problem?"

"My butt is in agony," he groaned. "Never felt such pain."

"Constipated?"

"No."

"Have you been having diarrhea."

"I told the other lady no."

"Anal intercourse?"

"God no!" The man's indignity was remarkable.

"Have you had any injury to your anus?"

The man was quiet for a moment before replying shyly and without looking at Dr. Dan. "I fell on a coke bottle."

"You fell on a coke bottle," repeated Dr. Dan in his sleep-deprived stupor. "Were you naked?"

"Yes."

"Did the coke bottle injure your anus, then?"

"Yes."

"Have you been bleeding?"

"A little."

"Are you otherwise healthy? No AIDS, no cancer, no intestine disease, heart disease, alcoholism, drug abuse, etc. etc.?" All negative or otherwise reassuring responses.

"Well, let's have a look."

Dr. Dan closed the door and grabbed a pair of latex gloves. Back then, latex gloves had talcum powder in them, to help them slide over the fingers. We have since discovered that the powder often poofs into the air, carrying some latex with it, and then is breathed into the lungs of the medical staff, initiating latex allergy. At one point, over 20% of medical workers had become allergic to latex because of this (me included). Latex gloves were now powder-free in the States.

Dr. Dan pulled the gloves down over his fingers with practiced ease, allowing the wrist of each glove to snap resoundingly on the flesh of his own wrist, an action that yielded a large poof of latex-laden powder that then floated lazily throughout the room and into the immunologically-primed lungs of the unsuspecting soon-to-be-allergic young doctor.

"I'll need to pull down your pajamas. Is that okay?"

The patient nodded his assent, and Dr. Dan took a sleepy aim at the now naked buttocks. With one hand he parted the pale fleshy cheeks. With the other, one finger dipped in warm water as lubrication, he gently poked around the outside of the man's anus. There was a small tear with just a little blood. Sometimes these tears happen when passing a large hard stool rapidly, and they can hurt like all get-out. Sometimes they happen during anal intercourse. Sometimes they happen when you fall naked on an outstretched coke bottle.

"You have a little anal fissure, Mr. Thomas. And a bruise. They can hurt very badly. You should keep your stools soft with laxatives for a week, and keep your anus moisturized with Vaseline. Drink lots of water and prune juice. If you do that, you should heal within a week. In the meantime, I can give you a prescription for some high dose ibuprofen to help with the pain. Can't give narcotics, 'cuz they'll constipate you, and that's the last thing you want."

Mr. Thomas lay still on the table. "Are you, umm, sure nothing else is wrong, doctor?"

Dr. Dan, sleepy as he was, was a very good doctor. The

patient's question caused his brain to jolt more awake. He remembered his first day in training as a surgeon. He had been taught that there are only two reasons not to perform a full digital rectal exam. Those two reasons are 1) no rectum, or 2) no digit. Dr. Dan looked at his hand and found the relevant digit: his middle finger. He looked at Mr. Thomas and found the relevant rectum. With the confidence of knowing that he would correct his error now by performing the full relevant rectal exam that he should have performed before, he re-wetted his still-gloved finger and went back in for the kill. "Let me check one more thing," said Dr. Dan as he parted the cheeks. And he checked.

Dr. Dan inserted his wet middle finger into Mr. Thomas' anus. He paused, and then inserted it farther into the rectum and then performed the standard San Fran Twisto, a maneuver which involved Dan contorting his whole body to allow his gloved middle finger to rotate essentially 360 degrees within the man's rectum, to feel every side for potential pathology, such as prostate lumps, stool impaction, etc.

As was soon to be learned, this man who had claimed to have fallen on the coke bottle (what would have been a standard case of Eiffel Syndrome: "I fell"), had actually not fallen, but in some other manner managed to have lodged in his bottom an old-style glass coca cola bottle. The bottom of the bottle had clearly gone in first and the open glass neck was the last in, but in it had gone. And into the rectum had gone Dr. Dan's finger. And into the open neck of the coke bottle Dan's finger had blindly and innocently proceeded. And then the San Fran Twisto screwed his finger into the neck of that glass coke bottle, creating that suction effect that caused his finger to get stuck, stuck firmly in the coke bottle that was rammed up the man's butt. The vacuum was strong. Dr. Dan calmly but to no avail worked to remove his imprisoned finger. He wriggled, he squirmed, he pried. Each time the coke bottle moved, the patient cried out in agony. Over a period of more than two minutes, Dr. Dan managed only to de-contort himself sufficiently so that his own back wasn't at risk of cracking. He then pulled a rolling stool over to the bedside with his foot, and sat next to John Thomas' butt, his finger still deeply ensconced within it.

"You have a coke bottle in your butt, don't you, Mr. Thomas."

"It's possible."

Dr. Dan nodded, non-judgmentally, as he considered his options. He knew from some childhood idiocies in his own youth, not involving any butts, how his finger would fairly rapidly swell within a coke bottle, making it nearly impossible to get out if too much time passed. When he had stuck his finger in a coke bottle as a child, he had been able to lick his exposed finger to lubricate the digit, which had helped him extract it. Dr. Dan quickly ruled out licking his exposed digit. He recalled that raising the bottle and finger over one's head would help keep the finger from swelling. He contemplated, only momentarily, the possibility of hanging Mr. Thomas from the ceiling, to keep the coke bottle and finger elevated.

Suddenly in a slight panic, he pulled again. Nothing productive resulted but another yelp of pain. With effort, Dr. Dan worked his stool and the patient's rolling bed over near the sink. There was some Vaseline gauze nearby, and he managed to grab it, open its packaging with his teeth, and lubed up his visible finger with the gooey grease. The net effect of his subsequent efforts to work his finger out ended with his finger more deeply inserted than before, and the coke bottle perhaps likewise more deeply inserted.

He pulled. Screams of agony. He lubed the anus and

pulled. Screams of agony. He San Fran Twisted and pulled. Screams of agony and prayers to Yahveh, Zeus, Thor and Jesus were hollered, followed by an extra prayer aimed carelessly and desperately at the Virgin Mary, "Sweet mother of Jesus!"

Dr. Dan looked over at the closed door. He looked at the phone high on the wall, out of ready reach. He chose the door. With effort, he, with his patient in tow, managed to open the door. He called for help. I was the fortunate one to be close enough to hear. Oh so fortunate.

I ran into the minor surgical room to see Dr. Dan—a man whom I looked up to with deep respect, reflecting my hope to be like him someday—with half his forearm visible, and the other half firmly applied between moderately flabby pink buttock cheeks. His face was red and sweat dripped from his nose and forehead.

"What, did he bite you, Doc?"

"Nice one, Eddie. My finger is stuck."

It came to me then. Ahh. Poor Dr. Dan. What fun I was about to have.

"Can't get it out?"

"I've tried. My finger is stuck in a coke bottle in Mr. Thomas' rectum."

I said nothing, but boy was I thinking.

"Eddie, I need you to call the surgical resident on call. Right away."

"I'm on it, Dr. Dan."

And I was. But I didn't stop at the surgical resident. It was one of the first times that I acted like an asshole. I figured Dr. Dan would need more help than just the surgical resident. So I called the anesthesiology team, the surgical ward nurses, the medical ward nurses, the OR scrub nurses, the night-shift janitorial staff, the three nearest firehouses, and every police precinct in the downtown area. By the time the resident had figured out that they needed to take Mr. Thomas' ass and Dr. Dan's finger to the operating room, I had lined up every awake person in Boston along the hallways all the way from the ER to the OR.

As Dr. Dan hunched over his patient, walking alongside the rolling bed, he smiled as the gathered mass of men and women who already loved him provided evidence of their appreciation of his existence by applauding, loudly and eagerly, for the entire duration of his long walk.

"Good job, Doctor!"

"Excellent diagnosis!"

"Obviously a superior grand rounds case. Please take pictures."

Sheila, our wonderful and beautiful triage nurse, who stood by the final corner that led to the operating rooms holding the hand of her fireman husband, simply said, "Nice ass, Dan."

Chapter 18

Fear of Flying

Everyone loves flying, particularly me. I am over 6 feet tall, so I particularly like being treated like a member of the either major species: cattle or sardine. I bitch whenever I fly, unless I am in business class, which I cannot afford.

There is nothing, nothing more valuable or productive in life than writing an angry note to customer service at an airline that has intentionally screwed you with their negligence, incompetence and utter failings. Every word you scribe or type you can be sure will be read and heed paid to it by the highest executives of the airline. Furthermore, their responses will be responsive, their answers will answer you, their apologies be sincerely apologetic, their explanations well-explained, and their concern for your continued business profound. They will care what you have to say. They know that it is important for them to understand the nature and degree of your anger and frustration. They know that you don't want to hear trite patronizing responses, and they wouldn't dare respond in a trite cliché patronizing fashion to a disgruntled customer. They will want to appease you with free airfare and free upgrades to business class, you can be sure.

Writing an on-line complaint is particularly fruitful of rapid and concerned response. You should always write a thoroughly detailed note to the airline when you are upset with them, because it is so effective, and will assuredly fix the problem so that it never happens again. Just as you would expect utility from writing to a U.S. congressman or a senator.

I have started taking Benadryl when I fly so that I sleep instead of pissing off the people next to me by bitching. Sometimes I forget to take this wonderful sleeping pill antihistamine brain-fogger, though. Sadly, I forgot this time, perhaps because I had booked my flight at the last minute. I was heading to a funeral of a friend—a sad fact but irrelevant to this story.

I had been stuck in the far back, bounciest, noisiest and latrine-stinkiest section of the plane, in the middle of the middle seats, squeezed between two enormous sets of shoulders that were coated with muscle and flab. Each of the men's sizable girths overflowed their tiny perches and bubbled into *my* tiny perch. My shoulders were forced up to my ears as I tried to sit back in my straight-backed semi-cushioned reminder of a puritan pew. The engine noise even beat on my head the way that a deacon would have smacked those who slouched in an old Presbyterian church service. My knees did not in any way fit between my hips and the seat in front of me. Usually, I could deviate one knee out to each side and encroach upon smaller people next to me, but on this flight the two gargantuan gorillas were already fully encroaching their obesities into my highly limited space. If the man squeezed into the seat in front deigned to lean his seat back, my kneecaps would be fractured and both my hips and my patience would be entirely knocked out of joint. I was utterly absolutely and in all ways miserable. It was a seven-hour flight and the damn plane hadn't even taken off yet.

There are things that no innocent human being should have to be put through. By "innocent" I mean very specifically those individuals who have never tried to get other people to do their bidding by using force or fraud. This is my only definition of "innocent" and it obviously excludes almost all politicians, as well as most people who vote for them.

One of the experiences that no innocent human being should have to suffer involves the position I found myself in right then. Given my innocence, how is it that I got stuck between these two massive bundles? I don't know, but I was sick and tired of it and I wasn't going to take it anymore.

I dropped my shoulders down from my ears to a more normal position, levering apart with all my strength the robust arms of the girthy gentlemen to my sides. I twisted my arms to push my elbows into their midsts and slowly applied increasing pressure. Each man noticed my effort and slid slightly away from me, but insufficiently to make any real difference on a seven-hour flight which would likely be a nine-hour flight with two hours stuck sitting motionless in the plane on the ground as the crew goes through pre-flight checks they should have done while we were boarding, and while awaiting a takeoff time slot in the overly-crowded takeoff time slot queue.

No, I wasn't going to take it. So I smiled at the man to my right and said, "Would you mind dropping fifty pounds, please? Your flab is preventing my breathing." To the man on my left, I said, "Would you mind disembarking the airplane and making an appointment at the airport liposuction facility? Your caloric intake has left no room for me to even sit in this seat that I paid for." I began coughing like I had tuberculosis and Ebola, and without covering my mouth.

But I actually of course didn't say or do any of these

things, because these men already knew they were fat and probably weren't any happier about it than I was. My telling them wouldn't help them be less fat, less expensive on my wallet through tax dollars extorted from me in subsequent treatment of their obesity-related diseases, or in any other way create value in the world. My using my medical acumen to diagnose them with Dunlap Syndrome (in which the belly 'dun laps over the waistband') wouldn't improve anyone's situation in the least. I gazed forward in the plane until I realized that there were no other available seats whatsoever. As usual with the airlines, they had me, as they had all the passengers, by the short curly hairs, and there wasn't a damn thing I could do about it. So I did something about it. I started writing a complaint letter.

There was no way I could write this complaint letter on my laptop, because there was too little room in front of my belly. I tried, but the laptop screen was still half-way closed, blocked from fully opening by the partially slanted seat in front of me, soon to be more slanted as the man in front would no doubt be attempting to fracture my kneecaps soon. Although I couldn't see the half-closed screen to work my computer, that mattered little, because my elbows had failed in their battle against the continental drift occurring to either side of me. My elbows were now pinned in front of my belly, with the only available space for my hands being either against the back of the seat that would soon attack me, or kept adjacent to my face. There was no way I could type.

I was going to type my note anyway. I will tell you how. But first, I decided to be optimistic and think of the bright side of my predicament. So, as the plane started accelerating up the runaway, I envisioned the plane lifting off momentarily and then crashing in a tumble of shattering glass, tearing metal, exploding fuel and screaming humans. What an optimistic thought, because there in my mind's eye I survived uninjured, protected from the trauma of deceleration, impact or flying debris by the two gargantuan soft pillowed cushioned airbagged masses that kept me as safe as if I had been encased in marshmallow fluff. In my mind's eye, I walked out of the residual bits of the wrecked aircraft and gazed over the scene of flaming devastation, grateful for the seating arrangements in which I now found myself. I smiled.

The plane was now solidly off of solid ground, soaring in the air. How it took off I know not, but I did note that as we climbed, the tail of the airplane was still substantially lower than the front, confirming that the tail end was weighed down by the two gentlemen displacing me from my seat, who were misbalancing the plane and risking an imminent flaming crash with screaming metal and twisting humans.

I turned toward my right, opened up the man's tray table and rested it on his belly. I leaned back against the man to my left. I prodded him with my now free left elbow to adjust his abdominal girth appropriately to serve as my lumbar support. I opened my laptop sideways and began crafting my note. I chose to ignore the bewildered looks of my seatmates as I fought back against their intrusion on my national sovereignty.

Dear Delta/USAIR/United/Northwest/Continental customer service. You suck. I think that phrase rather summarizes my feelings on the matter. You suck. You delayed my flight for five hours yesterday, blaming it on weather problems caused by global warming, and then finally cancelled the flight at midnight and sent us all home. You rebooked me for today on this current flight, which was delayed for two hours for lack of crew, although you blamed the delay on global warming so as to avoid financial culpability, and you placed me in the farthest back nether-regions of the aircraft, wedged between King and Kong, two sumo-wrestlers on vacation. The fact that I am immediately adjacent to the toilets would lead me to fear the resulting stenches which emanate therefrom, but fortunately that is not a concern because several people in the aircraft appear to suffer no compunction in simply passing their gas willy nilly while remaining in their seats.

Although my current level of comfort is the antithesis of pleasant, I still have the wherewithal to make some small suggestions.

> *1. Upon boarding, you should supply all passengers with red flags on sticks. As soon as seated passengers smell flatus, each should immediately raise his flag. As the flatulent miasma spreads through the region of the plane from which it emanated, the flags will rise in a gradually widening pattern. The observant and trained air hostess, using these visual cues, can quickly track backward the rising flags to find the criminal sociopathic passenger who decided to delight the rest of us with his flavor of the day by untimely giving birth to his previously unborn fart.*
>
> *2. Publicize how far apart your seats are fore and aft, and how wide they are. Compare this size to the size of the humans who actually exist in America and determine if your chosen seat size and humanity are at all compatible.*
>
> *3. Disempower the air hostesses, while empowering them. Take away their power to force us to turn off our Kindle e-book readers,*

our battery operated calculators, iPads, iPods, and laptops. Empower them to allow us to keep our seatbacks gradually reclined during takeoff and landing so we all don't have to sit for 25 minutes ramrod straight as if a glass coca cola bottle had been inserted, backwards, up our butts.

4. Provide small partial reimbursements on the cost of the ticket for each time your airline inconveniences a passenger as a result of your own cost-control policies, government regulations you didn't fight against or for which you actively lobbied, or for accidents that happen such as plane crashes or two overly expansive humans sitting in the same row.

5. Empower the air hostesses to be able to make the pre-flight announcements much more amusing. Let them be free. Here is what I think serves as an example of a good pre-flight announcement:

> *"Welcome aboard Delta flight 9857 to Boonesville. If you are not intending to go to Boonesville today, please take this opportunity to exit the plane. Please buckle up when seated, and if you don't know how to use the seatbelt, feel free to ask, you idiot. If oxygen masks emerge from the ceiling, put them on. They don't actually have any oxygen flow in them, as evidenced by the bag not filling up, so don't believe us when we say otherwise. Just put them on. In the event of a water landing, you are going to die. But we*

> *have life jackets under the seats because we are required to by act of the federal government. If you miraculously manage to survive a water landing, then God clearly has been with you and we can assume He will teach you how to use the life jacket under your seat. There is no smoking on the aircraft. The lavatories are considered part of the aircraft, so don't smoke in them. If you tamper with a smoke detector, we will allow the rest of the passengers to beat you up. If a terrorist starts trying to take over the airplane, please stand up in your seats, approach the terrorist, and beat the living shit out of him. If you all would show that gumption, we wouldn't all have to be strip-searched and rectally probed before boarding the aircraft. We know it is unpleasant to fly, but we will do our best to assure you at least have a tolerable flight. Our pilots and ground staff are being trained every day to keep the time you are stuck in this metallic airborne submarine to the barest possible minimum."*

I think that if you would follow my suggestions, you would have happier passengers and be able to brand your airline better. Right now, nobody can tell the difference between all you different airlines, because you all blur together under the category of SUCK…

Best regards,
Edward Marcus, MD

I didn't truly think my letter to the airline would be met with any response whatsoever. But a few weeks after the flight, I received a highly apologetic and empathetic electronically-generated personalized form-letter note in which they credited my frequent flier account with 7500 miles. That wasn't sufficient, so I sent my original letter to the airline again, and received another personal form letter of a highly empathetic and apologetic nature, in which they offered to improve the situation I had complained about and then provided me with 7500 miles. I sent the letter again, and received another 7500 miles. And then another.

One day, I am going try to make recommendations to improve a hospital, or a medical system or a health care law. When I do go to that effort, I am pretty sure that I won't even get an apologetic letter back. I expect instead that I will be viciously attacked by the entrenched interests, the pervertors of the law, and those holier-than-thou know-it-all fascist types. I sure as heck won't get any frequent flier miles, and I will probably lose my job, too.

Chapter 19

Lighting a Fire under the Match

So, there was this intern who I didn't like. A medical intern, a flea, a nerd, a geek, smart as a whip academically, but stupid as a ball bearing socially. He just wasn't a good doctor. He had a bad case of cranio-rectal synostosis, which prevented him from pulling his head out of his ass. Tom wore a pocket protector (really) and stuffed his white coat pockets with every medical gadget he could buy and crammed the residual available space with bits of notes and index cards. He was an engineer version of a doctor, thinking in perfectly straight lines. A laser beam of linearity. Black and white and nothing in between. There was more than just a touch of asshole in Tom.

There was another intern I didn't like. Cheryl had been a brown-noser in medical school. A gunner, gunning for grades. The woman cared about her grades much more than she cared about learning medicine to help patients. If a professor's test was considered by her to be unfair because he hadn't told the class what they needed to be prepared for, she would complain, but only if she had done poorly, which is the only reason why she would consider the exam to be unfair.

This type of doctor will spend her career caring about her career, avoiding making mistakes in patient management so that she won't get in trouble for making mistakes, and generally living her life in a perpetual state of fear and defensiveness, while using people to help her build her ego. It is like there was just a bit of asshole in Cheryl.

There was another intern I didn't like, who had a whole lot of asshole in him. He had a piss-poor outlook on life, perhaps because he was trying to do stuff he sucked at. Maybe he needed to have an optorectomy to disconnect his ass from his eyeball in order to overcome his shitty outlook on life, but maybe it was just because Dick didn't know enough to be a doctor. He was nearly clueless. Plus he was unethical. He would perform TUBEs—Totally Unnecessary Breast Exams. I don't know how he graduated. Yes I do. They don't fail students out after starting third year of medical school. He snuck through the first two years of book study, but sucked the big suck during his clinical rotations as a medical student. That Dick ended up at my hospital was a fluke of the Match.

The Match is a complicated monopoly process for assigning just-graduating doctors to the hospital in which they will do their residency. The primary purpose of the Match is to allow the hospitals to not have to negotiate with individual young doctors in regard to salary and benefits, thus keeping the hourly pay of the young doctors, who work 80 hours per week, lower than the pay of a Wal-Mart clerk. It is salary-capping enslavement. Because of the Match, no extra pay needs to be given for better young doctors who work harder. Given that Medicare pays most of the costs that hospitals accrue in obtaining and paying for resident doctors, one can see how the Match exists to help control Medicare costs. I think this bit of money-saving by Medicare by means of the salary-control of residents enabled by the Match is the only plan that the politicians have for preventing Medicare from bankrupting the federal government. It ain't gonna be enough.

The Match would be considered illegal collusion, illicit monopolism, and a variety of other corporate criminalities, had it been run by a cartel of big evil corporations. But the Match was set up for the 'benefit of all' and therefore spread all of that said benefit around, although I have never met anyone who benefits.

Anyhow, I disliked this intern because he was an asshole and sucked and yet got paid just as much as me, and I was at least slightly better than suck, so I should be paid, in a world that is sane, slightly better than the sucky pervert. But the world isn't sane.

I remember Match day well. It was less than nine months ago, after all. I had previously visited a half-dozen hospitals and interviewed with two dozen attendings and residents. They were all smart. They were all proud of their hospital. I was the second best student in my class of 150 in medical school, and none of these hospitals had any power to offer me any monetary or any other incentive to come be a doctor at their hospital. Not a one of them. The few times I raised the issue with any of the attendings, I was met with blank stares.

"I've been a pretty good medical student," I would say to Ms. Hutchens, the head of human resources at some third rate community hospital that had a fledgling family practice residency that had just been approved by ACGME and that they were trying to beef up in terms of reputation. She was the product of a progressive arts education at a progressive arts college somewhere, being taught by progressive professors who watch MSNBC, who are able to be professors because they are progressive and could therefore tolerate staying within the culture of a progressive arts college. The previous week I had met a similarly administrative person at another hospital who acted exactly like Ms. Hutchens but was the product of a southern bible college being taught by conservative professors who like to watch Fox News. Regardless of their supposedly radically different views, they each had responded precisely the same way to my questions to them, making me suspect that their actual views weren't very different despite them being in two supposedly very different camps.

"Look, Ms. Hutchens, I've received a grade of honors in every one of my classes except one, and all my clinical rotations so far. I have already been first author of two research papers, which have already been referenced more than thirty times each. I have interviewed at Harvard's teaching hospitals. I have interviewed at John's Hopkins. You want me and people smarter than me to come be doctors here, right? Can you not offer me an extra $3000 per year because I have proven that I am at least somewhat better than some other graduating doctors?"

The head of human resources would reply, shaking her head, "I don't think we want doctors like you here, who put money above the patients."

What a trite and ridiculous cliché type pile of bullshit. Look, you little hypocritical self-righteous woman, I would not say to her; look you psychopath who ignores that the biggest taking of life and biggest losses of dignity in human history occurred because of your philosophy; look you narcissist who tries to instill guilt into me for not being like you, so as to motivate me to be like you; look, I ain't playing that game. Screw you. If you want better doctors at your hospital, you will need to convince them to come work here somehow, and since you cannot compete on most levels, you better figure out how you *can* compete. I told you that for a measly three thousand bucks you could convince me to come here, and then you won't have to be saddled with assholes and perverts like Tom, Dick and Cheryl. But the notion can't even compute with you. You don't value better. You value equal. Okay then, I leave you to stew in your equalistic squalor.

But, as noted, I didn't say anything of the sort. I just *wanted* to say it, like so many before me have wanted to say it, but all of us have gotten embarrassed into not standing up against the moral failure of people like this human resource head, who dares to think that I care for money more than human life and dignity. I care so much for human life and dignity that I want both for everyone. I recognize that an honest wage for honest work is a good old-fashioned value to uphold especially in new-fashioned times, and especially in the medical system, for it encourages exceptionalism and improvement and brings out the best in people. And we want the best exceptional doctors, don't you think? But I couldn't speak rudely to Ms. Hutchens. I hardly spoke at all. I just nodded my head at her insult to me, and accepted it as the reality of the times.

But just before I walked out her door I found an iota of courage. I looked at her and said, "Three thousand dollars. Who castrated you so powerfully that you cannot even authorize three thousand dollars to get a better doctor for your patients? And tell me lady, who in this room is putting money above patients?"

But it wasn't just her. It is the whole system.

Before Match Day, all the fourth year students list their desired residency programs in order of their desire. They sign a contract that says they will go wherever they are told. The hospitals then list their desired interns in the order of their desire. Then a computer matches these lists all up in an attempt to maximally equalize everyone's happiness and minimally equalize everyone's pay, and on Match Day, we are all told where we will spend the next three or more years. Sounds fair doesn't it? But remember, it prevents any individual negotiations that involve money or benefits, and it assures a price control for salaries that prohibits encouragement of excellence. It was far worse than even the Baseball draft.

So I matched at the same hospital that I had worked for years, the same hospital within which I had done most of my clinical rotations during medical school. I knew the hospital well, I knew the staff. I knew the medical records system, and the morgue. I knew the cafeteria staff, and I knew the bartenders at the Horny Toad Pub next door. I hadn't even listed this hospital on my list of desired residencies. But that didn't seem to matter to the omniscient and omnipotent program in the computer that is the Match. The Match wanted me at this hospital that I knew so well. Who was I to argue?

And I was now an intern at my hospital, working my way through the brainwashing exhausting process of indoctrination into the flock of sheep. But I was still fighting that indoctrination.

Chapter 20

You Can Sleep When You're Dead

Another night in the ER. Here, I felt like a doctor. It was anybody's guess what might next come through the door. Back when I was a clerk in the ER, I always wanted to be a doctor. Now I was a doctor, and I was not uncommonly scared out of my pants and would rather be a clerk.

This particular week of ER work was an incredible albeit painful education. I was on the wound management team. During the day I worked with a retired Navy chief corpsman who knew his shit. I learned lots from him, fast, which was important because at night I was on my own. Fractures, sprains, lacerations all came my way. I would assist with any major trauma too. I was just like those surgical interns that I respected so much when I was a clerk, Dr. Dan and Dr. Barbara. If I got lucky, I might get my finger stuck in a coke bottle in a guy's bumhole.

Although I didn't know it at the beginning, this night was about to be a record-holder for the night in the ER with the largest compendium of resulting stories. Sadly, most ER stories are not pleasant stories with happy endings.

It was barely 6 PM when the first victim of inhumanity

came wheeling into the ER, surrounded by two paramedics, two EMTs, and a cloud of blood-red fog. The man's name was John Doe, as so many ER patients who are on the express train to death are coincidentally named. I wonder how their parents knew to name them John Doe. Could they by chance have known that the end of their grown child's life would be in the celestial transfer division of an inner city hospital?

John Doe came wheeling on a stretcher into the ER with an EMT sitting astride the man's hips and leaning forward over his chest performing CPR, like a man beating off angels. Press, lift, press, lift, pushing down on the man's heart to squeeze the blood around the dying body. But the blood wasn't going around the dying body, as could be seen each time the paramedic at the man's head squeezed the Ambu bag to inflate the man's lungs. Each time the paramedic squeezed, fine mists of bubbly bloody spray were propelled out of many small holes in the man's chest wall. Pressing, lifting, pressing, lifting just pushed blood from the man's heart into the man's lungs, which had quite evidently been air-conditioned by a 12-gauge shotgun blast at short range.

What had thirty seconds before been a clean white entranceway to our clean white emergency room was now a sea of blood splattered walls, blood splattered people, and red footprints spread along a floor that was now a blood-soaked slip-and-slide. The trauma team had been given only a two-minute warning of John Doe's impending arrival, because John Doe had been shot just outside the Horny Toad Pub right next door to our hospital.

Mr. Doe was scooped into the Trauma room, which rapidly filled with people, some of whom were doing work. I was one of the ones doing work. I felt his pulse. Zippo. I looked at the monitor reading the electrocardiographic leads that a nurse had just attached to the man's shoulders and hip. Noise and blips but nothing happy. I looked at an oxygen saturation monitor picking up an empty signal. I grabbed a pair of trauma scissors and sliced off the rest of the man's bloody wet shirt. A bottle of povidone iodine was splashed unceremoniously on his chest milliseconds before a large thick scalpel blade cut open his insensate chestwall like a clamshell, exposing in one flash his lungs and heart as his chest sprung outward like a jack-in-the box.

I was right on top of the man's heart and left lung. If they hadn't been obscured with thick red matted blood, they would both look like swiss cheeses. This wasn't the result of buckshot—which would only have left perhaps a half-dozen holes. This was like #7 birdshot, peppering the man's chest with tiny pellets propelled out of the barrel of the shotgun from probably less than four feet away. The center of the blast had hit the heart, his heart, John Doe's heart, the heart of this unnamed but real man, and this heart was oozing residual streams of a blood that was getting thinner every second as huge volumes of saline were forced through large bore IVs into his volume-depleted body.

The chief surgical resident and scalpel handler looked up from the opened chest with a sigh, catching the eyes of everyone around the table all at once. There was that moment of universal recognition and acceptance that John Doe was dead. Nobody moved. The hands that had been squeezing the IV bottles stopped squeezing. The hands that had been squishing the ambu bagged stopped squishing. The fingers that had been contorting into a vein a second IV catheter stopped contorting. The monitors stopped beeping, photons stopped bouncing, and there was nothing but a vacuous silence in the trauma suite. The trauma suite itself knew there was absolutely no chance of survival for Mr. Doe. The silence lasted precisely three seconds before the entire troupe that made up the trauma team began running around moving hither and thither and beating their chest and staring their eyes and shouting their shouts for this fluid, that drug, that device to be placed into this orifice, all in an effort to obviate to the extent possible the man's unequivocal 100% chance of being dead. The efforts went on and on, for a full forty-five minutes. Heart holes were stitched closed and lung holes were stapled tight. Blood products began pouring in, never quite as fast as they poured out. Pellets of lead were occasionally flipped out of the chest by highly-talented fingers that blindly bumped into them from time to time. The respiratory therapist was doing push-ups, the nurses were doing jumping jacks, and the doctors were running a marathon, barefoot and backwards.

After a sufficient period of time passed in which huge efforts were expended and nothing accomplished except for substantial proof that every effort had been made, the chief resident running the show decided finally that the show was over. He let out another deep sigh, put his kelly clamp and needle driver down, and held his hands up with his fingers spread in a gesture of acceptance of the defeat.

"Stop," he said to the respiratory therapist bagging the man's holy lungs. "Stop" he said to the intern (me) rhythmically squeezing the holey heart to keep the blood pumping around the dead man's dead body.

We stopped. When we stopped the man was no more dead than he had been forty-five minutes earlier, but now he was dead enough for the chief resident to declare him officially transferred to the Eternal Care Unit of Celestial Permanence.

"I am calling it. Time of Death 18:47."

I stood silent. We all did. For more than three seconds. Perhaps it was fourteen seconds. Fourteen seconds of silence to memorialize the man of whom nobody in the room had any memories. Then everyone at once, as a school of fish, turned from the dead man on the table and began milling around here and there, putting bloody cloth in the plastic bags for the laundry, bloody surgical paper sheets into red biohazard containers, and working their way to the sink to wash their hands, faces, arms, necks and all the other bits covered with what was once the man's life. I was last in line to the sink. The chief resident had gone out several minutes before to let the family know how hard we had tried, how we had tried oh so hard, how we had done everything possible, how there was nothing we hadn't tried to do, but that all our incredible superhuman efforts were still not enough, and yes, their relative had died.

I pushed open the swinging doors of the trauma suite and walked out into the ER hallway. Out of the corner of my eye, and far too late to react, I saw a trash can hurtling through the air straight at my head. It found its mark on my forehead, leaving its mark on said forehead and then clattering against the chickenwired glass of the nearest wall, leaving its mark there as well. I saw a man hurtling toward me. It was John Doe, raised from the dead, but wearing different clothes than those I had cut off of him with the trauma shears less than an hour earlier. The man ducked and threw his shoulder toward my declining head and caught me under the chin, smashing my teeth through my tongue. I was an object that stood between him and his anger. No, I was a target of his anger—an anger that stood between him and his grief and acceptance of his twin brother's murder.

The policemen who were somehow conveniently always around in the ER when they were needed tackled the man and had him handcuffed before the blood dripped off my forehead onto the floor. I went to the bathroom and looked at the mirror, trying in vain to distinguish my own blood from blood of the twin brother's dead twin brother. I washed as thoroughly as I could until I looked like a doctor from a television series as opposed to a butcher from a horror movie, spit some tongue blood into the sink, and then risked stepping back outside. All was calm. The angry brother was settled down and the police were removing his handcuffs. He was a big guy. I am glad there were no more painted saws hanging on the wall of the ER or I might have lost a cheek. He saw me and sheepishly smiled an apology, one which a man who is manly and non-politically-correct such as me could accept without further words or mention, and then he put his head in his hands. The grief had beaten his anger, as it is supposed to do.

But he wasn't a twin brother. He was a triplet brother. Later that evening, the Horny Toad Pub in which John Doe had been killed was burned down by the third, whose anger hadn't yet been replaced by grief. The next day the arsonist would be caught and the revenge on the bar would be all over the city news.

But tonight was to be a banner night, remember, and the results of the bar burning would affect many, including me.

Crispy critters, three of them. Horrible word. Horrible. Dehumanizing and unacceptable. Disgusting. How could the medical system ever come up with these terms? How could I use them? I thought I was a good guy, so no way would I use such dehumanizing terms. These three crispy critters were three firefighters.

"Dr. Marcus, I just called the trauma team. There is real trouble coming. They've called a third alarm at the Horny Toad."

The bar was burning. Everyone had gotten out of the Honey Toad safely, but the firefighters were trying to put the fire out before it spread to the hospital, our hospital, next door, which would catch on fire like the forests of California in a dry spell, packed as we were to the ceilings with the piles of medical record paperwork that doesn't exist.

When a person suffers a fatal injury from a building fire, they are suffocated by the smoke first or made unconscious by the carbon monoxide. At least we tell the families that that is the case, to help reassure them that there was little pain.

The firefighters are one big family. Even if they hate each other at the firehouse, which they sometimes do (just as family members sometimes do), they come together from all over the city whenever one of them is injured. Sadly, firemen do get injured. So do police officers. Although the firemen may sit on ass most of the time, they sure do have their moments, for when there is a burning building these crazy heroes run right into it while everyone else is running out.

The three men who were about to be wheeled in were victims of the spreading of the fire from the Horny Toad to a small Chinese laundry adjacent. The fire had gotten into the roof of the laundry, unbeknownst to the firefighters who were smashing a hole in the wall to get to the side of the Horny Toad. Three men were crushed under the burning rubble as the ceiling collapsed without any warning, and a blaze of fire engulfed them as an old cache of Stoddard solvent—used in days past by the dry cleaning industry but highly explosive—did indeed explode. Three men were crushed under burning wood and paint and flammable toxic chemical solvent that soaked their rubber clothes. Some unexploded Stoddard solvent traversed up their sleeves, as the chemical had been bred to do in seeking dirt and stains to wash away but now instead carrying its painful baggage of burning volatiles, scorching the skin of the innocent men who were innocent because they never initiated the use of force on others. These innocent men didn't have time to suffocate, and the burning

Stoddard solvent didn't release carbon monoxide to place them into a peaceful slumber while they were killed.

You could smell them coming in before the door to the ER even opened. There is no way on earth to inform you as to the nature of this smell by use of the printed word. It can be described only obliquely by means of the physiological responses it causes in those who smell it, which is a combination of an intensely pervasive nauseation, stinging in the eyes, hair standing on end, shortness of breath and abdominal pain, all in the setting of a deep, palpable despondency. The smell of burned human flesh triggers profound responses in a living human being, the nature of which must have been programmed teleologically, through millennia of evolutionary pressure, because they are so deep and trigger such prominent and instinctive emotional responses even when the cause of the smell is not known rationally. It is perhaps for this reason that doctors created such horrible terms as 'crispy critters' to somehow numb themselves against the deeply ingrained and profoundly despairing feelings that could utterly paralyze any human who had any empathy at all.

There was another intern standing next to me who smelled the smell, and didn't know what it was, but the instinctive emotional and physical response was evident as he turned as white as his coat and started to stumble.

"It's all right, Tim," I said as I slipped my arm under his, providing just enough stability to help him avoid injurious collapse as his body failed in its struggle to stay conscious. His heart had slowed profoundly, and I lowered him to the ground so that the little blood flowing around his arteries would have a better chance of flowing toward his barely alert brain. Within a minute of lying on the ground, his heart had started beating at a faster clip, and he started coming back to full function, with the residua being a profuse clammy sweat over his whole body.

"It's okay pal. You had a vaso-vagal episode."

"I passed out? Like an old lady?"

It wasn't the right time to joke, so I said, "You fainted, like a wimp."

Tim chuckled, embarrassed.

"Why?"

"The smell got to you. It happened to me the first time too," I lied. I hadn't passed out the first time I smelled this smell. Not at all. I had puked.

"Let's get you back in the game."

There were three stretchers now rolling down the hallway to a back room in the ER. The triage nurse had apparently seen them, and knew rapidly that there was no chance for any of them. But there was nonetheless work to do.

Tim and I followed the men down the hallway. The chief surgical resident was already assessing the men. The scene was as horrible as can be imagined. Three men with melted burned clothing adhered to melted burned flesh. I moved over to the second man, after sliding Tim near the first. Not only had my patient's eyebrows been burned off, but so had his eyelids. His hair was gone, his eyes were blistered and there was charcoal in them, or so it appeared. He moved not at all except for slight chest motion and a faint groan with each exhalation. Every square inch of what used to be his skin consisted of third and fourth degree burns. My eyes watered from the still rising smoke from the man's burned uniform and skin. They watered with tears. Tim's did too. The nausea was powerful, the emotions were abundant, there was fear, exhaustion, pity, horrible pity, and a sadness so profound as to be explained only by it emanating from within my very DNA.

Help him feel better. Help him feel better.

"Help him feel better, Eddie," the chief surgical resident who had earlier run the code on the air-conditioned John Doe told me.

How. How?

"Intramuscular morphine. Lots of it. He's in pain." The chief resident took a syringe from the nurse standing nearby, made no effort to squeeze out air bubbles, and injected the whole thing into the thigh of the third fireman whom he was standing near.

The nurse walked over to me with another syringe.

I took it.

It said 300 mg on it, written by hand in pen a few minutes earlier by a pharmacist who had been wise enough to be prepared for this need. Morphine. A very solid dose of morphine. A fatal dose most likely. But it would take the pain away with near certainty. Death takes pain away too.

I wasn't killing him. I was taking his pain away. The fire had already killed every part of this man, except his pain, which was evidently present. I had been taught once that there was no pain in these patients because these patients' nerve endings were all burned off. It was reassuring, but I didn't believe it. We had also been told before we did circumcisions on one-day old innocent baby boys that they sensed pain differently than older children and it was therefore okay to chop their foreskin off with a clamp and a scalpel without giving them any sedation or pain meds. That such a notion was obviously false was evidenced by the screams coming from the mouths of the one-day old baby boys as they lost the foreskin that their parents had so eagerly and desperately wanted removed before the child was even all the way out of the birth canal.

So I had no reason to believe that this man felt no pain. I

had every reason to believe he felt exquisite pain. And that he felt emotions that I couldn't imagine. Loss. Fear. Anger. Sadness. Anxiety.

Could I inject him with a potentially fatal dose of morphine? Would that be within my purview as a doctor? Any dose sufficient to take away his pain might stop his breathing too. And if it wasn't enough to stop his breathing, it probably wasn't enough to stop his pain. So, what would be the point of giving him a little, that might not be enough, when I could give him certainly enough to take his pain away and kill him.

I didn't know the man. I wasn't his wife, father, mother, brother or child. I didn't know his name. I didn't love him. I wasn't the person who could best make wise choices for him when he wasn't able to do so himself.

But I was the one standing next to him. There was no wife, father, mother, brother or child who loved him standing next to his bedside right now. His pain was in my hands. I imagined being him now, alert, in searing pain, immobile, unable to speak, hoping, so hoping that I wasn't burning in hell for all eternity, hoping that the faint misty image blocking the light still able to get through my seared eyes might be someone who could take away the agony.

I was the faint misty image of hope for this man. What would happen to his last little bit of hope if I walked away?

It wasn't black and white.

I injected a modest dose of morphine into the man's thigh, saving the rest, whispered into his ear that I would be right back to take his pain away, and moved quickly out of the room and up the hallway to the front of the ER.

There were six firemen and ten policemen milling around silently. Shuffling their feet aimlessly, powerlessly. They knew exactly what their friends' situation was. So did all the firemen outside still fighting the blaze.

The firemen all as one looked toward me as I emerged into their midst, hoping I would tell them what their friends' situation was, that situation that they knew so well.

"I am sorry, gentlemen." My voice barely worked. These were all men. They had to fall back on being men right now; they needed me to be a man, and I couldn't let them down. I repeated loudly in my deepest manly voice. "I am so sorry, gentlemen." They looked at their feet, all but one who looked at me, with eyes pleading. I approached him.

"I need your help. Now."

"Anything, Doctor." It was a title that I barely deserved. The firefighters lifted their heads again to look at me. I knew a couple of them.

"My name is Dr. Marcus. I don't know your friends. But someone needs to decide. Somebody who each would trust?"

Several men came over next to me now. They needed no more information. They saw the syringe in my hand.

There was a silent exchange of nods. Then the man who had looked at me so pleadingly took his hat off his head. The others followed suit.

"Do it, Doctor. We have known John, Howie and Joe for many many years. We love them. Do your job, Doctor. I promise you it is what they and their families would want."

I turned rapidly and moved with utmost haste down the hallway of wretched putrid singed-flesh smoke. Tim was standing next to his patient, with a syringe in his hand. The chief surgical resident was looking at him gently. Tim looked at me. I nodded at him, then moved to my patient.

We each injected our syringes into the thighs of our patients, who we didn't know.

But who we loved.

We did what doctors are supposed to do.

We took their pain away.

Chapter 21

But my pain was still there. I had never killed a person before, even though it wasn't me but rather the fire that had killed this person, that fire set by the arsonist that I knew not. I was happy that his pain was ended. The man was no longer worried that he was forever condemned to be in the third ring of the seventh circle of Hell, the place of perennial burning for those who had done violence to God. He was relieved of the fear, the anxiety, the terror, the dread. He was relieved. I guessed I was too. I wasn't.

My ER shift wasn't over. Remember, this was to be a record-breaking, record-making night for ER stories, ER pain, ER excitement, and ER shock. It took almost two hours before the other firefighters could come into the ER, but they all did. Then it was another hour before they had all ambled and milled out the door, each to their own support network, each to suffer their loss, and think about their lives. The families of the victims were being helped, to the little extent possible, by the network of friends and family that made up the fire department. Children, wives, brothers, sisters, and a mother.

No sooner had the last firefighter departed, and no sooner had the three men been removed from the ER to the morgue, did the next story begin to evolve. The ER still stank of putrid putrescence, and would for another twelve hours or more. When the day shift came to work, they would know the second they walked in that there had been crispy critters here overnight. Horrible phrase. Horrible dehumanizing phrase. How could we possibly use it?

I went to the minor surgical suite, my home for wound management. I washed my face and my hands. Not like Pontius Pilate did. But like Eddie Marcus needed to do. I needed to wash. My nose was still filled with the smoke from the men; my heart was still filled with the smoke from my soul.

The triage nurse walked into the room, through the swinging door. "Dr. Marcus, I got a doozy for you. You'll need help."

At that moment a stretcher rolled through the doors, with a man half-lying down, half bent up, squirming in obnoxious agony, holding a thick pile of bloodied sheets to his groin. He was probably in his mid-twenties, unkempt, with hair on his face where it hadn't ought to be and not on his scalp where at his age it had ought to be. His left hand was visible and bloody. His right hand was under the wad of sheets covering his groin. He was shirtless and, it seemed, pantless as well.

A policeman I knew from years ago walked in behind the stretcher.

"Hey Eddie, you finally became a doctor, huh?"

"Yes O'Reilly. I cheated on every exam and swore an oath I didn't agree with and they stuck a couple of letters behind my name. But I'm still the same moron you knew six years ago."

I turned to my groaning patient and said, "Sorry. I really am a doctor. My name is Dr. Marcus. What happened to you?"

The man groaned in response.

O'Reilly moved over and handed me a gallon-sized plastic Ziploc bag within which was a bloody mass of flesh and pine needles and dirt.

"Mr. Wilson got mad at his girlfriend."

I peered through the plastic of the bag trying to ascertain what I was seeing. It took but a moment to identify the bloody bluish pink mass.

"Mr. Wilson, who cut off your penis?"

Mr. Wilson groaned.

O'Reilly replied on his behalf. "He did it to himself. With a pair of kitchen sheers at his girlfriend's apartment. He threw it out of the window and it landed in a shrubbery on the ground, five floors down. I had to dig around for this. With my hands." O'Reilly's face was not pleased. Neither was O'Reilly's voice. Neither was O'Reilly.

I put on a gown to protect my bloodied scrubs from getting bloody, threw on a pair of powder-free latex gloves to protect my hands from getting penisy, grabbed a big wad of gauze sponges, and pulled back the pile of bloodied sheets to see the bloodied stump that had once served as the trunk of the man's former glory. It was oozing red blood with a small amount of residual arterial pumping. When arteries are cut straight through with a sharp object, they usually spasm closed, stopping hemorrhaging. When they are cut part-way through, or raggedly, they tend to pump blood until there is no blood left to pump. This man had cut his penis straight off, cleanly, with a sharp object, and was alive to groan about it because two of the three branches of the penile artery had spasmed tight. The third was the squirty one. I pushed the gauze down on the artery and reached around for a clamp. I thought to put some rubber tubing over the clamp jaws before gently using it to clamp closed the artery. That artery might be needed again, if the man was lucky.

A nurse, nameless and faceless to me at this point in the night, put an IV into the man's right arm, drawing off several tubes of blood into glass vials with various colored top plugs. Without any prompting, she would send them to the lab for a $490 standard set of bloodwork, including complete blood count, chemistry panel, drug screening, and HIV testing.

"Give him a liter of saline, wide open, will you Freda?" I said to the nameless nurse whose face I didn't know. "And can you give him a squirt of Demerol too?" She nodded her faceless face, as I contemplated what to do next.

I looked at the man's stump. I looked at the Ziploc bag. "Page urology please. And get some really cold water for me to put my spare penis in."

This man had a high cockroach factor. His ability to survive disasters and procreate were inversely proportional to any likely contribution to society. He was *Idiocracy* come to fruition. Urology came down and hosed off the man's cut-off hose, washing away the pine needles and the soil in which the pines had once grown. They were ruthless with young Mr. Wilson, showing him no respect at all, which was somewhat more respect than he might be deserved of at 1 AM upon dragging into the ER our slight and pretty female attending urologist along with a microvascular surgeon. These highly paid doctors were highly perturbed about having to reverse the man's highly destructive scissorwork. But they did. Over the next six hours, they sewed the man's arteries and veins together, plugged his distal corpus into his proximal corpus, twisted the relevant nerves into a braided hopeful knot and rifled his penile shaft with Frankensteinian sutures.

All of which ripped out the next afternoon, when the man got an erection because of clotting in his penile veins. So our pretty attending urologist spent another four hours fixing that mess, all so that the psychotic cockroach could procreate.

"Dr. Marcus, can you take a phone call?" It was 1:30 AM.

"Sure." I picked up the phone and pressed the blinking

white square indicating the likely line that was on hold for me, me, the brilliant young minor surgical family practice resident so knowledgeable that people would call me to help them with their minor surgical and wound management emergencies.

"Hello. I am Dr. Marcus. Can I help you?"

There was a silence on the other end of the phone before the silence was interrupted by a long, "Weeeeeellllll," from a tremulous male voice.

I patiently waited impatiently. Finally, to interrupt the long silence, and unable to generate the willpower to be evidently patient or obsequious, I pronounced the profound interrogative, "Ummmmm."

And my carefully considered 'ummm' elicited the response I sort of wanted, which was some information.

"My friend. He, weeeeeellllllll. He, ummmm." Interminable pause. Finally, "He shut himself in the dishwasher."

My medical and physics brain kicked in immediately. Those things were airtight. "How long ago did he shut himself in the dishwasher?"

"About 2 hours."

Moment of panic. "Is he out?"

"Huh?"

"Is he out of the dishwasher now?"

"Ummm. Yes?" said with a questioning tone.

"Is he breathing?"

"Oh, yeah. He's breathing."

"Is he conscious?"

"What?"

"Is he alert?"

"Oh, yeah."

"Why did he shut himself in the dishwasher?"

"It just happened."

"What, did he take the shelves out first?"

"Huh?"

"How did he shut himself in the dishwasher? Is he pretty small?"

Laughter. "No." More laughter and some tittering. "No, he is big."

I didn't have the energy, nor the imagination, to figure out the situation much further on my own. Other than the caller's obvious marijuana toxicity, I didn't have much more information than I had after the first prolonged statement of 'weeeellllll'.

"Look, what can I do to help you?"

"Weeeeellllll. He is bleeding, badly. He won't stop bleeding."

"Where is he bleeding?"

"Weeellllll. You know. From himself."

The 1:30 in the AM precognitive lightbulb turned on in my small semi-functioning brain. It couldn't be. Not twice in one night.

"From his PENIS?"

"Yeah. From his penis."

"He shut his penis in the dishwasher door?"

"Weeeeellllll, yeah."

"Was he doing the dishes naked?"

"Something like that."

I really didn't want to know more.

"What have you done to stop the bleeding?"

"We held a towel on it, pretty hard, for a long time. But when he takes the towel off, he starts bleeding himself again."

"Did any part of himself get cut off?"

"Yeah. There is a piece of himself in the dishwasher."

"Look, Mister. Your friend's injury sounds serious. He needs to come to the emergency room. Hold pressure on the wound and come as soon as you can. Bring the pieces of himself that got cut off too."

He never came in. Neither did his penis. Maybe he and his penis and his friend all went to another ER. Thank goodness, because had he come here on my advice, the pretty exhausted attending urologist would have become pretty pissy.

The night continued. It was time to move from front to back in the world of the mysterious male mind. I didn't realize until later that the rest of my night would be taken up by a trifecta of anal trauma.

"Lightbulb," said the triage nurse, shaking her head.

"In his butt?" I asked her, shaking my head incredulously, while believing it, remembering the coke bottle from years past.

"In. His. Butt."

"Oh my."

The man was wheeled into the minor surgical suite, lying on his side, groaning. He was holding his groin with one hand, and had the other hand behind him, defending his derriere. The groin often hurts when the rectum is stretched or injured—it is called referred pain. The hand defending his derriere—his efforts at booty-defense—seemed to have come a few hours too late.

"Hello, Mr. Friendly," I said to Mr. Friendly, who was about fifty years old, pudgy, balding, pale, with large pouty floppy lips, and eyes just a bit too close together. This guy wasn't getting laid. "What happened?"

Mr. Friendly shook his head, conveying with intensity the utter profound absolute humiliation of the situation.

"Did you fall on something?"

Mr. Friendly was in a lot of pain. He knew that I knew he hadn't fallen on anything with his anus, but he grasped at the straw and said, "Yes. I fell on it. A lightbulb."

For the moment I was going to let him live his untruthful lie. A case of what we call 'Eiffel syndrome' comes along now and again, and there was not a lot of point in pointing out the obvious lessons that such patients should learn from their unpleasant situations.

I examined the situation. His situation was dripping bright red blood down his pink left butt cheek. In medical parlance, this is written as 'BRBPR' or *'bright red blood per rectum'.* I wiped it off with a wad of gauze. The lightbulb in his butt wouldn't light again, because it was busted. Busted glass fragments in his rectum. Can you imagine?

There was no way I could perform a rectal exam safely without rubber gloves made out of steel-reinforced Kevlar. That thin glass of which lightbulbs were made would slice though latex with no more thought than went through Mr. Friendly's brain when he stuck one up his butt. I had no idea how the surgeons were going to deal with this rectal minefield.

Mr. Friendly had to have the lower part of his colon diverted to his abdominal wall through a stoma, through which he would have to poop into a bag attached to his skin for at least a few months. His rectum underwent partial resection and lots of stitching. He later developed peritonitis from the bacteria getting into his belly from his intestines, spent three weeks in the ICU, but lived to tell about it. Except I assume he never did.

It wasn't but fourteen minutes after turfing Mr. Friendly and his illuminated rectum to the general surgeons that the triage nurse marched back in to the room, laughing, but with a disturbed look.

"Eddie, this next guy has Eiffel Syndrome too."

"No way."

"I shit you not. A chisel."

"A chisel?!"

"That's what he says."

"Is he alive?"

"Very much so. I'll send him through x-ray first."

Which she did. The x-ray was on my computer screen thirty minutes later, and there was, indeed, a chisel in the man's rectum, and wherever else it might have migrated to. At least he had fallen on the handle end, and not the sharp end. Lucky fall.

"Mr. Frank, there is a chisel in your rectum."

"Yes, I know.

I was getting tired, and judgmental. "Why is there a chisel in your rectum?"

Mr. Frank said nothing. Neither did I. I stuck an IV in his arm, gave him a dose of Gorillacillin, and turfed him to the real surgeons, to put in their roster to fix up after Mr. Friendly. Shortly, Mr. Frank was out of my unkempt hair.

Within an hour, I was dozing, resting my head and unkempt hair on a counter in minor surgery when the triage nurse walked in.

"Dr. Marcus, you are *not* going to believe this."

A man rolled in on the stretcher behind her, head first. All I could see was his grey unkempt hair and that he was groaning and holding his groin. No way. Usually patients are transported feet first, but it was the wee hours of the morning, everyone is tired, and etiquette is forgotten. I forgot mine.

"Now what godawful insane apparatus did *you* stick up *your* ass?" I said to the man as the stretcher turned into its appropriate position in the center of the suite, revealing the man's face, which bore remarkable similarity to the face of the Dean of the medical school.

"Good evening, Dr. Marcus," said the Dean of the medical

school. "I seem to have an incarcerated inguinal hernia."

"Good evening, Dean," said I, glaring at the triage nurse, who was covering her mouth to avoid overt laughter as she walked out into the hallway. "I'm very sorry about the pain you must be in." And I *was* sorry. He was in lots of pain, and in some danger too. I was a sympathetic soul again, a doctor. Well, I was a doctor right now, but after my crack to the unrecognized Dean, I might not be a doctor in the morning.

I took care of the Dean, professionally, rapidly, recognizing that he needed surgery urgently, and calling the chair of the department of surgery directly. The Dean was treated with all the red carpet care one could hope for. They opened a second nighttime operating room for him, and brought in a second scrub and circulating nurse, just for him, so they could get to Mr. Frank's butt sooner too. My butt, like Mr. Friendly's and Mr. Frank's was on a sling now too, but after the stories that were going to emanate from this evening's ridiculous patient load, the Dean, even the Dean, couldn't help but laugh.

It was 4:30 AM when my anal trifecta was rounded out. As is said, you cannot make this shit up. This was the *magnum opus,* the *piece de resistance*, the *tour de force,* the *chef d'ouevre*. This was the case that, even in the absence of all the preceding ridiculousnesses of anal insertion and penile extraction encountered earlier in this historic ER shift, would make me, and this night, a mythical wonderment. If I was a hero for separating the Siamese Twins from the criminal justice system, I was a double hero for simply being present when this next patient rolled through the door.

The triage nurse walked in through the doors of the minor surgical suite and said, "Eddie, I am so sorry about the Dean. I didn't mean to suggest..."

I interrupted. "No problem. My fault. I was tired. I will be fired in the morning."

"No way. Everyone likes you, Eddie."

"Except the administrators, who all despise me. The Dean is the chief administrator, the head of the adminosphere, the bureaucrat extraordinaire."

"Well, I'm still sure it'll work out. Meanwhile this next patient stuffed something else up his butt. Three in one night. Unbelievable."

The man who was wheeled through the door, feet first, was lying on his side, groaning, and holding his hand over his buttocks. The only difference from most of my patients tonight was that he was groaning in French.

"Mr. LaPierre here has a problem he needs your help with Dr. Marcus," said the triage nurse as she walked out the door. "The x-ray will be on your computer in a second. I took the liberty..."

"Hello Mr. LaPierre. I am Dr. Marcus. What happened?" I knew what had happened.

"My bottom," he said in a deep French accent. It sounded like 'moi bwottoom'.

"What happened to your bwottoom? Is there something in your bwottoom?" I asked, confident that there was indeed something in his bwottoom and wondering if there was something in everyone's bwottoom.

"I fell."

"Of course you did."

I wheeled my wheeled stool over to the computer and clicked a few buttons to bring up the x-ray of his abdomen and pelvis.

His intestines were stretched and prominently gas-filled with unborn farts. But more notable, and readily visible on the x-ray was an opaque mass in his rectum, thankfully not in the shape of a chisel. I had no idea what it was. Tall and sharply pyramidal, with convexly curved sides. There were the radiographic outlines of two AAA batteries visible in the square base. I had to assume it was some kind of modern Eurodildo.

I rolled back over to Monsieur LaPierre's bum, grabbing some gloves as I rolled past them. I spun in the stool, pulling down his pajama pants and gazing at the orifice designed for egress not ingress. I pried apart the French cheeks and looked at the stretched, dilated French anus. No BRBPR. That was good. I squirted some surgical lube on my finger and dove in to immediately be greeted by a hard flat object, which, I learned later, was the aforementioned battery compartment.

I performed a San Fran Twist, feeling all around the rectal vault to ascertain the odds of extracting the foreign object from the foreign rectum without tying up the operating room again, given that Mr. Franks still hadn't even gotten in, nor his chisel gotten out.

I calculated that with sufficient force, perhaps a crowbar, I could extract the Eurodildo from the man's booty.

I added more lube. I stretched out his anus, blocking out from my hearing the accented groan that emerged from beyond. More lube, more stretch. Heck, I needed obstetric forceps to deliver this thing.

But with effort I accomplished my task. I extracted the foreign object. The object was not a Eurodildo. As it came out from his anus, Mr. LaPierre sighed a Parisian sigh of relief in French. Then his anus sighed a similarly loud sigh as the immediately subsequent gale-force winds of the previously unborn farts now emerged out of his patulous anus into the world, with their first external human contact being my face.

I looked at the foreign object I had removed from Mr. LaPierre. I looked up at Mr. LaPierre with renewed respect. He hadn't lied to me when I had asked him what happened and whether there was something in his bottom. He had simply said, "I fell." He was the first non-liar. For what emerged from his substantial analness was a toy model, a souvenir from Paris. It was painted red, and had green and yellow flashing lights, powered by two AAA batteries. It was pyramidal but tall. It was the Eiffel Tower. He had said, "Eiffel" not "I fell."

Mr. LaPierre had the first documented case of Eiffel Syndrome caused by the Eiffel Tower.

I would have been ecstatic, knowing that I forever would be able to regale my friends with this story, only I knew that I couldn't. No one would ever believe it. It was unbelievable. But you can't make this shit up.

Chapter 22

Bloody Diamonds

There are times when no matter how much you care, no matter how hard you try, no matter how many hours you work, no matter how much money you spend, no matter how many medications you run through veins, no matter how high tech the technology is, no matter what, your patient still dies.

And there are occasionally times when you screw up, the lab screws up, the bloodbank screws up, the radiologist, nurse, or cleaning lady screws up, and as a result, your patient dies.

And then there are the most common times, when you could have done more, could have worked a bit harder, been ten percent more vigilant, slept five percent less, known twenty percent more medical trivia, but you don't and as a result your patient dies and you blame yourself. But here is the secret: the patient was going to die anyhow. You could have been Dr. Zhivago, Doctor Livingstone, Dr. Pasteur, or Dr. Spock, or all of them combined in a big fat bespectacled mass, and the patient still would have died. As a doctor you can never work hard enough, know enough, be enough, to prevent the inevitable.

Life is a terminal disease. You might as well start mourning your impending demise right now, because here is the one certain fact: you are dying.

But you are also living, and since, even if you are a doctor, you can't do anything about the dying, you might as well do something about the living.

So I intended to do something about living, starting right now.

It would begin with smoking some beer and drinking some weed, buying a boat and sailing off in it, finding a beach in which to bury my toes, and finding my girl into whom I could bury my nose. I called up Nurse Maid.

"Hi Jennifer,"

"Hi stranger."

"I'm sorry I've been so busy. ER."

"I know."

"What is your schedule like?" I asked.

"When?" she responded.

"For the rest of your life."

Silence.

Silence.

"Eddie, did you mean to say that? Are you joking?"

"I meant it."

Silence.

"Call me later and ask me out to dinner."

It was 7 AM. I was at the mall by 9 AM looking for a ring.

The diamond engagement ring. What a scam. Until the early twentieth century, diamonds have been through history considered to be only of modest value. But De Beers in South Africa (not to be confused with De Bears in Chicago, or de Beer in de Bronx) controls the market for diamonds and locks up most of the stones dug up from the ground in order to keep the apparent supply of diamonds low and prices high.

De Beers initiated the whole concept of the diamond engagement ring in the US as one of the biggest marketing manipulations of the consumer ever. De Beers turned relatively common stones into what many people still today consider to be the epitome of the ultimate value. There are huge storerooms filled to the brims with diamonds, not to be released to the market so as to forever keep the prices as high as possible. Diamonds aren't rare. Diamonds are just a scam. And given that there are so many scams in the world, it is hard to consider diamonds special just because they are scam.

So, I would not buy a diamond engagement ring for Nurse Maid. I had to look for something else, something special, something out of the box. If we were to be married, I would not ask my bride to wear on her finger a manipulation of government-corporate collusions. Should the symbol of our commitment be a stone whose value was founded in fraud and promulgated with deceit? Hell no. I wanted to at least *start* with honesty.

But of what should the ring be made? What is honest, has real value, because of its beauty, its relative rarity, its consistent desirability by mankind throughout all recorded history. The answer is gold. Gold, out of which wedding rings are crafted for good reason. Gold is constant and doesn't react away or change. Gold has retained value for all of history. Gold is the perfect quantifier of human labor and productivity. Such persistent value retention is one of the many reasons why gold has always been the best form of money. Paper is just about the worst form of money, for it allows the printer of the paper to print as much of it as they want, without any real work. Whereas a dollar bill can now only buy what 3 cents could buy when the Federal Reserve was first created in 1913, gold has retained its value for millennia. How has this happened? Because the criminal government working with the criminal banks have made it specifically *not* a crime to steal your money by means of their printing new money. And, yes, you are right, this is a blatant and evil perversion of the Law.

I figure, along with Thomas Jefferson and a few other notables, that there is no power that the government has that is not derived from the people. So it must be true that I, as one of the people, have the power to print money, and like the government does, print as much as I want of it. I needed to buy a ring, made out of gold, and would need some printed money to do so. Several months earlier, I had undertaken the effort to figure out how to make money from nothing. It hadn't taken me long to figure out how incredibly well a color laser printer prints a scanned twenty-dollar bill. It took me a lot longer to find paper that was reasonably enough akin to the currency. At least it felt okayish in your hands and didn't show any lines when scribbled on at Wal-Mart with that special invisible magic inkpen that cashiers use to test large bills for 'realness'. That they are ALL fake doesn't make them any less real. The paper I found was the same stuff used in Chinese cigarettes. Not the cigarettes themselves, but the paper of the packaging that conceals within it the twenty sticks of toxic evil pleasure-producing smoky stinky nasties. Admittedly, obtaining a large enough supply of this paper was difficult.

It took me about five printing efforts to get what I thought was close enough to pass. Beautiful crisp twenty-dollar bills, in green, with some see-through watermarks and serial numbers that were useless, with words like 'This Note is Legal Tender' written on them—a cryptic statement that in actuality is the single largest factor in the destruction of the underpinnings of an honest economy. Nearby were the signatures of the Secretary of the Treasury and the Treasurer of the United States in order to make the bills so-much the more trustworthy. I was brimming in trust in my new found wealth, my new cash-cow, my deserved payment I was getting for my hard work in printing the bills. I wish I could donate some of this new real fake money to my preferred presidential candidate, but he wouldn't accept it, because he was too ethical.

Unlike the government, which could print these pieces of garbage willy-nilly without fear of reprisals, I was taking a risk. The government didn't like it when anybody else competed with them to print fake money. They didn't like it when anyone else created these pieces of paper garbage willy-nilly without fear of reprisal, so they created a fear of reprisal.

I was afraid. Of reprisal. But only a little. I was pretty certain that the Secret Service boys who seek out, arrest and prosecute counterfeiters wouldn't bother with me, given that I was only making a few thousand of these things. The main counterfeiters were printing out trillions of dollars worth of these things over at the Treasury and at the Federal Reserve, and loaning it all out to collapsing foreign banks and Wall Street Fraudsters. The Secret Service, which is a branch of the Treasury Department, sure as hell wasn't going to prosecute its own people, but I am sure they were nonetheless pretty tied up trying to arrest and prosecute those guys at the Federal Reserve who were competing with them for printing press time. So, although I was afraid of reprisal, I figured I would stay under their radar screen unless I got too cocky and started thinking what I was doing was good for the economy. Counterfeiting currency is only good for the people who do the counterfeiting. For the moment, I knew my printing press was only good for *my* economy, and for the economy of the ring finger on the left hand of Nurse Maid.

I carefully cut the freshly-printed bills out of the special cigarette paper with a dangerously sharp paper cutter. I sent the bills through the washing machine to make'em look old and therefore cleaner, and then started spending them here and there on things I needed, wanted, or could sell, in exchange for money that was just as counterfeit, but less likely to be noticed, because it was printed by the US Treasury instead of the HP LaserJet. It took just a few days of spending my fake stuff to collect enough of the real fake stuff to take to a jewelry store to buy a gold ring and a rock for Nurse Maid.

"So, what is the prettiest and not too flamboyant stone for an engagement ring?" I asked the flamboyant man behind the counter at the jewelry store that was at the mall.

"Diamonds. Every girl wants a diamond engagement ring," he replied pleasantly, on autopilot.

"My girl wouldn't be my girl if she wanted diamonds. She wants something different, pretty, and not terribly common."

"Certainly. How about colored diamonds? You can get them in just about any color."

"I want to stay away from diamonds."

"Do you know about the rating of diamonds? Carats, color, clarity, cut. Four C's."

"Yes I know about the four C's, but I'm not interested in diamonds."

"We have a special sale on the higher clarity diamonds today. Twenty percent off."

"Yes, twenty percent off after a nine-hundred percent mark-up. What stones do you have that aren't diamonds."

"I don't understand."

"I don't want a diamond engagement ring."

"But every girl wants a diamond engagement ring."

"I am not every girl."

"I see that, sir, but what I meant is that every girl wants a diamond engagement ring."

"My girl doesn't."

"Are you sure?"

"What do you mean?"

"Are you sure she doesn't want a diamond engagement ring?"

"She better not."

"Why?"

"Because I don't want to buy her a diamond engagement ring."

"Oh."

Shit. He had me. I had never checked with Nurse Maid as to what she would want. Bad me. Before getting married, I needed to learn that lesson. I was glad I did now. Of course that doesn't mean that I was going to actually *check* with Nurse Maid. All it meant is that I knew that I *should* check before making major decisions.

Tanzanite is what I decided upon. Tanzanite is beautiful and purple and shines and is much more rare than diamonds. And there was real specialness in Tanzanite. To get pretty radical, I had a couple of rubies, which also are more rare than diamonds, set on either side of the central Tanzanite stone. The effect seemed perfect. Totally not normal, totally radical, totally outside the box. I called it the 'Marcus Engagement Ring'. My initial plan was to print lots more just-as-real-as-real twenty-dollar bills and use them to buy the Tanzanite mines in Tanzania, start a revolution in neighboring Kenya to declare any of their Tanzanite exports as conflict stones, and then keep the Tanzanite prices wicked high by keeping the supply even lower than it would otherwise be. But then I thought better of it. Instead I would enjoy carefully planning how I was going to give this very special ring to my very special girl.

I put no thought into it at all.

At dinner, I was nervous. Outright nervous. I felt like I was on stage about to sing for American Idol with a goldfish stuck in my mouth. I don't get nervous unless I am anxious. And I only get anxious when I am nervous.

"What is wrong with you, Eddie?" Jennifer asked in her empathic empathetic Nurse Maidest soft-and-concerned voice, although she had a strong suspicion of what was wrong with me.

"What do you mean?" I asked, knowing exactly what she meant.

"You're jittery, and pale, and your knee is bouncing up and down."

"Oh. Sorry." I stopped my knee from bouncing up and down, stopped jittering and turned less pale. My knee started bouncing up and down.

"What are you interested in?" I asked, motioning to her closed menu. She was looking at me with amusement in her eyes. Her lovely eyes. Her caring eyes. Her understanding eyes. Those eyes that could read my mind. She picked up her menu while still looking at me, and flipped through it while still looking at me, paying no attention to the menu whatsoever.

"What's going on, Eddie?"

"Nuthin'," I replied. "Just hungry, I guess."

"Something wrong at work?"

"No."

"Something on your mind?"

"Always."

"My sister is having a baby. Isn't that exciting?"

"That's wonderful. She is a wonderful person. She will be a wonderful mom."

"I love babies."

"Yes, I know."

"Do you like babies?"

"Absolutely. You know I like being on the pediatric ward more than any other place in the hospital."

"Well, that's not what I meant. What I mean is do you like babies? Of your own?"

"I don't have any of my own, that I know of."

"Imagine a baby of your own."

"Okay, I'm imagining. A baby."

"Girl or boy?"

"Yes."

"Girl or boy?" slightly exasperated she was, and rightfully.

"Girl."

"Pretty?"

"Looks just like you."

Silence.

"So, yes, pretty as can be."

"Oh," Jennifer replied.

In a clear effort to change the subject, Jennifer changed the subject.

"What do you want out of life, Eddie?"

"Geez. You're coming up with some doozies to talk about tonight."

Jennifer smiled faintly and shrugged. "Look, Eddie, do you have something you want to tell me, ask me or give me?"

I shrugged back in return.

"Grow a pair, Eddie!"

And with that phrase, I was convinced. I grew a pair, overcame my fear of the unspecified indefinite, the certain uncertainty, the recognized unknowables, the indeterminate undetermined bits of future life, and acquired the commitment to commit. Sickness and Health. Richer and Poorer. Differences of Interests. Changes of Direction. Altering

Priorities. Radically Transitioning Preferences. Total Uncertainty. For As Long As We Both Shall Live.

Really?

REALLY?

Maybe she would sign a prenuptial. I hadn't accumulated much of anything prior to nuptials to reserve for myself except the ability to print unlimited amounts of fake money that was nearly identical to real fake money. That was actually a helluva cash cow, squirting out fake soymilk from its udders. But it was hardly something I could list on a pre-nup. Screw the pre-nup. Just jump in and pray it works.

I jumped. And prayed.

"Nurse Maid." I said. "Nurse Maid." I said. "Nurse Maid."

"Call me Jennifer."

"Jennifer," I said. "Jennifer," I said. The ring appeared in the palm of my left hand, stretched out across the table toward her, pleading, warm, inviting. The Tanzanite refracted and reflected the halogen bulb's light above the table, sending shafts of violet over us both. "Will you marry me, and stay with me through altering preferences, changes of interests, radically transitioning directions, certain uncertainties, in sickness and in health, for as long as we both shall live?" I looked into her eyes, hopeful, pleading, expectant.

"No."

I wasn't expecting that.

Chapter 23

Shock

I had to defibrillate my brain, which seemed to have its electrical currents running all haywire. The term 'haywire' to describe incompetent confusion was coined in the early 1900's in the Canadian legislature, but it applies equally well to the current US legislature and to my noggin after Nurse Maid rejected my offer. I was filled with uncertainty, had no clue of my direction, was full of sickness and had no health.

To figure out how to defibrillate one's brain requires one to have one's cognitive centers functioning at peak performance. As my cognitive centers were themselves fibrillating, I was caught in a Catch-22, which, although one of my favorite books, was not a catch into which I preferred to be caught. Blurriness clouded my confusion, but I could see faintly through the fog of my near pitch-black mind. There was a faint path I could travel.

"Umm?"

Jennifer looked at me with her intensely intelligent and caring eyes.

"Did you say you no?" I asked.

"Yes."

"You won't marry me?"

"No. Yes. No."

"What?"

"I won't marry you under your cynical view of our future."

"Huh?" Fog was not thinning yet.

"Eddie, I don't want to be married to you if in the future we have nothing in common, no shared interests, no shared values. In your view it may come to pass that the only thing we have is a commitment to stay with each other when we are sick. I think that sucks, Eddie."

"So what do you think you mean to be thinking?" I tried to convey what I was thinking of asking her, but I failed because I couldn't think. I remained in a slosh of mental miasma.

"Why don't we live with each other, and commit to each other for as long as we both shall want?"

"Umm. What do you mean?"

"I have never seen you so slow-witted, Eddie."

"Umm. What do you mean?"

"I'm sorry, Eddie. I didn't realize just how difficult this whole proposal thing would be for you. You are always so quick, so smart. Way ahead of the rest of the world, the rest of everybody."

"Yeah, well that ain't working so well right now."

"I'm intrigued that I've flustered you so much."

"I'm intrigued too. You're the first."

"Look Eddie." She smiled broadly, with concern in her eyes. "I love you too."

It dawned on me that I hadn't ever told her I loved her, even while proposing. Looking back on it, it seems likely that my brain was fibrillating the whole evening, and not just after she said 'no'. What an idiot. It proves what I tell people when they brag about their high IQs. People with high IQs are just smart idiots.

"I love you, Jennifer."

If you want to figure out what is most important to you, what you truly need, imagine what you would want to have, where you would want to be, what you want to be doing, and with whom you would like to be if the world were to be destroyed tomorrow.

I would want to be with Jennifer, with my toes in the sand on a beach, with a beer, watching the last sunset.

"What did you say before?" I asked her.

"Why don't we live with each other, and commit to each other for as long as we both shall want?"

"That isn't the standard liturgy," I pointed out.

"Nope."

"How does that work?"

Jennifer said, "It means that we have to work throughout our lives together to make sure we remain compatible and interested in each other's interests. It means we don't rely on a standard contract written by the State, with the State's rules, applied to everybody as if we were all the same. We don't have to abide by the traditions and dictums of any of several religions that started noble but were changed by the whims and machinations of humans over time. We make our own contract. Our own deal. Designed by us, for us, the two special people that we are. There will be bumps in our road. We have to find our way through those bumps on our own, not by being forced to stay together by a government contract, nor held by fear of the expense of a legal divorce, but by our own efforts to stay together voluntarily. We can have a noble relationship. It is what you would want if your brain weren't in fibrillation right now."

"Umm. Yeah. What you said."

But I was clearing up bit by bit. She hadn't said no to being with me. She hadn't denied loving me. She was willing to commit to me, and accept my commitment to her. But, like me, she wanted to commit on her own terms.

I loved her for it.

"So, Jennifer, I love you, and I want to be with you forever. Will you allow me the honor to commit myself to a process of being with you and striving with you for our mutual happiness?"

Jennifer grinned broadly and brimmed with sarcasm. "Now, *that* is a romantic proposal. How could a girl turn that down?"

It wasn't how I envisioned proposing to the love of my life. But then Jennifer wasn't a typical girl. Had she been, I wouldn't have fallen in love with her in the first place. She was way different, way more complete as a person, and had just proven it.

But having no legal marriage means being unable to file taxes jointly as a married couple, which means filing singly, which sadly means paying more money to the government. Fortunately, I figured that since the federal government had been ignoring the 10th Amendment for so long, I could start ignoring the 16th. To hell with taxes.

I gently placed the ring on Jennifer's finger.

I kept the receipt.

But only for the tax deduction.

Chapter 24

The Importance of Being Ernest

The little boy was turning red and screaming so much that he was not able to catch his breath. Dr. Blow held him down firmly as I sought a vein that might accept the intravenous catheter he so badly needed so he could receive antibiotics to treat the bacteria that probably were percolating through those same veins that were hiding from me so effectively. I hadn't even poked him yet. But fear causes more screaming than pain does.

Ernest had come from the ER because he wasn't looking quite right and was found to have a low white blood count. Upon arrival at the ward, his admitting nurse told me that he had some dots on his skin that either hadn't been there before or weren't noted in the ER. And he had spiked a fever. I did not like that one bit. Petechiae are like red freckles. They don't blanch when you press them, and when they appear with fever, doctors get very nervous. I was a doctor, I was very nervous, and I didn't dawdle.

The boy's blood pressure had been fine, so far. God I hoped it lasted.

"Good evening, Ms. Duncan." From the door of the room I

had introduced myself to the young mother holding her young child on her lap nervously sitting on the rocking chair next to the tall metal crib that looked rather like a jail cell. I pulled down my mask for a moment so she and her son could see my face. "I'm Doctor Marcus. I am here to help Ernest feel better as fast as possible, and to help find answers to questions about why he is sick."

Blow had taught me a version of that introduction, and I often used it. It is basically what is implied by the word 'doctor', and what the word 'doctor' used to mean to people before the profession mutated into a pandering sloth of sheep abiding by the dictums of insurance companies and political buffoons. In this fashion, I now quite often define the word 'doctor' to help a patient or a parent hear that I am not a member of the pandering sloth of sheep cavorting through the meadows of political brume.

Ernest's mom nodded, and I moved slowly to the small chair near the door, and sat myself, very small, within it, and then listened to his mother, while I interrupted only just enough for Ernest to get used to my voice, and slid my chair slowly over to him as fast as I could sneakily go.

"He was fine this morning when I dropped him off at pre-school. Totally fine. They called me to say he was acting tired and seemed sick. I had to take off work. I work at a bank. I got him. He threw up once, but then isn't eating anything anymore. He says "ouwee" a lot, but won't tell me where he is hurting."

I try not to use the words hurt or pain around children even when meaning "it won't hurt" or "no pain", because most children just hear the 'hurt' and the 'pain' part of those phrases. There is no more counterproductive phrase to use on a child than "this won't hurt" because all it does is activate their fear response, which is 90% of what pain is anyway.

"Is he a healthy boy in general?" I was a bit closer now.

Ernest's mom replied confidently, "Oh yes. He's strong as an ox. Never even had an ear infection."

"Anything medically wrong with him, ever?"

"No. Well, he doesn't have a spleen."

"Okay. Tell me about that."

"They told me he was just born without one. It hasn't ever caused him a problem." She paused. "I forgot to tell them that in the Emergency Room. As I said, he is an ox."

"Right. Never been in hospital before?" I moved closer.

"Oh no."

"Never had any surgery?"

"Oh no."

"Any allergies to medications?"

"Oh no."

"Has he had all his vaccinations?" A bit closer.

"Oh no. We don't trust vaccinations."

Oh no, I said to myself.

My experiences were limited, I know, and I know that scientists don't get it right all the time, or even most of the time, and I know that a vaccine manufacturer might from time to time try to hide some adverse effects, just slightly, and I know that vaccines affect the immune system, and I hear stories about children dying after vaccines, or getting autistic. I know. I know. My nature and strict rule is to never force people to do things against their will. But most vaccines are an amazingly powerful tool for health, and most vaccine manufacturers are doing good by creating them. If ever there was a role for artful persuasion in society, it is found in persuading, but never forcing, parents to vaccinate their children against formerly common severe communicable illnesses. Especially when the child has no spleen, and therefore has less immune protection from certain bacteria.

There has been a lot of stink lately about mandates for children to get vaccines for the virus that causes cervical cancer, which is basically a sexually transmitted disease. The company that makes the vaccine was a big player in convincing the states to initiate these mandates, this force. I don't like that one bit. That is not persuasion, but rather conspiracy to commit force. A sexually transmitted disease can be avoided without vaccination. One has to have a non-free-love mentality to avoid them, but many many people don't have a free-sex mentality, and there is no justification to mandate that their children be vaccinated against the virus that causes cervical cancer.

But then there are diseases that are transmitted just by being in the same room that someone with the disease happened to be in one hour earlier. No direct contact needed. Measles is one like that. Or being in the same class room with someone who is carrying meningitis asymptomatically in their nose. Or the same daycare.

Ernest was in the same daycare. And his parents, out of fear of vaccines, founded fear or unfounded fear, had elected to not vaccinate him against meningitis or anything else, it seemed, despite his own immunologic dysfunction. Maybe they had wanted to avoid autism in him, or some other disease that has been attributed to vaccines through anecdotes heard from other people, but I doubt those anecdotes highly, and the data—for what they are worth—back up my doubts. They had chosen to risk his life because they didn't trust the scientists and doctors. To some substantial extent, the scientists and doctors hold the blame because lately we haven't been out trying to help people feel better and answer questions, but rather out working with the system to save money or increase revenues for pharma companies or increase the power of politicians or whatever.

But the main fault lay with the parents who turned down the option of protecting their children because of their over-willingness to believe all the lay-crap in the press and to push aside as false all the scientific-crap in the press.

The fault that lies with the scientists and doctors is that they don't give credence to the lay. The fault with the lay is that they don't give credence to the scientists and doctors. There is no trust, because trust has been a major victim in the grab for political and economic power, in which honor and integrity stand in the way of both progressive progress and conservative conservation, and are therefore minimized and scoffed at.

So here we are. It certainly isn't little Ernest's fault that he didn't get vaccinated. It isn't Ernest's fault that he was in daycare because both parents have to work. It isn't Ernest's fault that he might have *Neisseria meningitides* bacteria swimming through his bloodstream like a nuclear bomb about to blow up, taking out his liver, his blood vessels, his heart, his lungs and the tissue surrounding his brain in the process. But it is Ernest who would suffer. Innocent Ernest.

My mission was to limit that suffering. I moved closer to Ernest, who was suspicious of everybody because in the ER they had tried to stick an IV in him, but couldn't. Had he had a fever in the ER, they would have been more nervous there. The petechial spots weren't there on his skin in the ER or they would have been more insistent about getting that IV in him. I hadn't seen the petechiae yet either, but the nurses had, and I had to move in more quickly than I would like in order to confirm it.

I moved the chair even closer to Ernest and his mom. He whimpered on my approach. He curled into his mother's chest and held more tightly to her long hair. I moved in close enough to touch him, and he somehow managed to immerse himself more completely into the protective flesh of his mother. I gently pressed the skin of his leg. He indeed did have petechiae. Sometimes petechiae on a limb comes from people using a tourniquet in the process of trying to stick IVs in it. Those type of petechiae are innocuous, but I didn't know where the ER had tried to stick him. I lifted up his shirt. I saw that his back was covered with petechiae. This isn't good. They sure as hell hadn't been putting a tourniquet around his chest. These weren't innocuous.

I gently pressed the hot skin on his back again to make sure that his blood flow to his tissues was okay so far, and it was. I snuck a little closer with my stethoscope to listen to his back. I could hear his heart through there. It was beating very fast. His lungs were breathing fast also. And now I was moving fast. I put my hand on his head and tried to move it a bit to see if his neck was sore, but he fought it. No more exam just yet.

"Blow," I spoke rapidly into the phone at the nurses station after excusing myself from Ernest's room. "Blow, this three and a half-year old is hot, has no spleen, no vaccinations, and he is covered in petechial rash. Cap refill is okay."

"I bet it is. I am on my way over." Blow had to come from evening clinic, a clinic which had been started by the administrators in order to attract more patients with common everyday non-life-threatening, uncomplicated diseases to seek our services instead of going to the community hospital that was so much better at dealing with common everyday diseases. Blow's clinic would be now filled with people who would be impatiently waiting their refill for hyperactivity medicine, or their cholesterol-lowering drug, but would be waiting a long time because Blow had to help me get this child with the non-common, serious, complicated, life threatening disease healthy before he up and died.

Upping and dying is something that can happen shockingly fast when *Neisseria meningitides* is floating around in the blood system of a child. If they have it in their brain—meningitis, it is often more readily diagnosed. When it hasn't gotten to the brain yet, it often gets missed and is at first thought to be a viral infection that doesn't need treatment. But it sure as hell needs treatment.

In this case, the ER doc knew that this child was a little bit sicker than he first looked. But he didn't know why. Given the information the ER doctor had, evidence-based medicine would suggest that the ER doctor send the child home with follow up planned for the next day. The ER doctor that saw Ernest had to jump out on a limb, risking chastisement from the administrators, risking chastisement from Ernest's parents when the insurance company refused to pay for the admission because it wasn't recommended to do so in some set of guidelines written by big-name experts who have never seen Ernest. The ER doctor who saw Ernest had to take a stand, and be a doctor. And he did. The ER doc had arranged for Ernest's admission against the advice and demands of reams of papers and paperwork and nameless distant statistics and cost-management programs. This act by the doctor was not just self-sacrifice on the part of the doctor, taking a risk on behalf of the patient. This was also self-preservation of self-respect on the part of the doctor, who absent this leap of anti-bureaucracy anti-collectivist anti-evidence-based-medicine faith would have not only been a sheep, but a sheared sheep, a sheared sheep that was in the care of a hungry perverted shepherd. This ER doctor had done what was right to do, based on facts and experience. It still can happen, and I was very grateful. And so was Ernest, although he didn't know it.

Blow had called the pharmacy and told them to hand-carry up to the ward some cephalokillemall antibiotic that Ernest would need fast, and that we would type the orders for it into the stupid electronic medical record later. The pharmacist had refused and insisted that Blow type the orders into the EMR first, because otherwise the computer wouldn't know how to bill the insurance company and it wouldn't give them access to the machine that spit out the medicine we wanted. Blow told the pharmacist to break into the machine and get the fucking antibiotic, but the pharmacist then referred to regulations and procedures. There were some really good people out there in the world. This pharmacist wasn't one of them. He was a true believer in the system. The system that sucks.

The too-few nurses were tied up with too-much elsewhere, and I needed someone who could hold Ernest down. So I had to wait for Blow before I could place the IV.

Blow had to prioritize typing a bunch of orders into the computer (which he is very poor at doing) over helping me get the child diagnosed and the IV in. There was a resulting five-minute delay in the IV getting inserted, but that was nothing compared to the 30-minute wait to get the antibiotics. Blow had prioritized correctly for the way the current system didn't work, but it would have been a big mistake in a system that worked rationally.

So Ernest was screaming, Blow was holding him down and mom was holding his free hand, and had her cheek next to Ernest lovingly. She didn't yet know that Ernest had systemic *Neisseria*, which would have been prevented had she made a different choice about vaccines. That didn't matter just yet. First thing was to get Ernest stable. Then the family might be stable enough to take the criticism that they would inevitably suffer from their own self-examination when the diagnosis was more confidently established.

I didn't hear him scream. I blotted the noise from my mind.

I have developed the ability to turn off and on that component of empathy that is emotional. When it is off, I remain rationally caring, but it is different. This scared little boy's screaming didn't invade my being and incite powerful emotions. At least I think it didn't. I was dehumanizing the cry from one of fear to one of a noise to be blotted out. Somehow I learned how to be numb when necessary.

Numbness is a survival skill. It is necessary when you need to cause someone pain, either for your own good—like the torturer in an evil spy game—or for the good of the person in whom you are causing pain. When it comes to little children like Ernest who will die without the IV that they don't understand, it is appropriate to make decisions for them that they would otherwise not make, to force them to undergo pain now in order to prevent pain later.

But how about for an adult, a friend with alcoholic liver disease, every muscle finely vibrating while he stands in front of you with alcohol on his breath at 10AM? Or harder yet, the sibling addicted to heroin? Force is not a ready alternative. The ethics are far from certain. Are these people sane? Are they capable of making their own choices? Who is to make that determination? What a slippery slope teetering on the edge of a cliff in an earthquake in the dark that is!

I ignored Ernest's scream. So did Blow. We were numb. But mom wasn't numb. Every pout, cry, tear and scream burrowed straight down into her soul, attacking the essence of her being, activating the evolutionary demand that she protect her child from pain and suffering. She was letting us cause pain and suffering in her child, and those cries of Ernest tore into her. But her rational mind, which in retrospect may have been wrong in her vaccination decisions, was strong enough now to recognize that it must squelch the ever-rising volume of emotional maternal nature that was blowing her speakers with its feedback. I was very impressed how well Ernest's mom handled this maternal torture.

I got the IV in with the first stick. The actual pain only lasted about 3 seconds. All the rest had been fear. Fear is powerful. It had power over little Ernest. It has power over us too. Our fears are very different and perhaps less primal than little Ernest's. We have fear of change, fear of the unknown. Ernest stopped crying as soon as the two evil masked men who had been assaulting him moved away, whimpered a bit as he recovered his personal sanity, and then settled into his mothers chest.

While waiting for the antibiotics to arrive, we moved Ernest to the ICU and got him ready for what could be a very difficult ride.

Ernest's blood pressure was falling. His capillaries were beginning to leak. Some of the thinner parts of his blood were leaking into his tissues, including his lungs, so his breathing was starting to be less effective and his oxygen levels were declining. He hadn't peed since arriving at the hospital. Soon, he was not fighting us anymore when we came near. And the petechiae on his skin were getting bigger, like bruises. All this was bad, very bad. Horrible. One wonders if getting the antibiotics into him thirty minutes sooner might have made a difference. The EMR didn't care about such things, because it was both emotionally numb and irrational.

In another twenty minutes, we were needing more help for sure. Blow called anesthesia and the pediatric intensivist. Dick Wad was by Ernest's bedside in no time, and took over managing his ventilation, fairly rapidly sticking an endotracheal tube down his throat while the intensivist provided the little bit of sedation that little Ernest needed at this stuporous point in his very big disease. Within two hours more, there were three intravenous lines in little Ernest, one tube down into his lungs, one tube down his throat into his stomach, one tube up his little penis into his bladder, and five different intravenous bags dripping into his vessels: a bag of platelets to help him not bleed, a bag of albumin to help keep his pressure up, a bag of epinephrine to keep his pressure up, a bag of dobutamine to help keep his pressure up and another bag of albumin to keep his pressure up. His pressure was not up, not up at all.

The *Neisseria* had taken out Ernest's adrenal glands as one of its first targets of destruction. The adrenal glands pump out adrenaline, also called epinephrine, to help overcome stresses, including severe illness. Ernest wasn't making any of his own stress-relieving adrenaline. The bacteria were continuing to make his blood vessels leaky, fill his lungs with fluid, and make his heart weak, and would soon be infecting the tissues around his brain.

Ernest wasn't screaming anymore.

It took three weeks of roller-coaster riding in that ICU. Despite all the risks of penalties and fines and censure from ACGME for overstaying my work hours, I stayed by Ernest's side, slept here and there in the call room or on a chair, worked my ass off and when there was nothing else I could do prayed hard that he would recover. Ernest temporarily died on three occasions, and lived near death for most of that period of time. But Ernest didn't permanently die. In the end, he recovered surprisingly well.

Blow never got back down to his clinic to see all the patients waiting for him. Several complained to the Dean about being abandoned.

Nobody complained about the pharmacist who was just

following rules.

Nobody sent a letter of commendation to the ER doc who had broken the rules to make sure that Ernest wasn't sicker than he initially looked.

But Ernest was okay. I would say that is all that is important, but that would be a lie. It indeed is all that is important to Ernest and his mom. But a couple of days, weeks, or months later, there would be another Ernest, for whom an ER doc might not take a stand, a busy nurse might not note some petechiae and rapidly contact an intern who understands its significance, a clinic attending might not want to risk angering his clinic patients and might therefore postpone coming up to the ward to see an only *potentially*-sick patient, a pharmacist who was a true-believer in bureaucracy might still not recognize the urgency, and because of any one of these failings, this next Ernest might die. And that would be all that is important to that Ernest, and that Ernest's mom.

Chapter 25

On Safari

I was back in the ER again. Some interns have a white cloud over their head, and get to sleep all night on their call nights and all the patients are healthy and no new admissions happen. Some interns have a black cloud and attract every bit of disease, catastrophe, calamity and plague to the hospital door as if these nastinesses know the interns' call schedule intimately. Interns with dark clouds get no sleep and lots of education on their call nights. Interns with white clouds get lots of sleep and no education on their call nights.

My cloud was black and white striped.

When I was on call, I attracted the zebras. Zebras sound like horses, smell like horses, but they aren't horses at all. In the medical world, zebras are the rare diseases that mimic common diseases and are therefore often misdiagnosed. When you hear hoof beats, look for a horse. But sometimes, it's a zebra. Zebras seem to like me. They like to ride past me and near me and over me and on me.

Tonight in the ER would be a night with zebras.

Hubie came into the ER. Hubie was a drunk. He was a homeless bum. I had known him for many years, and at some level I loved him. On cold nights he would arrange to have a fall and need to be picked up by the fire department off the street, and carted to the warm ER to get evaluated. On hungry days Hubie would manage to have a seizure and be picked up by the fire department off the street, and carted to the ER to get fed. On rainy days, Hubie would manage to have chest pain, and be picked up by the fire department, and carted to the ER to get dry. It was not uncommon to admit Hubie to the ER three or four times per week. In the winter, Hubie would use some saved up money to buy a round-trip ticket on an airplane and head south to Florida for a couple of months. I didn't envy the passengers sitting next to him, or even those in the same compartment. Hubie was fifty years old. Or maybe sixty. Or maybe seventy. He couldn't remember his birthday.

Most often, Hubie would come in to the ER on his own feet, to get a laceration sewn up, to have his sore feet examined, or some such. Sometimes he had to come up with some illness on the spot when asked by the triage nurse or administrator checking him in. He would stumble and come up with something and look at you hopefully. I remember one time when Hubie stumbled into the ER on his own steam. The night was wicked busy and the place was a zoo. The triage nurse was stressed and the system was strained. Out of the corner of her eye, Sheila saw Hubie moving in through the sliding glass doors. She turned immediately and said firmly and without equivocation, "NOT TONIGHT, HUBIE!" Hubie immediately turned and walked right back out.

But he got in tonight. Brought in by the fire department.

"Hi Hubie," I said to Hubie.

Hubie didn't answer. He just moaned. Usually Hubie was polite, addressed me as 'Dr. Marcus', and smiled guiltily and sheepishly as he recounted to me the fake purpose of his trip to the ER, after which I learned to simply ask for his real purpose. Sometimes, however, Hubie came in drunk out of his gourd, nearly unconscious, urine-soaked pants and sweat-soaked socks providing a noxious effluvium so overwhelming that the taste of the air subsumed the smell. Tonight appeared to be one of those nights.

"Ah shit, Hubie." I turned around and walked right back out of the room. In the past, I had examined Hubie probably twenty times, dutifully doing my duty. It was beyond the boy who cried wolf with Hubie. He was always never as sick as he tried to appear, usually not sick at all, but rather just a drunk bum looking for some comfort. This time, I had had enough. To hell with liability risk, to hell with doing the right thing and looking for the cause of Hubie's stupor and moaning. He was freakin' drunk and stinky. And after staying up all night for many nights working with innocent little Ernest in the ICU, I was pretty stinky myself, needed some comfort of my own, and had insufficient tolerance for the likes of Hubie.

I ambled on over to the nurse who would have the pleasure of taking care of Hubie. I was tired, I was cocky, I was beaten, I was foolish.

"Look, Mary. Hubie is zonked. Can you spray some Lysol all over him and let him sleep it off? Call me when he rouses."

Mary was an experienced nurse. She had varied tolerance for Hubie. Sometimes she was sensitive to him and caring, and sometimes impatient and frustrated. Mary was human.

I was walking away. Mary said, "Eddie, I'm gonna draw an EtOH level on him." It was a statement, not a question. It was a statement intended to tell me to type the order into the EMR so that the lab could do the blood alcohol test that she, the nurse, not I, the doctor, wanted. There was absolutely nothing wrong with this order of ordering. I would do as I was told and do what the nurse told me, the doctor, to do. Because to ever do otherwise is just stupid. I may be cocky. I may be foolish. But my mother didn't raise no stupid children.

Mary saved Hubie's miserable life that night.

Had I been cocky enough to risk defying Mary's credible authority, and denied her the blood alcohol level that she wanted to measure, Hubie would have died.

An hour later Mary handed me a slip of paper that didn't exist from the paper medical record that is against the rules to have. Now, guessing Hubie's blood alcohol level is a usual game for the long-time workers in the ER. Whereas a normal person might get utterly blotto with a blood alcohol level of 0.15%, Hubie could get to 0.50% without even seeming particularly off kilter, and that is a level that would kill most people. Hubie was blotto tonight, so the betting pool was much higher. The highest guess was 1.1% which was 0.05% higher than the ER all-time-record, high enough to pickle a mule or run you car engine. Someone in the Hubie pool thought Hubie tonight would beat out all other drunks that had ever traversed this ER. The game is played like The Price is Right. The person who wins is the one who gets closest to the actual measured alcohol level without exceeding it.

I had put five bucks on 0.85%. I had this strange notion that the result would be 0.84% and I would have been almost perfectly right but still lose out on winning the pool. That would serve me right for betting on somebody's illness.

I looked at the piece of paper, the lab slip that by hospital policy didn't exist.

"Mary, is this right?"

"Eddie, I am gonna hit you if you ask if I might have switched the blood vials with someone else."

"Any chance you switched the vials with someone else?"

Mary smacked me on the head.

"All right, let's go see him."

"Damn right, Eddie."

I tucked the lab slip that didn't exist back into the chart that didn't exist. The lab slip that didn't exist showed that Hubie's blood alcohol level was zero.

"Hubie, what's going on?" I said to Hubie as I walked into the room. I tried to rouse him from what appeared to be a pretty deep sleep. Hubie moaned faintly.

I took Hubie's shoulder and shook it back and forth. "Hubie. Hubie. Wake up. I need you to wake up!"

Hubie didn't wake up. He moaned faintly.

Hubie smelled horribly of urine and sweat and dankness and impossible-to-identify fetidness. Through the reeking stench it was hard to notice that the typical fruity scent of Hubie's alcoholic breath was not quite his normal. Instead he smelled somehow different.

I pried opened Hubie's left eyelid. The pupil was dilated and barely moved when I flashed a light into it. I opened up the other eye, the pupil of which was smaller and constricted with the light.

"Shit, Mary. I fucked up. We gotta get him into the Donut of Death. Hubie is blowing his left pupil here."

Now a pupil which is big and dilated and sluggish can be a sign of an intracranial hemorrhage—bleeding into the skull, or some other increase in pressure inside the head, and it meant imminent calamity. A gradually growing subdural or epidural hematoma—a mass of blood between the skull and the brain—is what I figured Hubie had: a big pile of gradually accumulating blood, probably resulting from a crack on his skull a week or more before when he had slipped on the pavement or gotten beaten up, that was compressing his brain, causing him to lose consciousness, and preventing him from even drinking. It would be fatal if not drained.

We stuck an IV in Hubie's arm and drew more blood. I gave him some mannitol to take some pressure out of his brain. Dick Wad came down and stuck an endotracheal tube down his throat to control his airway. We drew more blood from his vein and rushed him to the CT scanner, known by its friends as the 'Donut of Death', pushing aside several other patients who were awaiting their scans, and stuck his head in it to see how much and where the blood was. We had to move fast, because the neurosurgeons were wanting to get this blood out of his head and were already scrubbing up in the OR for his arrival there, assuming I had his head CT in hand.

I ran into the viewing room of the CT scanner and watched through the xray-proof glass as the big machine spun electronically around his brain. The insides of his noggin appeared on the computer screen next to me in detail.

No blood. No mass inside his head. No evidence of pressure buildup in his head. Just a very normal looking brain.

I wasn't experienced enough yet to figure this out.

I called the neurosurgeons in the OR to tell them.

"What else would blow a pupil?" I asked.

"Look it up, Dr. Marcus," was the answer.

I did. I went onto google, and looked it up. Google has all the answers, although many of them are wrong, and you have to be educated and smart enough to be able to figure out which of the answers are wrong.

I hadn't even begun reading my first google hit when Mary tapped me on the shoulder and said, "Hubie's lab. We got the new blood tests back. He's a little acidotic and methyl alcohol levels are high."

Shit. Methyl alcohol. Methanol. Wood alcohol. Hubie had been drinking wood alcohol. Toxic, not uncommonly fatal, commonly causes blindness. I looked it up quickly and found no evidence that it blows a single pupil though. The therapy for wood alcohol toxicity is treatment with ethyl alcohol, ethanol—regular drinking alcohol and the stuff that the government forces refiners to poison gasoline with now in a misguided effort to save the planet. Hubie got started on an IV drip of his favorite food: medical ethanol. The ethanol would help tie up the enzymes that turn methanol into toxic poisons and wash out the methyl alcohol and its toxins from his liver and kidneys and brain and optic nerve. It would clean out Hubie's system. It was what ethanol was good at. What it does for a methanol-intoxicated human is the entire opposite of what ethanol does in an internal combustion engine, which is to increase the amount of toxins, foul the gasoline, gum up the carburetor, destroy the rubber hoses and gaskets and take a perfectly good engine and make it fail miserably, all while making big agribusiness wealthy off the subsidies for corn ethanol and the mandates for gasoline to have 10% ethanol in it to destroy engines. It takes 1.06 gallons of gasoline to manufacture 1 gallon of ethanol, which is only 80% as efficient a fuel source as gasoline. So the carbon footprint of 10% ethanol in gasoline is much worse than the carbon footprint of pure gasoline. For those who cannot do math, this sucks. Ethanol in gasoline is a loser for the environmentalists who believe that carbon footprints matter, for the owners of small engines like lawn mowers and weed whackers and boat motors, for the owners of older cars, newer cars and non-diesel tractors, and for the owners of generators. Ethanol was a total loser for everyone except large agribusiness, politicians from Iowa, and small engine repairmen. And for Hubie, for whom ethanol had just saved his vision and probably his life.

The ethanol worked, and after a while, Hubie aroused, vomited, complained it was too hot in the ER, and said hello.

"Hi Dr. Marcus. What happened?"

"You drank some bad alcohol, Hubie. Wood alcohol."

"Oh. Barney gave that to me."

"Did Barney drink it too?"

"No. He said we shouldn't drink it."

"Oh." There was no point in asking why Hubie chose to ignore the advice of his hobo friend.

Hubie was sailing pretty nicely high on his intravenous ethanol drip. He was in his normal functioning Hubie mode now, with a blood ethanol level of 0.3 percent. These were Happy Hubie levels, about four times the legal limit for driving and about three times as high as usually needed to detoxify patients intoxicated with methanol. Hubie probably wasn't going to lose his vision. But his pupil was still blown.

"What's with your eye, Hubie?"

"Doc did that to me."

"What do you mean?"

"This morning, the ER doc put some drops in my eye so he could look for the things that were floating around in my eye."

"Ah shit, Hubie. You had drops put in your eye?"

"Yep."

That explained it. Nowhere was it recorded in the electronic medical record that in the ER twelve hours earlier, a doctor had put some pupil-dilating drops in Hubie's eye so that he could use an ophthalmoscope to look for the thing that Hubie said was floating around in his vision. These tiny bits of unneeded tissue bobbing around in the fluid inside the eyeball, swimming back and forth across one's retina and therefore one's vision, are appropriately called 'floaters', and are usually unimportant.

"Hubie, do you have something floating around in your vision?"

"Yep, Dr. Marcus." Hubie struggled to focus on whatever was wandering around within his own eye.

"Yep," Hubie repeated. "I sure do. It looks like a zebra."

Chapter 26

Fighting Darwin

It seems like lots of people like to fight that old bearded man from the HMS Beagle. And most of them are doctors.

A guy with dreadlocks came into the ER unconscious from heroin overdose. His hair had not been washed or combed in years, and it was matted and foul and gross and nasty. In contrast, his clothes were clean and new. The stinky matted hair was a choice he had made for some probably non-religious 'I am so Jamaica-cool' reason. All that being said, most people I know with dreads were pretty cool people. I couldn't judge whether this guy with dreads was cool or not, 'cuz he was mostly dead.

Heroin will do that to a man.

Darwin was doing everything he could to take this guy's gonads off the assembly line of the human gene pool. But here we were, the doctors, the superdeities, the *uberdarwins* deciding to overturn what nature had deemed proper. We would save his life.

All we really needed to do was keep him breathing for a while. There were two ways. The first was at least initially comfortable for him and easy—put him on a breathing machine and let the big H wear off. The second was hard on him but cheaper: dose him up with a Narcan regimen, which reverses the effects of the H almost immediately, and initiates instant and pretty miserable withdrawal symptoms, but no need for the mechanical ventilation.

I chose the Narcan. It was rough on him, but he would live through it, miserable and craving his drug of choice. But it would be quicker too.

And as soon as he could, he would make passionate love to his heroin again, that heroine of his own story, making romantic, divine love, the ultimate love, for he would love his heroin more than he could ever love a human. An affair with H was the ultimate love affair, and we in the ER helped make sure that love was not cut short.

In the ER, it was a night for very strange accidents, if you could call them accidents. By the time midnight had rolled past, there were several reasonable candidates for the Darwin awards—those special cynical awards granted to the people who improved the gene pool by the moronic choices they had made that most inventively led to their deaths or inability to procreate. The penile resections of my now nearly world-famous earlier ER night were certainly Darwin award candidates. Tonight there were no penile shortenings or losses, no testicular castrations, but rather only outright deaths.

One man was drunk and drove his car through a fence into a community swimming pool. The paramedics arrived just in time to pull his fully-drowned body from his mostly-drowned car.

The second genetic enhancement through negligent fatality was brought to our attention one hour later in the form of a man who had been mostly eaten by his pet dogs. It turns out that his hobby was breeding Pit Bull Terriers. They have a bad reputation for a good reason. The police had to shoot the damned dogs dead so that the EMTs could pointlessly get to what was left of the man, who had unsuccessfully attempted to hide behind his extremely high-end multi-thousand-dollar satellite stereo system in the back of his decrepit about-to-be-foreclosed-upon house.

The third tragic death was the man who was working on his car engine, his running car engine, with his garage door closed because it was too cold outside. He almost took out his whole family, although we were able to save them with the help of large amounts of oxygen to counteract their carbon monoxide inhalation.

The *piece de resistance* was the man who was trying to show off to his lover in their home's loft, which was used as an office with an open view of the rest of their apartment in an old open warehouse that had been converted to residences. The man playfully threw himself over the edge of the loft down onto their king size bed below. The problem was that the bed was a four-poster, with sharp pokes on the top of each post. The man overestimated his strength and underestimated the distance and didn't quite leap far enough. The EMTs had to use a chain saw to cut the post off the bed, but the sharp end had gone all the way through the man's belly to poke out an angle next to his lower spine. It had nicked his aorta and destroyed his spleen on the way through, and by the time the man had made it to the ER, with the post still impaling him, he had for all intents and purposes expired, although it took us 45 minutes of hard nasty bloody labor to prove that expiration to our *uberdarwin* selves. The music that the man had been playing when he leapt to his impaled doom was Brenda Lee's *Big Four Poster Bed.*

It had been a horrible devastating night in the ER, that is for sure. It was perhaps the worse night in recalled history, as far as death and destruction from separate incidents. But, I was a dark cloud with some zebra stripes. Darwin won all these battles tonight, and the human gene pool was improved, with enhanced survival characteristics each time he won. In contrast, each time we win the battle, the survivability of the next generation of humanity might be reduced. Most of the battles we fought against Darwin were not against the tragically moronic homicides of the self as described above. No, our longest battles against Darwin were in our efforts to keep children alive who, absent our intervention, wouldn't stay alive long enough to procreate.

Our war with Darwin was fought in the battles we engaged in to help a girl with cystic fibrosis live long enough to have a happy life, get married, and pass on her CF gene to her first and second child. Our enemies were the infectious diseases that we would no longer allow to kill children, and by saving these children we prevented the gene pool from clearing itself of those weaker elements that fall victim to bacteria and viruses. Each life we saved was a lost opportunity for the heartless forces of untamed nature to improve the human gene pool. Interfering with nature so frequently and in such an egregious manner should cause all doctors to feel guilty.

I don't feel the least bit guilty. I don't give one single crap about the gene pool. I care about each individual human, not humanity. Sure, we have totally interfered with nature. Modern medicine has pretty well eliminated natural selection in human existence. And good riddance. Nature has resulted in the extinctions of 99% of the species that have ever existed on the planet, and I'm talking long before humans were even a twinkling in their lustful lascivious ape-like ancestors' eyes. Evolution eliminates the weak, the unprepared, and the non-adapting.

For humans, evolution hasn't been stopped, not at all. But we are now in charge of it. Human evolution is now under the control of humans. We don't have to focus on the only thing that natural selection cares about—which is survival long enough to procreate. No, we can focus on an evolution that improves quality of life, and where appropriate, lengthening of quality life.

Whereas natural selection doesn't care much at all whether a woman lives past the child-rearing age, I bet she does.

Whereas natural selection could not care less if women have sex after menopause, I bet women care.

Although there's hardly any value to grandparents in natural selection, humans have given grandparents great value culturally, and as medicine advances further, great- and great- great- grandparents will have more and more opportunity to help enhance the quality of life of so many people. Grandparents remember living history. And nowadays, a generation without an understanding of the past has no future. That our generation has so little understanding of the past makes me worry about our future.

I don't feel guilty at all about beating Darwin in the war. I don't think he would want to win that war either.

"Jennifer," I said to Nurse Maid. "Do you want to improve the human gene pool by donating your genes to the next generation?"

"Are you asking me if I want to have a baby?"

"Yes."

"With you?"

"Well, yes."

"Now?"

"Hell no! We only just recently didn't get married. We have only just recently begun our life together. I'm not ready for a baby yet. But someday. I meant someday do you want to have a baby, with me?

"Eddie, you're crazy. Of course I do. I wouldn't have not married you and I wouldn't have agreed to stay with you for as long as we both shall want, had I not wanted to have a baby with you. We talked about it the very evening that I declined your offer of marriage, remember? So, yes, I would like that very much."

"Great. I'll put it on my wish list."

Jennifer looked at me quizzically, while I thought about my wish list. My wish list for life.

I had started writing my life's wish list when I was eleven years old. I wasn't a normal kid.

I remember it well. I wanted to play the guitar and piano. I wanted to be a doctor. I wanted to be a pilot and an astronaut. I wanted to help mankind progress in space. I wanted a boat big enough to sail around the world, and then use it to actually sail around the world. I wanted to help people have less pain in life. I wanted to understand the physics of the heavens, and understand humans. I wanted to write novels. I wanted to paint paintings.

My wandering chain of thought brought me to the three wishes I would be granted if I found a genie in a bottle on a desert island. The first would be to have the capacity to read, write, speak and understand every language ever in existence. The second would be the talent to play any instrument masterfully. The third, well, the third I hadn't figured out yet. Thank God I still had one wish left.

I knew that I was fortunate in my natural talents. I knew I had been given one helluva good hand to play in life. Most everything I did came easily to me. But I didn't suck off the teat of God-given gifts. I worked my living ass off. Things may come easy to me, but I don't go easy on myself. Success is only achieved when I say I have achieved it. And I haven't.

But I am not the only lucky one on this planet. Each and every one of us who is alive today is a lottery winner.

What is the chance that you would ever exist? In order for you, that special individual, to exist, an amazing statistically almost impossible sequence of events had to happen. What is the chance that it was that one special egg popping out of your mother's ovary that got successfully fertilized and implanted to grow up into you? Women mature about 20 eggs per month, but only one is released, usually. Over thirty years of fertility, there are 7200 eggs released. If you were an only child, you were a one in 7200 chance.

Then there is your dad. You were the product of your mom's egg blending with one very unique sperm. Out of 200 million different sperm made each day during a man's fifty-year fertile span, you were made from one. Your sperm was one of 3.6 trillion little spermies formed during your dad's life. Combine that with your mom's egg probability and your chance of being created was less than one in 25 quadrillion. Then, if they are right that only one half of fertilized eggs are implanted and carried to term, your chance of birth from your egg and your sperm becomes one in 50 quadrillion. But that is just the beginning of the math, for what is the chance that your mom and dad would ever meet in the first place and get together so that their egg and sperm would mesh to create you?

What is the chance that your mother would have been born, given the same sorts of stats for her mother's eggs and her father's sperm? Yep, one in 50 quadrillion. Likewise, your Dad had one chance in 50 quadrillion of ever being born. But these combinations of sperm and egg that created your parents could have only happened if *their* parents had won the celestial lottery and been born and met.

Your life, that you exist AT ALL, is the result of each and every one of your ancestors—without any exception—having won the biggest lottery in existence and then made choices that brought them together. Had any single one of those ancestors not won their one chance in 50 quadrillion lottery, or had they made different choices, you would not exist.

The probability of you ever existing quickly gets to be less than one in a google. There are less than a google atoms in the entire universe. Your chance of ever having been born is nearly infinitely small. So, wow. What a lottery you have won. You should feel very lucky indeed.

Or maybe, just maybe, you weren't lucky at all. Maybe you had help. Even sworn atheists admit that there is a teeny tiny chance that God exists. One has to wonder just how many quadrillion times more likely that teeny tiny chance is—that chance that an atheist gives for God's existence—than the chance of winning this celestial lottery.

Because if God exists, then your chance of having been born can be figured at, oh, about 100%, instead of one-in-a-google. And correct me if I am wrong, but you are 100% alive, right?

Chapter 27

The Touch of a Child

"So, which one of you enslaved young doctors want to do something different than graze on the same grass all year?" Dr. Blow had asked the entire intern class on the very first day of our orientation, just a week after medical school graduation. The scared, frightened, insecure, terrified, excited, stupid young doctors all stared at Blow, not knowing what to do, paralyzed in their brilliant mindfog. Blow had just waited, allowing the silence to be filled with awkwardness.

I had raised my hand. "I do." Apparently, the simple act of raising my hand—or rather my *ability* to raise my hand—distinguished me from among the remainder of the doctors, for Blow had taken me under his wing from that moment on. He had nurtured all my strengths and provided encouragement for my abundant sins ever since.

'Ever since' is the Liberian idiom for 'a long while ago'. And it would become relevant, because Blow's offer to the one intern who raised his one hand was to spend one month of his internship providing health care in Liberia, West Africa—a war-torn recovering country that was one of the poorest on Earth, with poverty rampant beyond the ready imagination of the average developed-world young doctor. Trash was scattered around everywhere, electricity mostly non-existent, running water rare, functioning plumbing rarer still. And the people were happy.

"It's the best place ever," said Blow, "because unlike Americans, the Liberians are *free."*

And they are free. The government has little power as yet, and taxes the income of people and businesses at only 4%. The people have a Constitution, similar to that of the United States, to protect them from government intrusion. It is weaker than the U.S. Constitution, but unlike the U.S. Constitution, it is not ignored rampantly by the government, nor forgotten by the people. The Liberian government owns the rights to anything underground, and trades the value to be found—gold, iron, and maybe oil—for the road and building construction provided by the Chinese, as those men from the East continue to invade Africa with economic vigor. Meanwhile the West, headed by the United States, dumps enormous amounts of free aid in exchange for _____. Yes, that sentence ended correctly, for the free aid is indeed in exchange for nothing. China makes deals with Liberia. In contrast, the US throws at Liberia freshly minted fake coins from our chariot as we ride by. All the while, the World Bank tries to teach the small Liberian government Keynesian economics in order to try to take more power over its people as had been so effectively accomplished in the West. Liberia's government so far resists. Two Liberian women had just deservedly won the Nobel Peace Prize, not to be confused with the Nobel Power Prize of the same name, recent recipients of which included Al Gore (for his work warming the globe flying around in his huge jet spewing hot air) and Barack Obama (for doing absolutely nothing at all).

Liberia is perhaps the one true success of the United

Nations' military forces. The United Nations generally has been a marginally corrupt organization, channeling money away from productive purposes and into non-productive purposes. However, that is far too simple a generalization. The UN is capable of doing good.

The deployment of UN troops to Liberia effectively stopped the chronic civil conflicts of the previous fourteen years—conflicts during which the most awful crimes were committed by leaders of various organizations seeking power by using force, fraud and the tactics of fear. Those days in Liberia were dominated by blatant force and evil. The West African nations had grouped together in efforts to halt the wars in Liberia, but their efforts were confounded by the illicit profit-seeking behavior of their own generals sent in to quell the violence. The generals from Nigeria and elsewhere connived with the government and the rebel leaders to rape the country, just as the rebel and government leaders of Liberia had been doing so well on their own.

In 2003, concurrent with and resulting from a massive UN military presence, the violence ended. The rebel leader Charles Taylor, who had been elected President on the slogan "You killed my Pa, you killed my Ma, I will vote for you anyway", was kicked out of the country and later arrested. No more bullets were fired. No more did AK-47 cartridge casings lay so thick on the city roads that you could not see the pavement. The piles of human skulls on the beaches, placed by families in memorial to the oh-so-many killed, gradually were removed and buried.

Over the subsequent years, the infrastructure slowly began to return. The capital city needs water and continuous power, but electricity now at least runs through some wires. The hydropower dam that provided the nation's electricity before the wars is being rebuilt. The Chinese have done a good job of repairing many of the destroyed roads. The Pakistani's, under the auspices of the UN, have built many strangely shaped bridges over the meandering rivers and rivulets.

Some of the doctors who had left are returning, so that now there may be seventy or so doctors in the nation of 3.5 million souls. In Liberia there is now one doctor for every fifty-thousand people. For comparison, in the US, there is one doctor for every three-hundred people. Health care is a challenge.

The doctors who are there have little time to teach, little time to try to change policy, little time to invest for the future. They are working extremely hard, just trying to help people survive.

Blow had been taking young doctors to Liberia for a few years, with the intention of teaching the medical folk in Liberia how to be technically slightly better doctors, and teaching the medical folk from the U.S. how to have a clue about life and how to learn to be a doctor at all. Sure, the U.S. docs who went for month-long trips to Liberia did some amazing good, absolutely. They often could see two hundred patients in a day, and of those two hundred truly save ten or twenty lives—with the rest not having been really in a life-threatening situation. In the US, a doctor might save one life per *month*, or even substantially less. So for a young doctor working in Liberia, there is real bang for the buck, no doubt.

It was February of my intern year, wintry and nasty at home. Slush on the ground and slush in the sky. Darkness prevailed, and depression was running the show. It was from this departure perspective that Blow and I boarded our airplane for the interminable flight in economy coach across the Atlantic to Liberia.

"I love being on airplanes," I said to Blow. I hated being on airplanes, as I may have previously hinted. Remember, I am six-feet two and over two-hundred pounds and I simply don't fit.

Blow was shorter and squatter, but also about two hundred pounds, so his knees fit better but his butt didn't so well.

"Why don't you get rich, Eddie, and then we can fly first class?"

"I am rich, in spirit."

"Eddie, what is your core value?"

"Ah hell, Blow, are you going to lecture me?"

"Nope. I just want you to remember your core value, because being in Liberia is hard, difficult, exciting, fun, and if it doesn't change a man's perspective, I don't know what will. If you have a core value that is good, you will want to put your experiences in Liberia within the context of the core value. If you have a crappy core value, then you need to be prepared to be turned into a useless piece of blubbering crap by how your experiences in Liberia will conflict with your crappy core value."

"What would be a crappy core value?"

"I want to make the world a better place by making sure everybody does things the best way possible. That is a crappy core value."

"Oh. But if I know the way to do something better than they do, shouldn't I want to teach them the better way? Isn't that one of the reasons we're going to Liberia?"

"Sure, but you need to teach them, not *make* them. First, don't be so sure you are right that you know best. See what they do first, and then understand it, and then after understanding it, compare it to what you would do." Blow looked at me, which brought our faces uncomfortably close together in that goddamned plane, and then quickly turned back looking forward. "Eddie, you have been taught a lot of shit in your life. You may not know what is shit and what isn't shit. Don't be cocky."

I was insistent though. "But if I know, really know something is right, don't I have an obligation to share that knowledge?"

"Nope. No obligation. But it sure would be nice of you to share it."

"So, what's wrong with wanting to make the world a better place by making sure everyone does things in the best way possible?"

"Are you going to be the one who determines what the best way is, Eddie? For everybody?"

I sighed a big sigh. "No."

"Right. You damn well better be the one who determines what is right for *you.* But you would be a right cocky bastard to try to decide what is right for someone else. Remember how you feel when the big G orders you to do something because politicians think they know what is best for you. I think you use loud swear words. Now imagine trying to take your knowledge of medicine and business in the USA and applying it to a culture and country and people utterly foreign. Like Liberia."

Blow had a point. I wasn't going to Liberia to teach all my brilliance. I was going to Liberia to learn how stupid and ignorant I was. His teaching me this, now, helped eliminate the cognitive dissonance I had which led me to be scared out of my pants.

"Don't worry, Eddie," Blow had read my nervousness. "You will learn what to do in the clinics of Liberia very fast. The medicine is pretty simple there. Nothing to fear."

Blow spent the next two hours of the flight talking to me about the diseases of West Africa, which I was supposed to have learned on my own in the preceding months, but hadn't had a chance to even lift a finger to begin. It really wasn't much. Diarrhea from bacteria, diarrhea from parasites, malaria, typhoid, burns, malaria, malaria, malaria, intestinal worms, malaria. Fever from typhoid. Cough from typhoid. Belly pain from typhoid. Fever from malaria. Belly pain from malaria. Diarrhea from malaria. And no diagnostic testing ability to differentiate the above causes of diarrhea and belly pain and fever.

"Pretty much any child with a fever or with belly pain you should treat for malaria. Probably treat the adults too. Treat acute diarrhea with antibiotics. Treat prolonged diarrhea with antiparasitics. De-worm everybody that you can. Watch out for typhoid, which can be tricky. Oh, and watch out for everything else too, although most of it is pretty much the same stuff over and over again."

This sounded not so bad. Very few diseases, little ability to distinguish among them, just throw the book at everything you see that looks bad.

"Sounds easy," I said to Blow.

"Cocky bastard." Blow said back, under his breath.

It wasn't so easy. Not at first.

Malaria could be in the brain, which would mean intravenous treatments or death. I was generally opposed to death.

I asked the air hostess for some water and took my daily malaria-prevention pill right then, to assert more fully my opposition to death.

The air hostess was not as young and attractive as she likely once had been. She looked like she had been with the airline forever, and forever is a long time. I reflected that I had promised both myself and the CEO of this airline that I would never fly their crappy airline again. Here I was flying on their cattle car. So I was cattle, not sheep.

Not much better.

But, the adventure would be great.

After listening to sixteen hours of continuous grumbling and hateful comments, Blow was tired of me and praising various gods for the flight finally coming to an end. We had bounced off the airport in Ghana on the way to Liberia, even though Ghana is not remotely on the way to Liberia. The return flight would also go through Ghana, again not on the way home. Apparently it had something to do with the FAA making rules to protect us from the world of people trying to kill us, but it added five hours to the flight, and that is a pain when you are six foot two. I would rather be dead. Almost.

We landed at the airport outside of Monrovia, the capital of Liberia. It was the poorest nation in Africa and it had the longest runway in Africa, built by the US government, that was so long that it had been the African emergency landing site for the Space Shuttle when that spacecraft had been operational. I asked, "So, what's the plan?"

"Well, we spend the next 30 minutes waiting in line to get through passport control, and then we play indoor rugby for 45 minutes with everyone else from the airplane to get our luggage, and then we yell at customs when they want to search our luggage, and then we get outside of the airport where I sure as hell hope my friend Joe is waiting for us."

"Who is Joe?"

"My friend."

Oh oh, it was going to be one of *those* conversations. Like Abbott and Costello.

I didn't always mind them, and I liked to cause them sometimes myself, particularly with administrators.

I probed. "How do you know Joe?"

"He knew me first."

"How?"

"Because he met me before I met him."

"When was that?"

"Not long after he met me."

"When did he meet you?"

"Just before I met him." I thought that was too simple a conversation for Blow, and I told him. "That is too simple a conversation for you. You are better than that."

"I met Joe here in Liberia."

"When?"

"When I was visiting Liberia."

"When?"

"About the time I met Joe."

The heat of West Africa hit us so hard as we emerged from the door of the plane that we stopped talking for a minute. I was grateful, for maybe the heat would interfere with the current conversation.

Blow was right about the line in passport control. At first we were about in the middle of the line. But somehow, we ended up being the last ones cleared. Bit by bit, all the people behind us found some other way through the stereotyped bureaucratic questions about whether it was a business or pleasure trip (Liberia was hardly a tourist destination), and then passport stamping with some illegible stamp that made nobody safer, but sure took time.

We walked through the passport control door into Hell. Baggage claim. Imagine three-hundred people packed in a room the size of a bus, mostly occupied by a single small baggage belt, steadily moving while being stacked four-high with enormous suitcases and surrounded by people stacked four-high trying to pull their bags from the bottom of that moving stack of bags piled four-high, all in a room with a temperature of 105 degrees, filled with stacks of people who have been stuck on a plane and haven't bathed in 24 hours. I didn't have to imagine it. I was living it.

A kind man who worked for the airport noticed the fact that I was American and clueless and helped me rescue my two large suitcases from the morass. Then with Olympic talent he managed to obtain Blow's suitcases too. Each of us brought one suitcase filled with personal items and one filled with medical supplies. The kind man helped us through customs where Blow argued loudly enough that they let us through the melee without making us open our suitcases and we emerged from Hell onto the pavement outside the airport to a crowd of eager people waiting for their loved ones to emerge. In that midst was Joe, whom Blow had met when he had met Joe, at the same time that Joe had met him, sometime in the past, somehow that I was never going to discover.

Joe was 5 foot 9, well fed, with a bit of extra paunch, and smiled broadly when he saw Blow. After a hug with Blow, he held out his hand to me, which I took eagerly, to be met with a Liberian handshake that consisted of a complicated maneuver including the snapping of fingers. Blow had taught me this handshake before, but I fumbled it badly and Joe laughed. "You will be Liberian soon enough."

Dollar bills emerged from Blow's pocket and were distributed among the dozen or so men who were eagerly helping us load our four suitcases into the back of Joe's white Toyota LandCruiser. Flights landing in Liberia were a big source of income for these men who fought to help the landing missionaries transfer their luggage to the waiting vehicles. At the airport—an hour outside of the city—there were no taxis. In any event there are no taxis anywhere in Liberia in which the average non-Liberian would be excited to ride. Liberian taxis are a) small, b) beat up, c) torn up, d) painfully uncomfortable, and e) filled with (and I am serious) commonly twelve people sitting on each other's laps. It is amazing how many Liberians can squeeze into one vehicle. What a Liberian calls a "fourteen-passenger van" would be considered by an American to hold six people with marked discomfort.

"How long is the drive?" I asked, feeling desperate for a shower.

"Just a short trip," replied Joe, which provided absolutely no information to me whatsoever.

On the road from the airport I sat in the back while Joe played loud African music with the most compelling bass lines I had ever heard, and carried on a conversation with Blow in the front seat, none of which I heard. The air-conditioning had begun to dry the accumulated dampness off my clothes, and I cracked my window to partake of the scents of West Africa: a sweet smoke of fresh burning charcoal, palm trees, rubber trees, diesel exhaust and gasoline generator exhaust, mixed with scents that I later learned were from cooking cassava and plantain.

Joe drove fast.

Very fast.

In Liberia, driving this fast is called "running".

We went running past the only speed limit sign in all of Liberia. It said 55MPH. We were traveling at well over 90. Joe drove expertly while looking at Blow most of the time and the road every few minutes.

A truck was far up ahead and a moment later was immediately up ahead. It was a tiny pickup loaded twenty feet high with bundles of blackened palm fronds swelling out to either side of the vehicle like a giant mushroom. It looked like it would fall one way or the other at any moment, which would cause great harm to the seven young men who managed to somehow be riding on top of the enormous pile, smiling and waving as we flew by. "That is charcoal," Joe said while turning his head toward me, which fortunately was in roughly the same direction as the truck as we raced past.

It looked nothing like the briquettes that I thought defined charcoal. More like big packs of mildly cooked leaves. But when burned, it smelled the same, of course without the lighter fluid. Charcoal and gasoline are the main sources of energy in Liberia.

"It sure is dusty," I stated the obvious. Dry dirt covered everything: the car, the road, the buildings, the charcoal, and everything. Dust followed behind the car like waves from a speedboat.

"It has not rained since November," Joe informed us. "Dry season is very dry this year."

"Global warming?"

"Just dry."

Joe wasn't dry. He took a long draw of scotch from a bottle sitting by the gear shift, then handed the bottle back to me. I availed myself, followed by Blow's generous partaking, which in turn was followed by Joe's, then mine, then Blow's. Then Joe again took a happy swallow as he slowed the car down to very fast from ridiculously fast as we drove past a military barracks and then slowed down to reasonable speeds through some more residential and commercial districts.

By 'commercial' I do not mean strip malls and gas stations. I mean fruit sold in shacks, miscellany sold in shanties, gasoline sold in mayonnaise jars and poured by funnels into cars, trinkets sold from wheelbarrows, charcoal sold from wagons, and simply overwhelming masses of people moving in and out and through the mazes of purveyors. Dust was billowing around us and flew all over, but the people were dressed immaculately. White shirts were brightly white. Dark pants were black and well-creased. I looked at my own clothes. Disheveled, wrinkled, splotched with bits of tomato sauce and chocolate and grease and dirt and dust and sweat and general foulness.

"What do you do, Joe?" I asked. "Blow doesn't tell me anything. He says it's best for me to learn on my own."

"I am a businessman."

"What business?"

"Right now, my business is driving this car."

"Which you are doing very efficiently."

Joe laughed.

"I start businesses. I make lots of businesses."

"What type of businesses?"

"Advertising. Transportation. Cell phones. Restaurants."

Blow chimed in, "Extortion, protection, gaming."

Joe didn't take it as a joke and said, "No, never. I never do that."

Blow added, "Joe has his hands in so many projects that he cannot even count them all."

"So," I asked Joe, "when did you meet Dr. Blow?"

"Just after he met me."

After a very long short trip of two or more hours, past amazing scenes of destruction and poverty, hope and exhaustion, sickness and joy, all punctuated by small oases of renewed wealth and recovery, we arrived at our fully walled-in and guarded compound.

The "White Compound" is called what it is called because the wall—which separates it from the thriving and very poor dilapidated village of which it is a part—is painted white. The buildings are painted white. The water tower is white. And it is a place where Americans and Europeans often stay, and they are, by coincidence only, mostly white. But that whiteness has nothing to do with the name. There had been a few white people on the plane, but since leaving the airplane, the only white person I had laid eyes on was Blow.

The accommodations were not dirt-floored, nor dirty. They were nice and spacious and comfortable and had toilets. Toilets that flushed. I was expecting much less, especially after passing the house for rent that had a sign in front that said "House for Lease—1200 square feet—3 bedrooms" and which consisted of a grass-walled, grass-roofed hut. So we were in the lap of luxury here, relatively speaking.

We offloaded our luggage with the willing help of the available willing help. Joe departed to go create new wealth for the nation and for himself, competing with all the government aid provided by the US and Europe.

Within a week, I would understand why the various western governments, particularly the U.S. with its huge invested dollars, had failed to benefit Liberia, or any other place in Africa. I would understand why all the money went down a black hole. I would understand why the private charitable organizations had better success in accomplishing things. And I would understand why the Chinese were providing the most help of all to Liberia. Within a week, I knew the following:

Most Liberians think about money differently than Westerners do. Money to a Westerner is a commodity to invest for the future, to save for hopes, and spend on needs. Money to a Liberian, as a generality, is something to be borrowed by a relative or friend, if it has not already been spent, and never paid back. There is no way to save or invest because if you are rich, you will be borrowed from, and if you refuse to be borrowed from, you will defy hundreds of years of cultural tradition and may be outcast. Only those people who defy traditional culture and think like a Westerner will risk becoming rich.

Additionally, money that is invested or given for one

particular purpose may be used for any purpose that the recipient determines is most important. If you provide a gift to pay for the digging of a well for an orphanage, the money may instead by used to pay for the hospital bill for the father of whomever received the cash, or for a new transmission on the broken-down orphanage van. This is not considered fraud by the Liberian, but rather prioritization. After all, the money was given and is no longer the property of the giver. Oh, it is totally normal and acceptable to ask the next donor for money to help dig the well that is still needed by the orphanage. The private charities, spending privately donated money, have figured this system out. The charitable western governments in their standard incompetence and lack of caring about the spending of forcibly-obtained tax dollars from their citizens, never figure it out, and wonder why things never happen the way they are expected to, and call it all graft and fraud.

The Liberian manner of thinking about money has been highly effective at keeping them alive during horrifically difficult times. It is a survival mentality, not a growth mentality. The classic American growth mentality will fail horribly, if—I mean *when*—the American inflated, fraudulent money bubble collapses and the U.S. economy is left in tatters while the bankers and politicians all move to the Caymans. Americans won't have a clue how to survive economic collapse. West Africans survive this sort of thing all the time.

It would take me a week to learn that stuff. But right now, three hours after arrival, all I knew was that I wanted a shower.

There was a shower in the bathroom that was attached to my room. There was no water, but there was a shower.

Instead of water flowing through the showerhead, there was a blue oil drum filled with water and a handled pail.

I took a bucket bath with cold water that smelled not quite as nasty as I smelled, dried off as best as I could with a thin white towel made out of textile sandpaper, and crawled into my queen-sized bed with its three-inch thick mattress. I sweated all night and woke up in the morning to a rooster crowing, and with five mosquito bites on my face that looked like zits.

We were served a delightful breakfast of scrambled egg, delicious fried plantains, and butterless toast grilled in a fry pan. It turns out that we would be served that very same delightful breakfast every single day without exception.

Clinic in Liberia is not like clinic in the U.S. First, most clinics in Liberia outside the capital have no electricity and no running water. So that was a change from my normal experience. Second, the patients commonly are responsible for keeping their own medical records. Third, nobody sues doctors, ever. Fourth, there is hardly any paperwork that has to be done, and sure as hell no EMR to assist with billing non-existent insurance companies. Fifth, there are no arbitrary rules. Sixth, I can be a doctor in Liberia, instead of a follower of centralized rules, a physician instead of a sheep.

I worked with Blow for the first day. Our first three patients had been having fevers for several nights, and their 'stomachs were running'—the Liberian phrase for diarrhea. We treated them for bacterial enteritis and malaria. The next young woman hadn't 'seen the moon' for three months. We diagnosed her with pregnancy and treated her for malaria. The fifth patient was a teenage boy complaining of 'craw craw'. We treated him for scabies and malaria. Blow only then started remembering to give a de-worming tablet to pretty much everyone. Might as well treat everyone for everything. Make a diagnosis, treat the disease, treat the ever-present malaria, and treat the commonly present intestinal worms. As

I mentioned, a typical day may have a single doctor seeing almost two-hundred patients. Rarely is there time for the so-important preventive services, although we tried to assure vaccinations at least.

Marriage and families are very important in Liberia, although fidelity is probably not the norm. Step-brothers and step-sisters are the expected, not the exception. Children are wealth in Liberia. Children provide care for the parents later. More children means more wealth.

It turns out that there is a lot of wealth—in the form of children—in the very poor country of Liberia. About half the population of the country are children. Happy smiley children who play with deflated plastic balls, a dolls head, a torn up stuffed animal. Immaculately attired by their cleanliness-conscious impoverished parents in the morning, they are a scruffly pile of dust and grime at the end of their day playing with their friends.

The two-year-olds are scared of white people, who appear to them as ghosts. But the four-year olds will call out loudly "White man, white man!" as we drive past their hovel of a home on the side of a dusty road, and chase the car smiling and waving, eager to just touch Blow's hand as it dangles out the window. White means money in Liberia, and it is true. The poorest of Americans (white or black or green or purple or pink or blue) is wealthier *by far* than the average Liberian. The poorest American has more opportunity to be healthy and well, *by far* than those in even the top tier of wealth in Liberia. Recovery from war takes a long time. Liberia had been one of the richest countries in Africa before the wars.

Most of the patients Blow and I saw that first day were children. By the time he and I were half-way through the day, I had learned much of what I needed to know to practice medicine in Liberia, but my problem was my inability to understand their version of English. The educated could make their English comprehensible to me. The uneducated were difficult to understand. It is thought that Liberian English is like slave English from the early 1800's in the United States, before the founding of Liberia by freed slaves during the first half of that century. Liberia is America's colony. Their English drops all final consonants, and a lot of the consonants in the middle of words too.

I walked outside the clinic to get some fresh hot air into my lungs, and a seven-year-old boy came up and held my hand as I walked.

"What's your name?" I asked.

He smiled a huge smile and said, "Mohammed."

"Hi Mohammed. I am Dr. Eddie."

"I know." Mohammed replied.

"How do you know?"

Mohammed just smiled up at me and squeezed my hand a little tighter.

We walked along quietly. There was a gentle breeze, the sun was high, and it was hot, but not oppressively. I was soaked in sweat from being indoors, where it *was* oppressive, but out here I started feeling better.

Blow, although fat and out of shape, was not nearly as sweat-soaked as I was when he came out and started walking with us. Mohammed reached over and patted his stomach.

"How many gayfoo you gah deh?" Mohammed said, in the lazy English of Liberian children.

Blow asked, "What did you say?"

"I seh, how many gayfoo you gah deh?" He patted Blow's paunch again.

I had no idea what Mohammed was asking. Blow had no idea what Mohammed was asking.

"Gayfoo. Gayfoo. How many?" patting Blow's stomach

again.

Blow laughed. "Are you saying I have a big belly?" he asked the little boy.

"Ahhhhhhh," laughed Mohammed. "You gah belly!"

Blow shook his head rather firmly. "No. I don't got belly." Then he turned to me. "The phrase 'Got Belly' in Liberian English means that you are pregnant." I couldn't help but smile at that. "I don't got belly," he repeated.

Mohammed got a little frustrated. "No belly."

We both shrugged and Mohammed ran off into the nearby jungle, known as 'bush' in Liberia. He was hidden in the morass of tangled plants nearly instantly.

"What on earth was that kid saying?" I asked Blow.

"How many gayfoo I gah deh," replied Blow, as if he had a clue.

"I wonder what a gayfoo is."

"I have no idea."

But Mohammed did. In a moment he came tearing back toward us, carrying something in each of his hands. As he came up to us, he gave us each a yellow-pink fruit. He smiled broadly. "Gayfoo. *Gayfoo."*

"Grapefruit!" Blow and I both said, simultaneously.

"How many grapefruit do you have there," I said, pointing to Blow's substantial midgirth.

"Mohammed. Dr. Blow don't got belly. He has five gayfoo in his stomach!"

Mohammed smiled his big toothy smile. There was a glow of light, a sort of energy field around him as he ran off to play with his friends.

Blow said, "Eddie, it's time to get back in there again."

"Let's do it."

The line outside the clinic door had grown substantially during the course of the day. The human telegram in Liberia is astoundingly effective. Word had gotten out that American doctors were in the village, and the diseases, and the people that had them, were coming out of the huts and bush like a flood. There were perhaps eighty people, many with children sitting on their laps, congregated outside the clinic, sitting on walls, stairs, on cement on the floor of the porch area. No one sat on the inviting grass.

"Ants. Biting nasty mean little ants are in that grass," Blow informed me. "Don't walk through that without shoes and socks and long pants and bug repellent."

I looked at Blow's feet, which were sockless. He wore sandals. I looked at mine. I wore socks and black shoes. His shirt was pulled free of his pants and hung loosely. He wore no t-shirt. My oxford shirt and my t-shirt were carefully tucked in to my sweaty pants. I wore a tie.

"Eddie, untuck your shirt. Get rid of the tie, open your neck. Tomorrow, no socks. Wear sandals. Let your body breathe. Let the air circulate over your skin. Then you won't sweat like a stuck pig."

"Why didn't you tell me this before?"

"You have to realize the box you have been living in before you can confidently get out. Even you. You who are so much outside the box, in so many ways. But you still have been living in a box of dressing like an American doctor in the United States. You didn't even think what would be suitable in Africa, did you?"

Blow had me figured. Better than I had myself. I like to try to think for myself, but I had failed in this instance, for sure.

Inside the clinic I fixed my attire as per Blow's instructions, stuffing my t-shirt into my backpack along with the tie I would not wear ever again in Africa. I left my oxford hanging out of my pants for the rest of the trip.

Then I noticed that traditional African garb is indeed open

and loose and allows for airflow over the skin. It made sense.

In the afternoon, Blow let me work by my own self, but I was slower, mostly because of translation problems. I had no x-ray machine to look for fractures in injured children. I had no blood test equipment to look for anemia, leukemia, porphyria, thrombopenia, electrolyte imbalance, or any test for any blooditis. I had no way to do bacterial cultures for wounditis, urine tests for urinitis, skin tests for allergic skinitis, stool tests for stoolitis or any testing at all. In my management of the patients, I had to rely entirely on each person's dysfunctional partially-comprehensible history, my physical exam skills, and hope, spit and a prayer.

"It's a malpractice clinic, isn't it Blow?"

"Damnsolutely it is, Eddie."

"But we saw about two-hundred patients today, in one day. That's pretty amazing."

"Do you think you diagnosed most of them right?"

"I don't know. Probably."

"Probably is pretty good. You treated lots of people for malaria, which they all have, all the time. So you know you got that one right. And worms. Most have worms, so you will have gotten that right most of the time. And the water is so risky here that most diarrhea is bacterial enteritis, so you probably are getting that one right too. Sure, you overused antibiotics. Sure you over-de-wormed. So what?"

"But I could have missed something, like a brewing appendicitis."

"Sure. If you missed an appy, so would all the other doctors that the kiddo could have seen."

"What other doctors?"

"Precisely."

"But it's still a malpractice clinic."

"Sure it is. But it's better than a nonpractice nonclinic. It's actually awfully good, overall. You kicked butt today. You got into the swing of things. You made best guesses after thoughtful evaluation. Caring best efforts. Old style medicine. Do you feel like a doctor?"

"Damnsolutely."

Damnsatively.

I spent three and a half weeks in Liberia. We de-wormed orphanages. We de-wormed villages. I saw children with horrible burns from the open fires that are so prevalent for cooking. I cared for pregnant moms, newborn babies, an old wise town chief, an old wise businessman, an old wise female politician, an evangelical seemingly-reformed rebel leader and hundreds of others with interesting and terrifying tales of their lives, some of which I was able to hear during the rush of the clinical work, but most of which I learned after hours at the restaurants, nightclubs, masonic meetings, Sunday church services, and other venues.

God seems to like to spend time in Liberia, and miracles happen everyday. And every day there is another 'so-called coincidence'. I will tell you about just one of these, now.

I met the head of the Catholic hospital on the outskirts of the capital city. Catholic had stayed open during the entire war, even when the big US-government funded hospital--called JFK (after the JFK of John F. Kennedy fame), had closed down for the duration. The head of Catholic Hospital was busy, and she was appropriately skeptical that I was of any value at all to her hospital, but made time to chat with me and show me around. We talked for an hour and she told me about the frustrations of trying to provide medical care in such a resource-limited environment. At the end of our time together, she was telling me how the generator could not be run all the time because the fuel was too expensive. Power was only available part time from their generator, and a huge amount of their tiny budget was spent on fueling it. The government hospital—JFK hospital—was just a mile away, and was on the fledgling new power grid supplied from a large diesel generator in the city. She wondered with some desperation: why couldn't Catholic Hospital get on the power grid? She had tried to get in touch with the power authorities, to no avail. There were tears of frustration and exhaustion in her eyes as she told me this, and we hugged, and as I said goodbye I knew there was nothing, absolutely nothing on the face of the planet I could do to help her with her electricity problems.

My very next stop was at the nearby JFK Hospital, where I was to meet the head administrator there. I found a building that looked like an admin building. There were seven men sitting on the stairs, doing nothing, just living, which is a common pursuit in Liberian afternoons. I approached one of the men, I believed at random.

"Hello. My name is Dr. Eddie Marcus." I introduced myself, which I had learned was very important to do in Liberia.

"Hello," he told me his name as we reached our hands out to shake and snap our fingers, which I was now moderately accomplished at accomplishing.

"Can you tell me how to get to the hospital administrator's office?"

This man was the first person I had spoken to since saying goodbye to the head of Catholic hospital twenty minutes earlier. The man kindly showed me the way. We talked as we walked. I asked him what he did in Liberia.

"I am the Chairman of the Board of the Liberian Electricity Corporation," he told me.

It was a helluva so-called coincidence.

This really happened. You can't make this shit up.

He and I talked a bit more, and not long after, Catholic Hospital was on the power grid.

My time in Liberia was filled with such coincidences. I learned not to plan quite so hard, because my plan wasn't necessarily the right plan, and my plan had little chance to be carried through to completion. I learned to go where the winds blow you, and find out what you are supposed to learn, and pay attention to the education that you will inevitably receive by just listening.

It is said that the rational mind must dispense with spirituality. I would say that the rational mind should consider spirituality as a high-probability reality.

Chapter 28

Blowing smoke

It was one of the unique aspects of my residency program that it requires all interns to have one month dedicated to research. I am pretty sure the Dean will eliminate that requirement soon to make more doctors available to help compete with the community hospitals to provide run-of-the-mill patient care. Other than the fact that I used to work the ER in this hospital, and went to medical school here, this research month was one of the reasons I was glad to stay for my training at this hospital. Not because I wanted to do research, necessarily, but because I wanted to try it a few times while the trying was good.

In medical school, nobody tells you that the most important choice you need to make is not what specialty you want to work in, but an unexpected and more basic choice—do you want to be a clinician out in regular practice, or an academic physician? That is the first and foremost decision. In either path, you can be a neurosurgeon, plastic surgeon, general surgeon, pediatrician, family practice doc, dermatologist, radiologist, ophthalmologist.

"I want to help people. There is no way I am going to be a

lab rat," says one fourth-year medical student.

"I always wanted to see patients. I like seeing patients. No research for me," says another.

"I am 250,000 dollars in debt. I can't get that paid back on an academic salary. I need to earn real money," says a third.

None of them understand. I don't know of any medical student that really understands the issue. Academic vs. non-academic medicine. They involve totally different mentalities. Although both are semi-self-destructive, self-effacing, selfless, and masochistic, they represent totally different lifestyles.

Imagine you are in middle school, and decide you want to be a doctor because some nice doctor did something nice for you that made you feel nice and warm and fuzzy. Or because you liked watching ER, Scrubs, House, or M*A*S*H on television. Or because your parents think that the only acceptable careers are professional and you don't want to be a lawyer or a priest or a rabbi. You embark on a journey that is long and intense, and it *will* affect how your brain functions biologically. It will change your brain's hardwiring. You will have to work hard for four years of high school so that you graduate high in your class and get into a good college. In college you work very hard so that four years later you will graduate with excellent grades and honors, so that you can get into medical school. In medical school, you work hard for four years so that you can graduate with distinction and get your choice of residency training site and specialty. You work interminably long hours for three to five years during residency to learn medicine and excel so that you can be a good doctor as well as to get the best fellowship in order to subspecialize. You struggle and toil for three years of fellowship, so that you can practice in the field of your choice. The day after you finish fellowship, you move to the clinic facility and start seeing patients as a practicing subspecialist on your own. At the end of that first day, you go home to watch Kim Kardashian Take New York. The next day, you see patients. Then you go home. And you do that for the rest of your career, each evening going home after completing your work, each morning going to the clinic to start your day's work.

You have spent your life since middle school working for goals on about four-year timelines. Four years to finish high school. Four years to finish college. Four for completion of med school. Three to five years to complete residency. Another three to get through fellowship. You have become completely hardwired for these long-term goals, programmed to function on several year horizons. Always something to strive for, a goal to propel you to keep working, to keep caring. That is, until that day you finish fellowship, and start in your daily grind of clinic. What is the long-term goal for you now? To get vacation time? To lower your golf handicap? To get a whole weekend off without interruption before starting the daily routine again on Monday? Perhaps it is to maximize your patient population, which will conflict with all the other goals. Most likely, all of a sudden there is no long-term goal. But your brain is hardwired for such a goal. Your brain needs it like a heroin user who got addicted in childhood must have heroin to feel normal. You have been biologically altered by the process that you began in childhood, and you have to have it. So you create a few artificial long-term goals. Like golf handicap improvement. But that is not satisfactory at all. You spend your career wondering why you are dissatisfied, blaming it on the government, the scum-sucking ambulance chasers, or on the health insurance system. Sure, you may be dissatisfied for those reasons, because the government and the insurance system do indeed suck. And the lawyers are not deserving of comment. However the answer may lie in yourself, and in the cognitive dissonance between your now day-to-day 7 AM to 6 PM job which is the reality of your professional life, and how it simply doesn't mesh against a back-drop of a biologically programmed need for long-term goals.

Academics have such long-term goals, all the time. Their job is not day-to-day at all. And, even if you don't think of yourself as an academic, after four years of college, four years of med school, and three or more years of residency, you will have spent eleven years fully immersed in the mentality and culture of centers of higher learning. You *will be* an academic.

And an academic mentality in a day-to-day job will be a major struggle.

So, you have two choices to optimize your happiness: accept the reality of your academicness and try academia for a career, or be a day-to-day clinician, but put serious and early effort into finding a long-term goal within your profession that will keep you coming to work happy day-to-day. Work to become the Senior Medical Correspondent for ABC news or one of the other major brainwashing media outlets. Start a project to help get sustainable health care to those who need it somewhere else in the world; build the largest most productive specialty practice in your state. Work to get government to stop fouling up the medical economy. Terraform Mars. Then when you accomplish your chosen long-term goal, immediately find another.

Then you will have a chance to be happy in a world that is filled with unnecessary potholes filled with unhappiness.

My first step in my plan has been to decide if I want to be a professional academic. And for me, that means deciding if I want to be focusing on teaching others how to be doctors, and on researching new treatments, cures, and preventions for diseases. I had done some research before and during medical school, but I wasn't running the projects completely then. I needed to do some research project that was stem-to-stern my own. From idea to hypothesis to development to funding to accomplishing to getting the answer to the first question. All by my own effort. Do I have it in me?

I had an idea. We have been told by academic researchers that chocolate does not cause acne, that such a thought is a myth. It was proven to be a myth by means of the classic clinical scientific testing system: they blinded people (not really *blinded*) as to whether they were eating chocolate by sticking the chocolate in swallowable capsules so that they could neither taste nor smell the chocolate. They had matching placebos that just had sugar and flour in them that they could sneakily give to half of the people. No one, including the researchers, knew whether a person was getting the chocolate or the fake, until the special code was broken at the end of the study.

Then they counted zits.

The people who were swallowing chocolate everyday (but didn't know that for sure) didn't get any more zits than the people who were *not* swallowing chocolate everyday (but didn't know *that* for sure). *QED*. Chocolate doesn't cause zits.

The dermatologist and pediatricians and family practice doctors all hit the streets to try to correct the ages-old outrageous and unsubstantiated fiction that chocolate causes zits, backed by the power of the evidence-based medicine of the recent well-publicized paper showing without any doubt that chocolate doesn't cause acne. Armed with such confident scientific knowledge, the doctors assured struggling teens that therapy for acne control no longer involved dietary wisdom, but rather one must buy products produced by pharmaceutical companies. And damn if many of those products don't truly work. They do!

But I get zits when I eat chocolate. They didn't enroll me in that study the academics did. Maybe I am different than the average person. Maybe Joe Pimple is different. Perhaps Joan Blemish is different too, as well as Tom Carbuncle, and his uncle Tim Furuncle, and Dick Goophead, and Peter Papule and his twin brother Peter Pustule, and maybe even Theresa Whitehead. Maybe they are all different, and maybe they respond to eating chocolate by getting zits. They all think that chocolate gives them zits, so when a doctor tells them it doesn't, they have two choices: 1) stop believing in their own deductions and observations—which is a recipe for denigration of self-worth if there ever was one, or 2) realize their doctor is an unlistening jerk—which bodes poorly for the doctor-patient relationship that already is on thin ice, especially with teenagers of the millennial generation, whose skepticism and cynicism is appropriately heightened by all the fraud in the world about which they should be skeptical and cynical.

But there is a reality. There is a very real placebo effect that may be causing these special people who get zits when they eat chocolate to get zits when they eat chocolate. Is that placebo effect relevant to me? If so, does it matter whether the chocolate is causing the zits because of certain oils being exuded from my body only to be digested by the unfriendly bacterial skin flora which get gas and fart into my pores to initiate the pimple, or whether it is just my mind, knowing that I have eaten chocolate, that somehow neurologically initiates the pimplistic process? Maybe it does matter if I know. For if I knew that it really was placebo effect causing me to have zits, maybe my brain could overcome that. And if it is a true effect of the chocolate (which it sure as hell is because I am too cocky to be influenced by the placebo effect), then I can avoid chocolate before my planned weekends in bars trying to pick up girls, which I don't do anyhow because I love Nurse Maid.

Or maybe it is only certain chocolates that cause zits in certain people. You see there is no way that the scientists who studied chocolates and zits could have examined all the various forms of chocolate: Godiva, Nestle, Hershey, Cadbury, Ghirardelli, Lindt, and the product of the four hundred other chocolatiers in the world, each with their own mixture of butters and oils and sugars and cooking times. There is no way that the academics investigated all those.

And there is no way that in their studies of chocolate the investigators investigated all the people in the world either, and it turns out that each person is different. Let's repeat this highly obvious aphorism, unquestioned precept, universally recognized truism, this absolute adage, that is so often entirely ignored by the academic purveyors of evidence-based medicine: *each person is different.* Again, the purveyors of evidence-based medicine must live each day with horrible cognitive dissonance, because they know that everyone is different, but try to treat everyone the same.

So, I wanted to seek the truth, for me. And by seeking the truth for me, identify a means for seeking the truth for every other individual me that was out there.

So, I made a plan. But I needed to get funding. Part of being an academic researcher is applying for funding from the National Institutes of Health, which proudly proclaims that it supplies ninety percent of the medical research dollars for the nation. Now, last I looked, the NIH doesn't make any money, so I don't know how they can claim that they supply ninety percent of the medical research money. But I guess they do.

So, because the national government controls the purse strings, legally, ethically, or illegally and unethically, I needed to learn how to get some. I had to learn what to write, and how to write it and I needed to write something legally and ethically or illegally and unethically, depending on my perspective on the NIH.

It actually didn't come easily to me, because I am not a natural grabber of stolen loot, unless I, like Robin Hood, had a chance to steal from the thieves and give to the people who had been robbed. If I took money from the NIH, I would be stealing from the thieves, but not giving it to those who had been robbed. I would be doing research with it that I, not the person whose money had been stolen, thought was worthwhile. That isn't right.

So I suffered cognitive dissonance myself as I began my application for NIH funding. I wrote and pondered and pondered and wrote.

"How do I go about assuredly getting an NIH grant?" I asked Blow.

"Assuredly? The only way to get it assuredly is to meet with your congressman."

"No, really."

"Really. Political influence is the only way to have confidence in getting government money."

"How about without using political force. Is there a way?" I asked hopefully and dejectedly.

"Probably."

"How?"

"Probability," Blow replied sternly.

"What do you mean?"

Blow shrugged. "I mean that getting NIH money to fund your research is a game of chance. It's a roll of the dice. You have to roll it over and over again. Roll it often enough and you usually can win."

"How do I roll the dice?"

"That's not the right question. The right question is what

number do you bet on"

"Huh?" I asked unknowingly.

"Say you got two dice, what is the most common number that comes up when you roll them?"

"Seven."

"Right. Seven comes up way more often than any other number. So bet on seven."

"How."

"Well, plan on writing a grant for a project that there is no foreseeable way of the outcome ever helping anyone. NIH loves that."

"Like what?"

"Pick a pet protein that no one has ever heard of. Have it be deeply hidden inside a cell where few, if any, medications can get to it. Have higher levels of it make one disease get better while causing another disease. Make sure that there is no way to know exactly what good will come for a human as a whole from increasing or decreasing its levels. And make certain that there are all sorts of interacting systems that are affected by what you do to try to affect the level of your pet protein. Then genetically engineer a mouse to not have the protein and then try to figure a way to cure that rodent that you made sick in the first place."

"Why?"

"Because then the scientists who review your application at NIH will love your thinking, because you will be studying something that sounds very scientific even though nobody cares about it and nobody can do anything about it or would ever want to. And importantly, you can have a nearly unlimited supply of other questions that will pop up during your studies, that will be important for you to spend more taxpayer money on to answer, prompting the NIH to need more money to support you, prompting them to get more money, prompting them to have more power. That is how they ended up funding 90% of the medical research in this country."

I was quiet.

"That is the NIH." Blow spoke quietly and looked out the window.

"I don't want to engineer mice to be sick."

"Okay," said Blow. "Then at least title your application using words that the NIH likes a lot."

"Like what?"

"Like nano-anything. Or Evidence-based-medicine. Or AIDS or breast cancer."

I pondered, "I want to study if chocolate causes zits."

"It does. Study over."

"But everyone says it doesn't cause zits."

"It does cause zits. Everyone knows it."

"But the scientists say it doesn't"

"Well, they must be right then."

"But I want to prove them wrong."

"Okay, prove them wrong."

"But I need money to prove them wrong."

"Okay. So, do an Evidence-Based Study of Biomarkers of Nanotube-Induced Breast Cancer in AIDS Patients."

"But I don't want to study breast cancer in AIDS."

"Okay, so write your grant application about of the effect of Alfaromeo Deacetylase on Tautomers of the Histone Complex in Sprague-Dawley Rats."

"What? Why do that?"

"I thought I told you already." Blow seemed exasperated. "Because the NIH loves to fund studies of rodents and of irrelevant proteins in parts of cells that you can't target with medicines or in any other way, thus allowing no possible therapeutic advance to come from the knowledge, which is created at great expense for knowledge's sake and then immediately lost among the pages of the fifty-thousand medical journals because nobody, absolutely nobody cares. That is the perfect NIH grant application."

"But I just want to study chocolate and zits!" I reiterated.

"That doesn't matter. You are rolling the dice. If you win, then you can do whatever you want with the money, as long as it's ethical."

"Really?"

"Well, not really. But the NIH doesn't seem to give a Sprague-Dawley rat's ass what happens to the money they dole out. You can study dandelion bead bracelets and their effects on Alzheimers if you want, once you put your bullshit grant together and get it funded."

"I don't like this."

"Neither do I. Tell you what," said Blow, "maybe you should be honest and forthright and tell them what you really want to study."

"That is more my way."

"Okay, then how about your application being, "The Effects of Nano-chocolates on Biometric Evidence of Hyperexpansive Acneiform Tumorous Lesions in Adolescents."

"That I can do."

"Good. Ethical morass has been forded."

"What next?"

Blow told me what next. He taught me the stereotyped format for applying for NIH grant money. He taught me the lingo, and he taught me the tricks and shortcuts and buzzwords and necessary patronizing. It was a substantial amount of paperwork, but no more than one would expect when applying for a loan from Fannie Mae or Freddie Mac.

"When you are writing, think of your audience. Who

would you want to read your grant and make decisions about it?"

I replied, "A family practice doctor, like us, who knows adolescent medicine, or a nutritionist. And a dermatologist too."

"Good. But no chance. Your grant will be reviewed by a Ph.D. in chemistry, biology, or nano-tubology, with no knowledge of nutrition or dermatology, who never gave a crap about the zits all over his face in high school, and who doesn't have a clue about medicine, adolescent fears or crises, or the importance of clarifying whether eating chocolate prevents clarifying acne from the face. You will need to convince this guy that your medical research is more important than the research of the guy whose application is all about preventing breast cancer in AIDS using nanotube biomarkers. If by some strange freak stroke of luck you get a dermatologist to read your application at the NIH, then you might have a chance, if, and only if, he or she hasn't already decided that chocolate is innocent, because she was an author of that one paper."

"Would a scientist actually be biased, prejudiced like that?"

"Hell yes," replied Blow. "The biases in academic medical research are powerful, because these folk don't want any threat to the very thin web of support that they have created for their fledgling or not-so-fledgling scientific reputation. Anything which calls into question their own research will not readily get through them into the NIH funding cycle, that's for sure."

"But who cares about chocolate and zits?" I asked, meaning, "Who cares enough to try to stop the research in it?"

"Nobody cares much about chocolate and zits."

"I do."

"Okay, go study chocolate and zits."

"But I need to get the money to do the study."

"Then ask your Congressman to put it as a line-item in the federal budget, right among funding a war with Iran, ethanol subsidies, a bridge to nowhere, Obamacare, and studying the effect of methane in cow flatulence on global warming."

"Are you saying my project is pork?"

"It would be if it were in the federal budget. It won't be considered pork if it is just a later entry within the NIH sub-budget, which Congress never looks at."

"I don't want to study pork. I want to study chocolate."

"It is really the same thing if you are asking the government for money that it shouldn't be giving out, cuz it's broke."

"But they control ninety percent of medical research money in this country."

"Yes they do."

"So what do I do?"

"Well, you can find the other ten percent."

"They won't care about chocolate and zits."

"You're probably right about that. But you care about chocolate and zits."

"Yes I do."

"And other people who think they get zits from chocolate care too, right?"

"Sure they care."

"Then get them to fund the study."

I replied, "They won't."

"Sure as hell right they won't. Because they don't care."

"So what do I do?"

"You fund the study yourself."

"On intern pay?"

"Can't happen," Blow smiled. "You can't even afford

chocolate on intern pay. You should fund it with the income from the frigiproppers that you sell to the hospital."

"Actually, I sell the frig'o'graphs to all the hospitals in the area now."

"And someday, they will pay you for them, I suppose. Use that money to pay yourself back for the money you put into this chocolate boondoggle."

"But it's not a boondoggle. It's important to people who eat chocolate."

"Not important enough for them to pay their hard-earned money to find out."

"And the Frig'o'graph money is for African children."

"Are they more important than your chocolate research?"

"Yes."

"Point made."

"But I might be able to get NIH money, huh? That money isn't going to Liberian orphans. It'll just go to some other researcher studying some useless protein in a useless animal model. So I should try for that money, huh?"

"Sure, because your chocolate boondoggle is plenty important enough to spend other people's hard-earned money on. Isn't it?"

Blow had me there. It wasn't important enough.

"Okay, so I'll drop this. It's not important enough to pursue."

Blow stood up, his face filling with redness and he spat out words in anger. "No Dr. Marcus, it is VERY important. It is one of the most important things you can study."

I sat silently, in complete confusion. Was Blow jerking me around? I had never seen him joke with such powerful emotions.

After a minute, I said, "Ummm. Why? It's just chocolate and zits."

"No it isn't, you idiot! You're taking on the system, can't you see that? And the system needs its ass kicked. You need to teach doctors that a study doesn't give the answers needed to help a patient. And this is very important, because these studies—such as the one about chocolate that taught everyone that there was no way chocolate causes your zits or my zits—are already being codified into law by the federal government. Pretty soon, if you tell a patient that chocolate causes zits, you will be a criminal."

"That's insane."

"Tell me something in this crazy country that is not insane."

Blow had a point.

So I got to work. I wrote up the whole NIH application, got all the forms signed by the administrators, consumed hours and hours of a secretary's time, pissed off and bothered everyone who I needed to help me so that they would supply to me all the paperwork that NIH required, and submitted the application through the NIH electronic application system which never works. All in all it took two weeks of hard effort, which consumed two out of my four weeks of my research month. After I had submitted the application, Blow brought me a champagne bottle.

"Congratulations!" he said, in a congratulatory exclamation of my job well done.

Neither he nor I were on call, so I started popping the cork. "Stand back!" I gently eased the top third of the cork out of the bottle mouth, and aimed it at the ceiling. I eased further. Soon it was eighty percent of the way out and still no gratifying POP. I nudged a bit farther and the cork fell out limply on the floor.

"Water." Blow smiled as I poured the dead clear contents into a convenient sink. "And the day you get the NIH money, I will give you a champagne bottle filled with piss."

I put the bottle down. "What is my chance of getting the money?"

"About twelve percent."

"Not more?"

"Nope, you didn't even try to roll a seven. Instead you foolishly wrote a grant about something you cared about."

"When will I get champagne?"

"When you produce something worthwhile, without stealing someone else's money to do it."

He was hurting me. "When will I hear from NIH?"

He replied in what seemed to be a totally uncaring manner. "Well it takes them four months to even look at the application, at least. You'll hear something about four months after that, and if you get lucky, they won't reject it completely, but will ask you to revise it. You will miss the deadline for revision though, because they take so long to review your grant in the first place, so you have to send in your revision at the next cycle four months later, which they will take eight months to get back to you about. So, let's see, you might get funding in the middle of your final year of residency."

"That's deflating."

"It's the government."

"The NIH has very smart people in it. Lots of them."

"It sure does," affirmed Blow. "No doubt. Some of the best and brightest medical minds in the country are there."

"Then why can't we expect NIH to be more than just competent, but actually stellar?"

"You can expect it, but when you get really smart people together and give them power, there are two potential bad outcomes. The first is that they are completely stumped by the bureaucratic system they are in, so can't get anything productive and sensible accomplished. They are stymied. This is the most common."

"Sounds like a huge waste. What's the second bad outcome?"

"The second is worse. They might, and sadly often do, think that getting themselves together with other smart people gives them moral authority to use all their groupsmarts to make rules and policies and dictums to make sure that everyone else abides by what they know is so smart, and now they have the power to do it. You can get all mad and worked up and call it all sorts of nasty names, like narcissism, fascism, or some other kinda of 'ism, but sadly, it is just realism. It is rule by experts."

"Expertarchy," I said, making up a word to compete with 'oligarchy'.

"That is a pretty good term, Eddie. We are living to a great extent in an Expertaucracy. We have a giant bureaucracy run by the narcissistic experts whose expert comments and statements and predictions are used by the narcissistic power-grabbers to justify to the masses their increasing power-grabs. They say that we need experts to tell us how to do everything and the non-politically powerful don't feel competent enough to argue. The experts use the power of government try to create an Expertopia in which the experts make the rules we all are forced to follow, and that is not just the NIH, Eddie. It's pretty much everywhere now. In the end, we just get a giant totalitarian Idiocracy. It's at all levels, from the federal government, to corporations, to public and private schools, to our own university and most hospitals. It has inculcated itself into our culture far beyond just the government."

It was exhausting even to contemplate. So I didn't. The last two weeks of my research month I spent working in Blow's laboratory, learning how to make a breath assay for marijuana.

"Why do you want me to make a breath assay for marijuana?" I asked Blow.

"So I can make money selling the test to parents who want to know if their kid is smoking weed."

"Why do you care?"

"I don't, but parents do. They need to know so they can help their kids figure life out. As long as marijuana is illegal, most kids won't tell their parents if they are using it."

"But marijuana is pretty harmless in the big scheme," I noted.

"Sure, so why is it illegal?"

"I have no idea. Why?"

Blow sat back and said, "You won't believe it."

I was quiet.

"In the mid 1930's there was a bunch of illegal aliens coming across the Texas border from Mexico. Except back then, they weren't illegals. They were just immigrants. But the lack of illegality didn't stop the racism and anger, especially during the Depression. So there were all kinds of laws made to make it unpleasant for Mexicans, including making marijuana illegal, because it was thought they liked to smoke it after a hard day in the fields. Also, some rich bigwigs considered hemp to be a threat to their wood-pulp paper manufacturing businesses, so these fat cats chimed in to help get hemp growing made illegal. The government bent to racist and corporatist pressure and took unconstitutional control over marijuana and hemp and made it illegal nationally."

"So, why do you want to help parents enforce the national government's illegal laws?"

"I don't. I want parents to have the power of knowledge to help raise their children in a world that is full of various intoxicating compounds, full despite all the laws designed to make drugs unavailable. The drugs are there. Let's help parents work with their own children, and not rely on the bureaucracies in the raising of their child. That's the point."

So I worked in the lab. I worked hard in the lab for the next two weeks. Nurse Maid almost forgot who I was, because I had been at the lab so much. But in the end, I came up with a breath assay for marijuana.

Blow and I tested it. Several times. And then some more times, just to make sure. We had to make sure it would work to detect small exposures as well as large exposures.

It worked for both.

So, it turns out that I like research. I can do research. I can be an academic. It is good to know it so early in my postgraduate medical training. Research months are good.

Blow and I patented the test, and he is working a deal to sell it to the State of California, which plans to mandate the presence of the test in the houses of all teenagers. And he sublicensed it to a company for sale in Florida, where, unbeknownst to Blow, it will be placed in all the government-run public schools to try to nab kids on Monday mornings so that the schools can keep the kids in fear.

"Well, you can't win them all," sighed Blow.

Chapter 29

My Groupism

It turns out that I am an assholist. I didn't realize it at first, but Blow taught me one day, and he was right.

"You are an assholist," Blow said one day, without a hint in his demeanor that he was joking, as he interrupted an important conversation we were having about how useless the high level administrators in the hospital are. It was pretty much the same conversation as always.

"What?" I was hurt. I respected Blow so much. And he had called me an asshole without, as I mentioned earlier, the faintest hint in his demeanor that he was joking.

"I said you are an asshol*ist*."

I heard him better this time. I think.

He repeated for my edification. "Eddie, you are an assholist. A proponent of assholism."

"Like racism or sexism, you mean, except that I discriminate against assholes? Do you mean that I am prejudiced against assholes?"

"Right. And wrong."

"Huh?" I prodded.

"Exactly," Blow replied. Blow chuckled inanely. So did I.

I pondered and contemplated in my contemplative manner of pondering, and had to admit that Blow was right. I wasn't thinking at my fastest for some reason that right now I wasn't a fast enough thinker to figure out.

"But Blow, I always thought that prejudice is wrong, and I don't think I act wrongly."

"I agree that prejudice is wrong, but you aren't prejudicial. You aren't *pre*judicial. You are *post*judicial. Based on evidence, you have judged them to be assholes, and then you choose to behave poorly around them. After rational judgment you discriminate against being friendly with them."

"But we are all taught that discrimination is wrong too. And I don't feel wrong."

Blow rolled his office chair the five and a half feet necessary to cross his entire expansive office, so large that we both barely fit in it, so worthy of a faculty member of his prominence. He rolled all the way over to his bookcase, in which sat a dictionary. He flipped through it and started reading:

> *"Discriminate: to note or observe a difference; distinguish accurately."*

I absorbed the definition. Slowly.

"Okay," I said. "So discrimination can be okay. It means to distinguish accurately."

"Yes, but it also has taken on in common usage an entirely new meaning, which is the notion of making decisions about someone based on a group to which they have been assigned in some fashion.

> *"Discriminate: to make a distinction in favor of or against a person or thing on the basis of the group, class, or category to*

which the person or thing belongs rather than according to actual merit"

I pondered again. "Well, that definition does suggest that discrimination sucks. Like we are all taught."

"Sometimes. If you discriminate in order to choose wisely among options, that is good. If you discriminate unwisely, based on superficial criteria or group classifications, that is bad."

I was being preached at.

"I get it, Blow." I said, getting it.

"In any event," said Blow, "you are an assholist."

I do discriminate against assholes, the nature of such people I determine postjudicially. But I don't group them into one giant group of assholes, because assholes can be so individual. The thought of a giant asshole group made me laugh again for some reason. I wasn't able to think fast enough to understand why I laughed, which I didn't understand, for some reason.

My discrimination somewhat involves not wanting to associate with assholes. But mostly my discrimination takes the form of actively trying to stop assholes from accomplishing anything assaholic that they are attempting to accomplish. I am a postjudicial discriminatory anti-asshole assholist with an agenda. I think this is a totally fair description of me.

"But what makes you so sure about your definition of asshole?" probed Blow, thankfully only verbally. I remained fully clothed in case the verbalized word 'asshole' and the non-verbalized word 'probe' might together create some sort of subconscious behavior on the part of Blow, who at the very moment was, like me, heavily under the influence of the research study we were scientifically performing to study my new diagnostic breath test for cannabis inhalation. Come to think of it, maybe that was why my brain wasn't thinking so well.

"Assholes are assholes. It is self-determining and self-defining."

"Ahh," responded Blow in his always usually wise way. I feared he might go Socratic on me.

"Do you know any assholes who sometimes aren't assholes?" asked Blow, as he went Socratic on me. Well, as long as he stayed Platonic, it was okay.

"I suppose," I supposed.

"Well, how do you deal with them when they are not being assholes?"

"I don't."

"You don't deal with them?"

"Right."

"When trying to improve behavior, it is wise to reward good behavior and punish bad behavior."

"Yeah. So you want me to be nice to them when they aren't being assholes, huh? To help reinforce their non-asshole behavior in a positive way?"

"I didn't say that. But you certainly do punish them when they are being assholes, so you might as well do the obverse."

"Obverse," I laughed, clueless.

"Obverse, the other reverse opposite, but kinda the same, from another angle. If you reward their good behavior with your pleasant presence, it will be memorable to them, because most of the time they think you are an asshole. It will be much more impactful than just being an asshole when they are being assholes which they will come to expect and therefore won't have impact."

"Wait. Are you calling me an asshole?"

"No, you are an assholist. But *they* think you are an

asshole."

"Why do they think that?"

"Because you're not a sheep. They can't control you. Therefore you're an asshole."

"But *they* are the assholes."

"Of course they are. That is why they think you are an asshole."

So, it seems that I'm both an asshole and an assholist. I would have to discriminate against myself in the future so that I wouldn't be discriminatory. I would try.

In the meantime, I was on a roll as an assholist.

And it wasn't just individual assholes whom I apparently despised and reviled and discriminated against postjudicially. If a group of people (whether good people or assholes) got together in said group, and the group was an asshole, I would treat said asshole group with equal despicability. I would not discriminate against, or in favor, of an asshole, just because it was a group.

"What do you think about switching insurance companies," Dick Wadley was saying to me as we sat on the call room sofa a few nights later watching the temporarily-repaired television and letting our brains die.

The television was proclaiming that you could save $450, or more, by switching from Progressive to Geico, or from Allstate to Progressive, or from Geico to Allstate, or from State Farm to any of the above, or vice versa. Except this is not what the ads really say.

"Have you called them?" asked Dick.

"What, that insurance company?"

"Yeah. Can they really save you money like that, or are they just lying?"

"They aren't lying. I'm sure what they are saying is the truth."

"But they can't all be cheaper than the other ones."

"Nope."

"Then at least a couple are lying."

"Nope. They aren't lying. They're just assholes."

"Whatdya mean?"

"The ads say that the savings of the people who *switched* was $450. Most people don't switch. The ones who do switch do so because they save money."

"Ahh, said Dick Wadley as he retreated to the bathroom to perform horrible and egregious acts of flatulence in anticipation of Nurse Maid stopping by to say Hi to me.

Which she did soon thereafter. Remember, Nurse Maid doesn't appreciate odors emanating from non-hospitalized persons, and Wad's ability to create vicious scents in High Fidelity olfactory stereo was legend now, so I cut her off at the door and guided her safely out of the toxic region, down the elevator toward the cafeteria. We chatted for fifteen minutes over coffee. Damn, she was beautiful.

After a bit, we braved returning to the call room. The Wad had been paged away, leaving only minor destruction in his wake. The volume of the olfactory stereo had been turned down sufficiently that Jennifer only crinkled her nose slightly.

We sat down together on the couch, my arm around her, and just breathed each other's presence for a few minutes. Soon, Jennifer reached over for the always-missing remote control that miraculously was not missing just then, and made an attempt to flip the television over to a channel that wasn't professing the glories of whatever pile of crap they were always trying to sell you.

But it was to no avail. The first channel she turned to was selling nutraceutical capsules that promised to support heart health.

"What the hell does that mean? Support heart health??"

Jennifer asked with modest disgust.

"Absolutely freakin' nothing," I replied, with more than modest disgust.

The next channel was selling another set of pills in a bottle, this one claiming to 'support the immune system'. Another entirely meaningless statement used to sucker in the unsuspecting, thoughtless and insane.

"Eddie, you hate evidence-based medicine, yet it can be used to combat these scams."

"I don't hate evidence-based medicine. I hate how it has been perverted. I'm a big fan of the original intent, which was for doctors to use the best evidence to assess the likely effectiveness of various medical interventions, and then use that information in concert with the very individual and personal information from your patient to help make the best decisions for the care of your individual patient. The MD's who write the practice guidelines, and the insurance companies and governments that enforce the guidelines, keep forgetting about the 'individual patient' part of it. That's what I despise. Oh yeah, I also hate how the authors of the guidelines call them guidelines so that they sound not mandatory, but how the government and insurance companies and lawyers all enforce them, thus making them mandatory."

"Don't forget to breathe, Eddie."

I remembered and then Jennifer asked, "But it would be good to have evidence based medicine used to test these claims from these companies that sell snake oil to support the immune system and cardiac health, wouldn't it?"

"It sure would. But it won't happen. The companies that sell that stuff sure as hell don't want to test it using real science, because their stuff might not do much. They are assholes. Their stuff might work wonders for some people.

But we won't know, because they won't test it. Hell, to me, buying something completely unproven is pretty stupid. But to others, it is sensible. As long as they are spending their own money and not mine, it doesn't bother me much. Some of these remedies have been around for thousands of years. It is hard to argue that they *don't* do something of value."

"How can you measure if it supports the immune system or supports heart health?"

"I don't think you really can. I think they just make some leaps of faith from what's known of the chemistry, and make untestable claims."

"Shouldn't they be forced to prove their statements, like drug companies are?" Jennifer regretted the question instantly, for she knew that an assured way to work me up was by suggesting that anybody should be forced to do anything they hadn't previously agreed to do.

I replied in one of my most wise moments, "Let's not get into that. The whole system is a scam and filled with assholes, and I don't want to get worked up."

Instead of getting worked up, we snuggled up on the couch, kissed, petted, cuddled more. Life was good. Very good. She smelled so good.

Her lovely scent covered up the stench that still slightly persisted from the effluvium that had emanated from Wad's asshole, and her gentle voice and lovely eyes removed from my brain the stench from the assholes advertising on television.

Jennifer was my remedy for assholes.

Chapter 30

Bureauxidative Stress

I wondered if I could bottle the essence of Jennifer and sell her as a remedy for assholes.

I decided against it, and instead decided it was time to embark on another business venture.

"Blow, I was thinking that I do need to make some money, at least so I can pay you back what I owe you. I want to create a new product and sell it to people who will pay lots of money for it."

"So do I," answered Blow.

"Well, I'm serious."

"So am I."

Blow continued to write in his patient's chart that didn't exist because it was made out of paper. After a minute, he looked up at me.

"What are you wanting to invent, create, market and sell?"

I shrugged. "That's where my idea gets rather thin."

"Eddie, you're better than that. Come back to me when you got a handle on something."

It took me a few days, but then I came up with it. Oxidative stress. The nutraceutical companies were always talking about treating oxidative stress using anti-oxidant mixes. New stuff was coming out every day; most recently the entrants were compounds that supposedly turn on the human body's own anti-oxidant systems. Oxidative stress has been a major buzzword in the wellness world, but not only there. The MD world pays a lot of attention to oxidative stress too. The MD world has no therapy for it, but it sort of wishes it had. The nutraceutical companies and herbalists and naturopaths were way ahead of the MD world in this field.

Oxidative stress is the gradual, slow, burning of your tissues. Not your Kleenex, but your biological tissues. This burning leaves scars, damage, dysfunction. Oxidative stress seems likely to play a large role in the process known as aging. Oxidation is always happening in your body, and is always balanced by reduction. Reduction is what most of the anti-oxidants assist with. The real chemistry involves transfer of electrons. The oxidizing molecule receives the electrons from the molecule that gets oxidized. The oxidizing molecule itself then gets reduced. In our usual metabolism, Oxygen accepts electrons from Carbon and Hydrogen, thus oxidizing them, while the Oxygen itself is reduced. For every oxidation there is a reduction. Perfect balance. Throwing a lot of anti-oxidants doesn't change that balance. In fact it cannot.

However it does change something else. You see, although oxidative reactions are constantly happening in the normal process of body function, oxidative *stress* happens when valuable parts of your cells are getting oxidized. These are like accidental burns. Atoms are pretty stupid, and once they are on the move, they might knock electrons off any molecule that they happen to bump into. If they bump into a bit of glucose, the glucose will be oxidized and the metabolic system will create energy from that. This is how we get energy from food. If however, they bump into a molecule that is part of normal cell surface functioning (in other words, *not* food), that molecule is changed and won't work to keep the cell functioning. If too many of those molecular injuries occur, the cell dies. Enough cells die, and scar forms. And you age.

Oxidative stress is when your systems accidently oxidizes bits of you that you don't want oxidized.

There were billions of dollars of dietary supplements being sold in the country to lessen oxidative stress, supposedly lessening the rate you age. People don't want to age, so they buy this stuff like crazy.

And sure, the stuff that is sold indeed are anti-oxidants for the most part. Some are actually misguided oxidants being sold as anti-oxidants by companies that don't understand the chemistry, but that is less than thirty percent. Most are actually anti-oxidants, which for the most part means that they are reductants. They give up their electrons to the most common recipient of electrons (which is oxygen), so that your healthy cells don't end up giving up their electrons (thus getting oxidized). That is the point, at least. But, the question is, how much do you have to bathe your cells in Vitamin C, Vitamin E, Selenium, Uric Acid and all those other juices before the cells are less likely to be oxidized than the supplement? How can an individual know if they are taking the right mixture of anti-oxidants, or the right dosage? How can they measure how fast they are aging, to see if all the expensive supplements are doing anything for them other than lightening their wallets?

Likewise, losing real weight (not wallet weight), and exercising well, more probably should help reduce oxidative stress. But will it do so in YOU, or Joe Pimple, or Joan Pustule? Or Tom, Harry or Dick? How do you know?

Well, you need to be able to measure it.

"Blow. I want to create a way for people to measure

oxidative stress in themselves."

"Now, *that's* a good idea," replied Blow enthusiastically not caring at all, as he scratched some black pencil smudges from under his fingernail. He was writing in a non-existent paper chart again, using forbidden and therefore non-existent pencils for his daily patient progress notes.

"Come on, Blow, what do you think?"

"I think it is a fine idea. How are you going to do it?"

"I don't know. But let's figure it out together."

"It's gonna cost money. Lots of money."

"Thank God you and I have lots of money."

"Do you?"

"Well, no, but I've been promised lots of money, because I'm a doctor."

"Right'o. You ain't learned much yet, have you. But okay, let's do it."

Blow finished up with a few more patients while I waited for him at the nursing station reading the daily news on the internet. There was a story about passive-aggressivity as central to the modern female's method of controlling her man, vs. manipulation as the modern man's method of controlling his woman. Apparently no longer is it violence and withholding of sex that were the coins of the control realm. The next article was a comparison of the 'Me generation' to the 'Millennial generation'. Thankfully, I didn't have time to read that article right now, for I needed to sit and wait for another thirty minutes twiddling my thumbs with nothing to do, and that was taking up all my time.

I looked at the people on the ward. The nurses typing on computers. The doctors typing on computers. The transport team and phlebotomists typing on computers. Everybody was going to suffer from QWERTYitis. The scary thing is that these people were writing in the non-existent paper records the same things they were trying to type into the electronic medical records, so there was hardly any time left for actually hanging out with the patients. Some of the computers were on wheels, and would roll around on them from room to room as the doctors got together for rounds. One of my friends worked for one of the companies that sold most of these R2-D2 rolling computers to the hospitals for implementation with their medical records. Now *that* seemed like a good business to be in. He was making money while I was not. I was proud of him.

After a while, Blow finished up with his end-of-day quick rounds, and came over to me. I like end-of-day quick rounds. When I do them, I just run into each room and check on the patient and make sure things are okay. I don't write notes, I don't do anything other than just be the caring doctor that I really am. Blow does the same thing, but sometimes writes notes. It takes time, but it is good time. The best time. I love just chatting with the patients. Helping them. I like that. So does Blow. But I wasn't on service now, and didn't know the patients. So Blow got the fun.

"Let's go." Blow motioned to the door of the ward. We went.

Pizza and beer for me. Pizza and Pepsi for Blow.

"So, you want to measure oxidative stress in patients."

"In people, not patients."

"How about in people *and* in patients."

"Maybe."

"Why maybe?" asked Blow. "You don't want to make a test that patients can use?"

"If we make it for patients, it will clearly have to go through FDA. FDA is unpredictable and whimsical. Can't trust them."

"It probably has to go through FDA anyway, no matter

who you design it to be used for."

"Why is that? The nutraceuticals don't go through FDA." I pointed out brilliantly to Blow.

"Are you a nutraceutical? No, you are making a medical device. There is a specific law that Orin Hatch rammed through Congress a long time ago that excluded food supplements from regulation. But his law didn't exclude drugs or devices from regulation."

"How can the FDA legally prevent me from making a test for oxidative stress?"

"They can't. But they can prevent you from selling it."

"Where is that in the Constitution?"

"Nowhere."

"So how did they get that power?"

"Stop being an idiot, Eddie."

I stopped being an idiot. I knew damn well how FDA was illegally empowered, and that we would have a choice of sucking up to them and following their inane bureaucratic dictums, or try to sneak illicitly around them.

"Let's sneak illicitly around FDA," I told Blow.

"Agreed. Are you ready to go to jail?"

"Sure."

"Me too. Didn't used to be, but now I'm more than willing."

"You're pretty beat down, aren't you? I haven't seen you pissing off anybody in the hierarchy lately. Have you mellowed?"

"No, you were right the first time. Just beaten down."

That feeling was common among almost all the rebel doctor non-sheep that I encountered. The rebel doctor non-sheep were rare and survival for them was difficult. The seemingly successful among them had to isolate themselves from the system to the limited extent possible that was compatible with making a living, and then numb themselves to the otherwise horrible feeling in their guts when they inevitably had to work with the system. So 'isolated and numb' became the general feeling of the rebel doctor non-sheep. I felt bad for them. I felt bad for Blow. I felt bad for me.

But I was numb to feeling bad, so I continued the conversation in what I thought was a productive manner.

"So, let's create a breath test for oxidative stress."

Blow looked up from his pepperoni and nodded, waiting.

"So a patient breathes through this tube and a number spits out on the screen, showing how much oxidative stress he has."

"Brilliant. How? What are you going to measure in breath?"

"How about oxidants?"

"If you can do it, it will tell you about the amount of oxidants, not the amount of stress. The oxidants could be causing no harm."

"How about some chemical that is only formed by oxidative injury of cells?"

"Now that sounds good. What chemical are you thinking about?"

"No clue."

"I don't know that chemical."

"Neither do I."

"But whatever you measure, watch out because there will be environmental and bacterial and dietary contaminants. Most likely whatever you measure will be lying to you."

Blow was silent. I was silent. We silently contemplated.

Then Blow said, "How about we measure carbon dioxide?"

"Huh?" I asked.

"Sure, carbon dioxide is certainly an end product of oxidation. That, and water, are the two end products of oxidative metabolism of carbohydrates and fats. The more you exhale of it, the more oxidation must have happened in your body. And the more accidental oxidation must be happening to your cells too, don't you think?"

"Sure," I said hesitantly, expecting a trap. "But most of the carbon dioxide won't be formed from oxidative *stress*."

"True, but *some* of it will."

"Probably a tiny fraction."

"Yeah, but the rest of the CO2 is a toxin to the environment, at least everyone has been taught to think so, so they will think that it is bad."

"People aren't that stupid, Blow."

He looked at me with his eyebrows raised, and said nothing.

"Blow, I don't want to defraud people."

"Says the very same man who invented the frigopropper."

"And the frig'o'graph. I am not defrauding anybody with that stuff. I'm just supplying the services that people who have been defrauded by their own foolishness think they need."

"So, what is different about using a breath carbon dioxide test and claiming it's an oxidative stress test?"

"It isn't an oxidative stress test. That's what's different."

"And your frig'o'graph is a solution for global warming?"

"No, my frig'o'graph is a means of keeping refrigerator doors from being kept open too long to save the ozone layer, which is all that I claim. The frigopropper wedges to which you refer are only used in summer, when it is hot, to keep the refrigerators open to resolve global warming."

"I miss the subtle differences," replied Blow.

"So do I."

"Okay, so you admit to taking advantage of people's stupidity, right?"

"Only blatant stupidity."

"Well, what's different with my idea? Only totally stupid people will believe a test for breath carbon dioxide will tell them about their aging."

"That's not true," I interrupted. "I think smart people who don't know about science will be suckered into using it."

Blow interrupted. "It's spelled S-K-I-E-N-C-E. The second C is silent."

I ignored him. "Look, Blow, I get your point. If anybody wants to use this test to determine their own personal carbon footprint and the effect that their very living and breathing has on the environment, then I am all in favor of selling it to them. However, if they are using it to truly try to figure out how to slow their aging process using diet and exercise, then we would be doing a disservice."

"Oh the moralist appears," Blow chimed. "You are both a moralist and an assholist. I understand you more and more."

"So, what can we *really* measure, Blow. What will be real? What will truly tell people how fast they are aging?"

"A clock."

"A clock. Thanks."

Blow swallowed another chunk of cheese and pepperoni, no doubt substantially increasing his oxidative stress, although we had as yet no way to prove it.

"Skip the breath test," Blow suggested.

"Should we test urine, blood, what?"

"We actually need to put a clock into the patient somewhere, that measures their oxidation rate. That's what we need to do. A clock that ticks each time it gets oxidized."

I thought about that a bit. An oxidation clock would only be oxidized by misguided oxidants that were bumping into the clock, just like they would bump into the cell membranes.

Blow said, "Most people notice they are aging by their skin changing. So how about we stick a redox probe on their skin?"

A redox probe measures oxidation-reduction potential, or the drive for electrons to move from one place to another. It wasn't necessarily crazy. These devices report back to the user a level of oxidation potential that can be tracked and monitored. If it is high, that means more oxidation.

"I think I like it, Blow."

We finished our pizza and I went to work. Work almost entirely now consists of sitting at a computer, looking stuff up on the internet. So I did that. I looked up redox probes and found a quarter of a zillion. I found a few that might work on the skin. I ordered a few of them. I waited.

After waiting, they arrived. I played with them. I taped them to my skin. They spit out numbers. I didn't know what the numbers meant, but they were spit out. I did things to affect my skin's pH, (dropping vinegar on it, exercising) and the numbers spit out changed in the worse direction. I smeared myself with anti-oxidant goo bought at a store, and the numbers spit out of the machine changed slightly for the better.

Damn. This was making sense.

I called an engineer friend and got him on board. We put it all together, and we made a company and we got financing and we built the product and we started selling it and lots of people wanted it and lots of people liked it and people began to use it to better manage their skin care and then FDA came and shut us down because we hadn't followed their unconstitutional rules.

Screw FDA. I gave the system to my Chinese friend from college and he is selling it in China now. I'm supposed to get a piece of the action. I'm gonna keep my income offshore so that the US government can't tax it since all they did was obstruct it. The Chinese have much nicer skin than we have here in the United States. At least they do now.

Chapter 31

Movies, Ice Cream, and Heartaches

Jennifer and I sat on her couch staring at the idiot box waiting for it to turn on. I was excited because I had just given Jennifer the romantic gift of a new Blu-ray disc player. Previously, she only had the antiquated DVDs, but now, she had the razzledazzley Blu-ray. Cool, High-definition Blu-ray.

The problem was she had a twenty-year old television that was incapable of showing anything in high definition.

Despite my so-called intelligence, I am an idiot. But I marched on. I got the Blu-ray plugged into her television, which I wanted to throw out the window, and plugged in the first Blu-ray movie, rented today for one dollar from a machine outside a Seven-Eleven that was owned by a company that would probably go broke in the next few years, just like Blockbuster before it. These companies were going to go under from the creative destruction of the capitalist system, which is so embodied in the fabric of the internet. The internet, and its inherent freedom, was making the world wealthier and better. What a great thing. The people who hate freedom don't like the internet. The people who don't think clearly and keep putting the people who hate freedom into power *did* like the internet, but as noted didn't think clearly, so keep voting for people who hate the freedom that the internet can help bring about.

The Blu-ray revved up and we waited. It revved a bit more as the disc spun inside its guts and while its brain digested and translated the digital dots and dashes being read off the spinning disc.

We waited.

Finally, it popped up with a screen that told us, for more than sixty seconds (I counted) that Interpol, yes Interpol, would be called in to arrest us if we copied the disc or showed it to our friends. Another message came up after this, telling us that the FBI would investigate us and fine us $250,000 dollars. I tried to skip this message by pressing the fast forward button, but was prohibited by the disc. I tried to skip the message by pressing the 'top menu' button on the remote, but was prohibited. Another sixty seconds went by.

Then came the previews, which the Blu-ray disc would not allow us to skip. Five of them. No, SIX of them. Boring previews that we didn't want to watch. There was no way to complain about this. There was even less value of complaining to Blu-ray than of complaining to the airlines. But with Blu-ray you can't even get free frequent flier miles. Blu-ray sucks. That is my new motto. I would persist on feeling this way forever, until I forgot to feel that way a few minutes later.

Finally, we got to our movie, but within thirty seconds of it starting, Jennifer needed to pee. I paused the movie and went to the refrigerator for a couple of beers. Thirty seconds was record time for the first pausing of the movie. Jennifer didn't care too much about movies.

"Don't pause it," she would say to me as she walked out of the room during the most critical portions of a movie, when all the relevant secrets would be revealed. Somehow this frustrates me, just a bit.

I don't think women care about watching movies. I think they just want to be with their man while he watches movies. I wonder what women think about while their men watch movies. My brain is not sufficiently vast to comprehend the complexities of femaleness. I am a man and therefore make no pretense that I can understand a woman.

Because I am a man, I understand women pretty well, I think. They aren't all the same. That is the first thing I understand. Most women are *way* more worthwhile than most men. But at the same time, the typical woman *thinks* she is much less worthwhile than she really is, while the typical man thinks that he is much *more* worthwhile than he actually is. The American culture, and perhaps the world, is strange this way. This seemingly natural but nonetheless horrible misbalance between actual value and perceived value has somehow contributed to the insane empowerment of men over women throughout mankind's history (note it isn't *womankind's* history).

Thank God women have so much power over men. Else we men would be in charge of the place. That would suck for us all.

The movie was horrible. It never seemed to start. And I don't mean that it was just the interminable previews that were delaying its start. I mean that once it started, it didn't start. Two couples stuck in an apartment arguing about how their two eleven-year-olds were fighting. We both watched, shockingly bored, for forty-five minutes before we finally came to our senses and turned off this horrible movie that I had rented. Maybe just after I pressed the stop button there was about to be a murder or an earthquake, an alien attack or *something*. Maybe we missed all the good parts of the movie, I don't know. But I feel good, because my action, albeit forty-five minutes delayed, probably prevented a murder, alien invasion, or natural disaster. I am a hero.

"There is a new movie I want to see in the theater," Jennifer said. I didn't want to see it. It was the movie version of a teenage book series that was very popular but wasn't about vampires.

"Okay," I said. "Let's get Thai food on the way and maybe we'll be late for the movie."

Jennifer knew better than to respond to me. But she did so anyway. "You don't have to go."

"But I want to," I lied. I pride myself on being honest. Why do I lie to the woman I love?

"Why do I lie to the woman I love, Jennifer?" I asked Jennifer.

"Maybe you will like the movie," she ignored my question while paying close attention to it and spending the next fifteen minutes in relative silence likely contemplating it.

We skipped the Thai and got to the movie theater just in time to pay eleven dollars a piece to watch seven previews that for the life of me I couldn't figure out how to fast forward through. The movie started and within three minutes I was feeling nauseated. The director of this teeny-bop girl science fiction movie version of a science fiction book series that every teenage girl in the country had read for god-knows what reason apparently decided that he wanted to wiggle the camera constantly. It was the wiggle-cam method of filming taken to extreme. This constant wiggle, combined with the fact that every teenage girl in the country had packed into the theater to see this movie, leaving Jennifer and me in the only available seats, which were in the second row, made me feel like I was in an amusement park where they take you on a roller coaster ride in a little movie theater. Nauseating.

I moved to stand in the back of the theater so I wouldn't feel like I was on the space shuttle attached to a global roller coaster. But it didn't help much. Twenty minutes later I needed a meclizine pill to counteract the vertigo. Jennifer lovingly left the theater with me and we went home and made dizzying love.

I hear from teenage girls that the movie was awesome, and full of all sorts of scenes of kids killing kids. Great stuff, these movies.

I had the next day off, so we went to the art museum. There was a big sign there saying that the 'Works of DaVinci' were on display.

I walked up to the first docent I saw. "Hi. You have some works of DaVinci here, or so the sign says."

"That's right," replied the slightly overweight, slightly-overly-made-up volunteer in her red jacket. "Just upstairs there, and to your right."

"Do you also have the works of DeRome?" I asked.

She paused before responding. "I don't think so."

"How about DeBoston? Or DeParis, or DaBeijing. Any works by them?"

"I don't think so, sir," she said with growing disdain.

Jennifer had pulled me away just in time to prevent me from asking the lady about whether the museum had any works by DaMoscow, DaTokyo, DaCleveland, DaSanDiego or DaSanFrancisco. So I guess I won't know about whether the museum had any such fantastic artists on display.

Jennifer and I climbed the stairs and went to our right to find a dozen amazing works by Leonardo, who hailed from Vinci. Leonardo's full name was Leonardo di ser Piero da Vinci, which means Leonardo, son of Piero, from Vinci. For 'The DaVinci Code' to be a sensible title, the book would have needed to be about a code written in the town of Vinci. But then again, it must have been sensible because that book has sold more copies than the Bible.

Tonight I hoped to listen to a symphony by DaBonn, perhaps his 9th, the choral symphony. Or perhaps I would instead listen to a piano concerto by Wolfgang Amadeus deSalzburg. Or I would read Hamlet by William DeStratford-upon-Avon or perhaps read some of said bard's sonnets. I could study the works of the famed psychiatrist Sigmund DaVienna.

After fifteen minutes in the museum, I disappeared for a bit, leaving Jennifer on her own. When I returned, I was pushing two wheelchairs. Jennifer groaned when she saw, but she sat down in one and I in another, and we spent the next four hours comfortably wheeling around the museum, reading all the informative placards, soaking in the art hanging on the walls, but speeding by the bullshit that was also hanging upon the walls, laughing and loving the opportunity to live. At the end of our time in the museum, our feet didn't hurt, we weren't tired, we were full of energy. The wheelchair is the way to enjoy a museum.

We went to the zoo for the afternoon. Picked up some wheelchairs at the entrance. The wheelchair is also the way to enjoy a zoo.

That night Jennifer was full of energy about the animals. She loved animals, the way she loved children, perhaps. She loved the innocent, the truthful, the naïve.

"Did you see the chimpanzees on the right? They were going crazy, jumping around and shouting at each other! They were arguing, like a husband and wife."

"Or a gay couple, because they were both female."

Jennifer starting pretending to be a chimpanzee, hooting and hollering and wildly jesticulating.

She looked so ridiculous that I tackled her onto the bed,

hooting and hollering and wildly testiculating.

I couldn't deny that I loved this woman.

At 5AM I awoke, a minute before my alarm would go off, like usual. I turned off the alarm so it wouldn't bother Jennifer, and groaned out of bed, moaned to the bathroom, whimpered through my morning ritual, and lamented as I dressed. By 5:30 I was on the road, by 5:40 I was picking up breakfast at the cardiac-surgery-market-expansion-greasy-fast-food-restaurant-with-golden-arches drive-thru window, and by 6:00 I was on the wards, ready to do my job for the next forever.

I had twelve patients to round on today. About average. Plus I was on call tonight, although I would have to take a mandatory nap sometime in the afternoon. I wasn't allowed to be at the hospital so early, because I would exceed my mandatory maximum patient-care period, so I would just lie. I would say I came in just at 8AM and magically knew all about the patients' needs for the day for when rounds started, also at 8AM.

Sadly, Blow wasn't the attending on the wards this week. The attending was Dr. Henrietta Stuff. Dr. Stuff was a smiley and friendly woman who knew her stuff. She was no slacker by any means. But she was completely mild mannered. She had been assigned to volunteer to be the Director of the Family Practice Residency Program after Dr. Blow had voluntarily been fired by the goats of ACGME. She didn't like being the Residency Program Director. I have never met someone like Dr. Stuff. Except I met her.

"Dr. Marcus," she asked me on rounds. "What would you like to do for Mrs. Johnson today? Any changes?"

I replied, thoughtfully, "Well, she hasn't responded to the antibiotics we started yesterday for treatment of her kidney infection. She's still having high fevers, so I think that we should change her antibiotics. Perhaps try a different cephalokillemall antibiotic instead, or maybe Gorillacillin."

"That's an idea," Dr. Stuff responded. I later learned that her phrase '*That's an idea*' meant that it was a *bad* idea. "Has the lab told us what bacteria is in her urine yet?" asked Dr. Stuff, who certainly knew the answer to her own question, but was pimping me.

"Not yet. Maybe tomorrow morning."

"How long does it usually take for a woman to respond to antibiotics when she has a kidney infection?" she pimped me again.

"I would think that the fevers should be coming down after 24 hours. No?"

Dr. Stuff responded smoothly, "Well, Dr. Marcus, that may be true in some patients, but I find sometimes it commonly takes three or four days for the fevers to settle in kidney infections. Perhaps we can wait before changing. Give a little time?"

"Okay," I said, finding it very wise to sometimes commonly agree with smart gentle attendings who chastise with such subtle eloquence as Dr. Stuff had just chastised me.

By the next morning, with no change in therapy, Mrs. Johnson would be without fever and eager to leave the hospital.

But back to rounds. Dr. Stuff liked to see the patients herself, the old-fashioned way. Her system was to collect computer, lab and radiographic data available, go see the patient to collect additional data from the patient, and then make decisions. This old-fashioned way was very different than how modern attendings lead rounds and teach doctors to think. Nowadays, most doctors on teaching rounds sit in a room and go over all their patients' data, make decisions, and then go see the patients in order just to confirm that their decisions weren't way off the mark. By the time the attending saw the patient, the orders had already been entered into the EMR order system, and the medical momentum was flowing, and only a major difference of opinion about how the patient looked, or what the patient wanted, would likely change the medical momentum of that day, until the next rounds, when the patient's wishes and desires might be brought up twenty-four hours later, if those wishes and desires were remembered.

Now, the interns, like me, see the patients before rounds, as long as we lie about the hours we work on the forms we have to fill out every day for the ACGME JCAHO Nazis. But we see them at 6 AM when they are sleeping, and not uncommonly before they have had their morning vitals taken by the nursing staff. We sneak into a darkened room, creep up to the bedside so as not to wake our patient, quickly listen to the heart to make sure it is still there, and quickly listen to the lungs to make sure they still have a carbon footprint, and then sneakily sneak back out the door. It is always best to let patients sleep, because they get better when they sleep, and their pain is less, and their fear is less, etc. So it makes sense what interns do.

However, when it comes to rounding time with most attendings, it is only that intern's brief unconscious contact with their patient that provides actual human-body related information for rounds.

Dr. Stuff would have none of that. We all had to stand and walk from room to room.

"But what if other patients hear what we are talking about? Doesn't that cause privacy problems?" asked one of the medical students.

Dr. Stuff replied gently, "Yes it does. So we should speak quietly. And if there is something sensitive, speak even more quietly." She pointed around to the fourteen people gathered around her on rounds. "Whether desired or not, if you are a patient in a teaching hospital, there are going to be some people here who know about your problems. But if you are a patient here, you also have lots of people who are thinking about you and caring about you and around to help. It is much easier to see your doctor at a teaching hospital like ours than at a private non-teaching hospital, where the attending doctors have to be in their clinics all day and there aren't any residents."

We talked, gently and calmly about the patients outside each door. Then we all went into the room, after Dr. Stuff knocked, and we listened as Dr. Stuff talked with the patient, listened to the patient, learned from the patient. If there were relevant physical findings which were either of import in the management decisions or educational to the team, they were demonstrated, as discretely as can be with fourteen people crowded in a room.

She would then talk a little more with the patient, hear from the patient any preferred therapeutic paths, and we would depart the room, close the door, and discuss such plans. It was then the intern's job to go back, after rounds, to discuss with the patient what we were hoping to accomplish, and see if they agreed. If the patient didn't agree, it was our job to find out why, talk to Dr. Stuff if necessary, and by all means abide by the patient's wishes. It was also our job to do our best to convince the patient that our plans were wise. But it was never our job to insist.

Rounds took a lot longer with Dr. Stuff. After rounds, we had much less time than usual to spend typing into the electronic medical record, document hours worked by us, or number of times vomited on. We had less time for didactic lectures and less time for lunch. But, we had much more time with our patients. And we learned. Dr. Stuff was awesome. She resigned from the clinical staff in frustration over ACGME a few months later and opened an ice cream factory in Hong Kong.

Medical students learn in different ways. But they all are taught in the same way, likely for expedience sake. In typical medical school we have two years of didactic lectures filled with anatomy, biochemistry, physiology, histology, microbiology etc. Then we have two years seeing patients before we graduate. Most of the stuff we learned from lectures and books in the first two years is initially forgotten when we get to clinical rotations. But then it comes back, in pieces, pieces that are relevant to the care of each patient. We don't tend to forget a patient. We don't forget a real human patient. We don't forget his anatomy, biochemistry, physiology, histology or microbiology. We don't forget his psychiatric state, or his metabolic state. Somehow, we remember all the nerdy science stuff when it relates to a flesh-and-blood human being.

Some schools have developed systems from day one of medical school to teach medical students based on one patient-at-a-time, entirely. These students get no initial classes filled with lectures on blackboards and powerpoints, but rather jump right into seeing patients.

"Hi Ms. Smith," said one of these very lucky special medical students as she walked into the hospital room during her first year of medical school. "My name is Molly Certainly. I am one of the medical students, here to learn from you and help you where I can." It is a nice canned introduction, but honest and effective. She spoke confidently.

Medical students are generally scared out of their pants. But they are excited to be seeing patients. It is true for the students of the traditional teaching pathway as well as the students who are as lucky as Molly to be in this special type of teaching environment, which is an expensive method of teaching so only the best students get offered the opportunity.

I was standing out in the hallway outside Ms. Smith's door, listening to the student surreptitiously. One of the jobs of interns is to teach students.

Now there are two ways that this conversation could go, I knew. The hoped for way I will present in normal typefont. The actual way I will present in *italics.*

Mrs. Smith smiled welcomingly at Molly, who still stood near the door in her short immaculate white coat stuffed with little books and niftily-lit medical gadgets that she had been given earlier that year across the street in the medical school building. "Come on in further, young lady. I will teach you whatever I can. I have all day."

Ms. Smith grunted and scowled at the young useless non-doctor who was probably even more useless than the real doctor, who had been in earlier and who was completely useless. "Be quick. I ain't no damn guinea pig."

Oh wonderful *crap,* I thought to myself outside the door, with happy *horror and concern for Molly.* Molly's patient today certainly was an amazing *horrifically bitchy* patient. It would be a good learning experience for her, that was for sure.

"Thank you," said Molly. "Mrs. Smith, can you tell me why you are in the hospital?"

The kindly Mrs. Smith replied, "Come on in and sit down. There is some room here on the bed. I am here in the hospital because the handsome young doctor in the emergency room told me that my heart wasn't working right, and that you all would try to fix it." She scooched her frail body over on the bed to make room for Molly to sit.

"How the hell am I supposed to know?" the scowly bitchy Ms. Smith responded to Molly's question, shaking her head in

blatant disgust. "You're the doctor, not me." She paused. "That doctor in the Emergency Room was an idiot. Totally missed my diagnosis. Had to wait for the specialist to get called in. Heart specialist. They should have called him in first, right away, and maybe I wouldn't be like this." She lifted a massive butt cheek and farted.

Molly moved over to the bed and sat on the bed next to kindly Mrs. Smith *while I, without being noticed, slid a rolling stool through the door and placed it immediately behind Molly so she could sit as far away from the bitch Ms. Smith as possible.*

"Can you tell me more about your problem?" A nice open question. A good interviewer will start with open questions and let the patient talk about whatever the problem is. If you make too many assumptions, you can miss important pieces of the puzzle. For example, Molly could have said, "Can you tell me more about your heart problem," but that would have forced the diagnostic conversation down the heart path, when there may be some valuable information to be had elsewhere. Good for Molly.

"I haven't been feeling well for many months. Lightheaded mostly. I think I have passed out a few times," the pleasant Mrs. Smith told Molly. "Most recently Jack woke me back up. He was slobbering all over me."

"I keep telling my doctor, over and over again, that I been sick. But he never has any time to listen. Keeps giving me pills and sending me home. I have no energy at all, I passed out when I got up to piss during American Idol last week. Woke up with Jack all over me."

"Who is Jack?" asked Molly a bit thrown off by the image.

"My little bichon frise." Mrs. Smith reached and found a picture of a white mop of a puppy sitting on her lap in happier times. "Do you have a dog?"

"Jack. You know, Jack Daniels." Ms. Smith pursed her lips in

obvious frustration at Molly's ignorance. "Jack Freakin' Daniels. How old are you? Have you even finished school yet?"

Molly shook her head indicating that she wouldn't be acquiring a dog, at least until she finished medical school.

"What other symptoms have you been having?"

"My heart flutters sometimes. Like when you first fall in love. Out of the blue, at the darndest times," replied Mrs. Smith with a distant expression of forgotten joy on her angelic wrinkled face as she gently squeezed Molly's hand.

"Can't you read the chart?" Ms. Smith shook her head in anger. "I told the idiot in the ER all this stuff already. I told him last night, and some other people too. My heart gets puppitations when I get upset." Ms. Smith was upset. She glared at Molly who sat fearfully against the far wall by the door.

"Do you have trouble breathing when this happens?"

"Just a little. It feels strange," replied Mrs. Smith. "But the handsome doctor in the Emergency Room said that would be fixed when my heart got all back in order again."

"Can't you listen? I told you already that I feel like I am suffocating when it happens. I tell everybody that, and nobody listens. Doctors these days don't pay attention. You learn that, missy! Learn how to pay attention." Ms. Smith pulled up one of her other prodigious buttcheeks, squinted her eyes, and coughed out another bit of flatulence.

"I am sorry you aren't well, and that you have to be in the hospital." Molly was expressing heartfelt sympathy. I was impressed with this young student.

"You're very kind. You are going to be a wonderful doctor, Molly," Mrs. Smith said warmly.

"Are you done with your questions yet? The Kardashians Take New York is coming on now." Ms. Smith punched her remote control repeatedly with stubby fingers to try to tune in her favorite ungodly totally useless unbelievably

unconscionably stupid and wasted television show on the face of the planet. She started staring at the television and rapidly drifted into telehypnosis.

"Molly," I called into the room. Molly nodded and smiled at her patient and excused herself to come out to chat with me. "You're very good with your patient interviewing skills."

"Thank you Dr. Marcus. My patient is, well, very interesting."

"Yes. You'll need to go spend a lot more time with her. I think you have a knack for getting even the most difficult patients to be cooperative and helpful. Just keep showing that sort of empathy and your patients'll love you. Even the nasty bitches." I nodded toward the door. "Now, your education involves you going off and reading and learning everything you can about heart dysrhythmias."

"That's right," said Molly. "Can you give me a list?"

I knew this drill. I had been one of the first of the fortunate students like Molly, when this education was first tried out here at the medical school. Molly started writing, recording what I was saying. "First, get to the anatomy lab and cut up a heart. Learn the gross anatomy of the heart completely. Second make sure you know the heart's electrical conduction paths. You can find those in the books. Third, get to the histology lab and memorize cardiac cell types. Fourth, talk to the pharmacology department and they will give you the syllabus for rhythm disturbances and you need to read it. Then also get a full updated list of dysrhythmia medications and make sure you understand how each one works, and try to memorize some dosings. Fifth, you need to take ACLS—Advanced Cardiac Life Support. This is where you will learn how to identify dysrhythmias and resuscitate patients when their heart stops. Imagine as you learn that you are going to need this information to help Ms. Smith. Sixth, you need to learn the complications of heart dysrhythmias, blood clots, strokes. Not in detail, because you will learn that material with another patient sometime. Seventh—this is a good time to learn about pacemakers. Get the Idiots' guide to pacers, and read it. Then, eighth, I want you to go the psychology mentor and ask her for the best short resource about dealing with different personality styles in your patients. Read it. Ninth, I want you to figure out what YOU would do to help your patient. Tenth, I want you to teach me everything that you have learned. Meanwhile check in on Ms. Smith everyday and get to know her. You have ten days. Now go!"

Molly was off and running. Her work was cut out for her, that's for sure. She was a self-motivated student, the kind I would want to be my doctor someday when unmeasured oxidative stress had aged me. She would go consume as much information as possible about her patient's condition, and the mentors in the various pre-clinical basic science and clinical science departments would help her one-on-one. This was self-motivated learning, with support. And it made for great doctors, because they learned fast and always with their patient in mind. Thus they remembered. It was faculty-intensive, but effective. The regular students would learn the histology (tissue anatomy) of all the organs during one semester. In contrast, Molly would learn the histology of the heart now, the kidney when she had a patient with kidney disease, the brain when she had a patient with brain disease. She would learn always in context of a very real patient that is hers. And teaching me what she had learned would help consolidate her knowledge, and resuscitate my own fading knowledge.

I liked teaching. At least this way. It was fun and for me efficient.

As I walked away I couldn't fail to notice the vibratory

excrescences as the nasty mean Ms. Smith blasted off another abrupt intrusive convoy of miasma from amidst her abundant buttcrack. It is too bad the pleasant Mrs. Smith didn't exist. Hopefully Molly would get to the heart of the matter and figure out why Ms. Smith was so bitchy. I have found that almost all people are good at heart, even when their heart is not working right, and if they seem like nasty people, it is often because their heart has been broken, is hurting, is lonely, or was badly wounded sometime and cannot quite recover. I picked Ms. Smith for Molly because I think Molly has it in her to help heal Ms. Smith's sick heart.

Chapter 32

Making Money the Old-Fashioned Way

"I need to make more money," I told Jennifer. "And I need to know how much I am making with each thing I do."

"Start another business. Maybe one that does something valuable this time."

"I think mandatory nap monitors are valuable," I retorted, with a bit of anger that I didn't have. I couldn't keep a straight face and tried to stifle my laugh.

"How can I help?" asked Jennifer as she handed me a napkin.

"Help me come up with ideas. What ideas do you have for valuable businesses?" I asked Jennifer, hopefully. It was good conversation, even if it didn't pan out with my creation of the next Intel, Microsoft, Exxon, Enron, Fannie Mae or Madoff Investments, LLC. "What is needed in the world?"

I was still in scrubs, but Jennifer was dressed in a marvelously sexy pair of blue-jeans that fit her just right. We were about two miles from the hospital awaiting our nice meal at the Flaming Wok Chinese Restaurant. We had a Flaming Chinese waiter who wokked up to our table. His black pants were unconscionably tight over his nearly non-existent butt, and his white silk shirt highlighted the purple strands falling from his very strangely coiffed Asia-doo haircut covering a head that was almost as wide as his narrow scrawny shoulders. This was not a handsome and fit American gay male. This was a freaky technoflamer who was hard to look at without making a diseased expression similar to the expression one makes when there is rectal urgency during dinner with the Queen.

We were having dinner served by a queen of Taiwan, there was no rectal urgency, but the facial expression I struggled to suppress was sufficient to make Jennifer laugh despite her best effort not to, and that made her feel bad because she didn't want to insult the Flaming Chinese waiter or his wok.

"Can I get an order of fried dumplings and a diet coke?" asked Jennifer.

"Same here," said I, watching Jennifer in her effort to suppress her laughter at my effort to suppress my reflexive urgent rectal face.

The waiter asia-flamed away from the table squeezing his little buttcheeks as he wokked, out of habit, rather like the way people purse their lips when they see somebody sucking on a lemon. I am a fan of homosexuals. I just have bad reactions to anybody who stereotypes themselves. And this asia-gay waiter sure did stereotype himself.

I had to admit there were many people to whom I responded negatively based on their own self-enhanced stereotypicalness. Please don't think I judge people on their innate or uncontrollable human characteristics, but at this point in my internship, I had become a bit of an asshole and was quite quick on the draw in terms of judging people on their choices. And the choice to hyper-aggrandize one's stereotype in order to maximize your assignment to some group or other is worthy of being a point of judgment. It is de-individualization, an intentional effort to place yourself as a cog in a group as opposed to an individual human being, and I just don't respect that process in any way. And there are so many who do this.

First, there is the superflamer, whether heterosexual or homosexual it matters not. I am sexual-preference blind. Then there is the doucher. The doucher can best be visualized with an example: Harper Twadsdale. Harper Twadsdale, or Harpy as he was commonly known, was a patient I had seen in my continuity clinic earlier in the day from the undergraduate university. He was nineteen years old and full of himself and full of his fraternity. He wore a Lacoste shirt with two, not one, stitched-in polo horses above his left nipple, buttoned up too high on his neck, and carefully selected to be two sizes too small, thus accentuating his well-exercised and tanned torso that he clearly wanted everybody, male and female, to notice. He wanted the females to notice so as to increase his chance of getting laid, thus impressing his male friends. And he wanted the males to notice to increase the chance of impressing his male friends, which had nothing to do with getting laid. Harpy Twadsale was a stereotypical richboy fraternity doucher who drove a BMW and whose motivation in life was to impress people who were supposedly friends but weren't. I felt bad for the kid, told him he was a doucher, and that he should work to impress himself, not his doucher friends. I think the kid needed to hear that much more than he needed to hear that his blood pressure was okay and he could play JV Lacrosse again this year. Although my clinic day had been very over-booked, I spent a lot of time with this very healthy young man, hoping to open his eyes to the universe outside Doucheville. Nonetheless, as he left the exam room, he flexed his pectoral muscles to make his chest look bigger in his Lacoste shirt as he walked past each nurse on the hall, female or male.

So, we got the flamers and the douchers. Then there are the punks. Leather jackets, tight pants, skinny bodies. A bit of goth, a bit of the Fonz, a bit of James Dean, and a bit of the six year old that falls down, skins his knee and wants his mommy while holding back his tears. Something missing in the parenting realm of those kids, I always thought. Not bad parents, but something missing. So they reach out by making themselves look like the punks that are stereotyped on television, and they mope in my clinic, and mope in the hallways and mope through life.

Flamers, douchers, punks. But there are so many more. There are the business-students who like to hyper-stereotype too. They wear expensive suits that look like dookie on these kids whose faces appear to be fourteen years old. They might as well cover themselves with bumper stickers that say 'College Republicans'. Maybe a power-tie over a pink shirt and blue sportscoat would work for them. These kids will smile and nod their heads knowingly when you talk about rich and powerful people whose names you have made up because they don't exist. Then you have the Poemians—pronounced as either PO-HE-ME-AN, or as POEM-I-AN—these are the English majors focused on poetry who try to look like John Lennon in his later years and who will feel good about themselves for caring about the poor while never creating any wealth and therefore never doing anything to beat back poverty. The Poemians like to exaggerate their poutiness when someone walks by whom they want to not impress. And the hunters, overweight, dressed in blue jeans and camouflage shirt to conceal themselves in the woods so that the deer they are planning to shoot don't notice the blaze orange hat and vest that they have to wear to avoid being shot by other people in camouflage and blaze orange. The strange thing about their cross-purpose garb is that the deer can't see the blaze orange worth a darn, but they can see those blue jeans as brightly as the lights above a baseball field. My favorite of all time is the girly-girls who have brought on the resurgence of the aerobics garb of the 1980's. Tights that climb up the girls' bumcracks, and ankle warmers. That garb makes the bicyclists' tight-fitted clothing all covered with free advertisements look tame, despite the fact that they want to look like they are racing the Tour de France even though they are in downtown America. At least the bicyclists' ridiculous pants have padding sewn in the butts for comfort. Of course one might ask why don't they just pad the bicycle seat more?

"Eddie, what are you thinking about?"

I had apparently been lost in my prejudicial postjudicial grouping of stereotypes far longer than I had intended. Jennifer smiled and frowned at the same time. I don't know how girls do that.

"I've been watching you for several minutes, Eddie. You were, like, way gone."

"I'm sorry. I was thinking about people. People are very strange. Why do so many people dress up in strange clothing to go out?"

"Yeah. Like why do people wear scrubs outside of the hospital? Is that so you can look cool and proclaim 'Look at me, I am so cool, I am a doctor.'"

"Hah," I replied, "you know there isn't anything cool about being recognized as a doctor. Not anymore. I think the businessmen look at me and think *'future employee'*, and multiply my wages by one hundred to set their baseline starting salary." I looked at my strange totally hyperstereotypical clothing in which I was dressed and in which I went out: green thin cotton pajama-equivalents clearly inappropriate for any setting outside the hospital or perhaps the bedroom. I was way worse than the Asia-gay or even Harper Twadsdale.

"Don't ever wear scrubs in my bed," Jennifer said, reading my mind as she tends to do.

"Fine by me. I won't wear scrubs, or anything else, in your bed. What were we talking about?"

"Starting a business. One that creates value. Not just something that skanks off people's stupidity."

"So, no more organic green businesses?" I asked, wondering if the love of my life would try to prohibit me from doing my part to save the planet from all the idiots trying to destroy it.

"No more green businesses, Eddie."

"I can't sell people filtered tops for their 2-liter Coca-Cola bottles to absorb the CO2 that bubbles out, and thereby help reduce Coke's carbon footprint?"

"No, Eddie, you can't."

"How about Pepsi?"

"Nothing green, Eddie. It is just too hard for you to behave yourself in those situations."

She was right. I looked at a baby who was sitting in a high chair at the next table, sucking on a lollipop. Before internship and before being infected by the contaminated medical system, I never used to think this way, but now I wanted to take the candy from that baby.

"Don't you dare," commanded Jennifer.

I wouldn't.

"All right," I tried. "How about we start a company that makes signs for cars?"

"Oh no."

"Yeah. Listen to this. The signs are made out of these little

LED lightbulbs and fit in your back window. There is a keyboard up front, next to the driver. Whatever you want to say to somebody behind you, you do. It will allow communication between drivers of cars, in ways that will prevent the need for middle fingers and horns."

"What sort of things would you want to be able to say, in your sign?"

"Imagine this. You are stuck in the left lane behind a guy in an Oldsmobuick driving sixty, adjacent to an 18-wheeler loaded with chickens on the way to Colonel Sander's house. For five minutes you are stuck behind this guy in the Oldsmobuick who is clearly going way too slow on the highway. You've honked. You've flashed your lights. You have yelled loudly through your windshield to ask him politely to move. You have tailgated him, only 10 feet back from his bumper. You have had no opportunity to pass him, and you've been very patient. Finally, as you climb a hill the chickens slow down just enough to allow you the opportunity to risk your life by swerving into the right lane just in front of the truck, floor your engine, and get in front of the slowpoke in his Slowmobile in the left lane. How can you teach him? How can you help him learn how dangerous his driving is? Well, you put on your sign and have him read, 'Left lane is passing only. Please stay out of left lane otherwise.'"

"By that you mean 'Fuck you, you little shit', don't you Eddie?"

"Not at all." But I did. "I mean to educate people, not start wars. Look, there's nothing on the planet more dangerous than slowpokes in the left hand lane."

"Yeah, everyone agrees with that. So why don't you make a petition to get the State Troopers to stop pulling over speeders, and instead pull over everyone who drives too slow in the left lane."

"Jennifer, I was working on just that. I was going to run for governor to make that one law. But then I realized that I don't think the government does much well, so I figure I had better take this on myself. With signs. I sell people lighted signs for their cars. Get them made in China for forty bucks. Sell them for $180. Great deal, huh?"

"Is it legal?"

"I don't know. Freedom of speech, no? Maybe we can sell them to cops first. That way the cop cars can drive past people and tell them their tail-light is busted without having to pull them over. Once the cops have them, other people can buy them, right, since the cops can't do anything that the people can't do, right?"

Jennifer was bored. "Okay, so the road-rage-inciting car signs are one idea you have. What others?"

"Jen, you're supposed to be coming up with something too. Your turn. We're in this life together, after all."

As I said this, for just a flash of a second Jennifer's face changed, revealing something that was either hopeful or fearful. I couldn't tell because I was a guy and therefore relatively autistic compared to Jennifer. Had I made such a facial expression as hers, she would have been able to write a three-page description of the underlying communication so revealed, whereas I would draw a picture of a blank.

"Okay," Jennifer said. "I will." She thought for only a few seconds before coming up with a great idea.

"Okay, so, guys like to hang out with guys and do guy things, right? But their womenfolk like their guys to be attentive and do girl-things with them. Like shopping, listening to emotional conflicts, etc. So the guy blows off his friends, and goes shopping with his girl and listens to the emotional conflicts, which then, being a guy, he tries to resolve. He tries to fix the problem. Fixing problems, as any girl knows, is utter lunacy and *not* at all desired or requested. So the guy gets in trouble for being unsympathetic. He blows the day with his friends, and blows it with his girlfriend too. It's crazy."

"So, what is your solution?" I prodded.

"How about 'Gay Buddy Enterprises'?"

"Tell me more."

"You get a bunch of gay men, truly gay men, not Bi- or fakers or temps, with just enough flame to be believable, but not so much as to set off your hyperstereotype alarm, and hire them out to the men to supply to their girlfriends. Gay-buddy. Each needs to have a personality that provides for a good shoulder to cry on, a friend to tell secrets to, an advisor to help buy shoes. Pay the gay buddy $100 for the evening, and then you get to go hang with the guys, lose no points with your lady for being autistic and trying to solve problems, and everybody is happy. Plus you create jobs for gay men."

"Yes, the gay man, a member of an economically-depressed minority who have horrible problems with unemployment and who mostly live in poverty."

"Eddie, be serious."

"Okay. I am serious, now," I said, now seriously.

Actually, I thought, and "Actually," I said, "that's not a bad idea at all. We could have a Gaybuddy Match.com that could connect eligible hetero-wives with homo-buddies. It would be listed under "Men seeking Men for Women." This had possibilities.

Jennifer, ever the good soul, chimed in, "We could get a celebrity spokesperson."

"We could get a dozen celebrity spokespeople," I espoused, in an espousement which could do nothing other than to cause both of us at the table, and then several others from surrounding tables, to start naming all the gay celebs we could list.

"Ellen DeGeneres."

"Needs to be a guy, don't you think?"

"Neil Patrick Harris."

"Nathan Lane."

"Ian McKellan," called someone from the next table.

"Who?"

"Magneto from the X-men."

"Oh."

"Harvey. Harvey someone."

"Harvey Fierstein."

"Independence Day."

There was a pause before Jennifer said, "Clay Aiken."

"Boy George."

"Not a good choice for spokesman, you think?"

"George Takei. Mr. Sulu," shouted a woman nearby.

I whispered, "Probably Mr. Sulu isn't the best advertisement either."

"Elton John?"

"God, he would be perfect. But I doubt we can afford him."

"What's wrong with a woman spokesperson, Eddie?"

"What, like Martina Navratilova?"

"No, like a heterosexual woman celebrity. One of the people who would be the beneficiary of the service. A semi-happily married woman whose husband is known to be all man. Like Melanie Griffith."

"Who's her husband?"

"Antonio Banderas."

"Ooh, excellent. Let's call them both."

"I am on it," said Jennifer.

"Or Tom Hanks and his wife. Ummm...Rita Wilson."

"Are they still together?"

"Who knows. It's Hollywood."

"Gay Buddy is gonna go live. www.gaybuddy.com. I can see it now."

And I could see it now. Unlike me, Jennifer could make things happen.

Jennifer made things happen. Four months later, Rita and Melanie spent a day in the city making the first three commercials for us, all for a piece of the action. The demand for gayness was high. We put our ads in the newspaper. The applications came in. Jennifer and I had to interview and fully vet the potential gayployees on all our days off. After that, we hired a gay management team, took in a gay investment round, and became part of the .dotgay bubble. Antonio and Tom and Elton all bought shares and became spokesmen. Men of all preferences everywhere celebrated and women were happy. Now *that* is wealth creation.

Chapter 33

The Donut of Quality Improvement

Doris-Doris had been talking to Jennifer. I didn't hear what she said at first, but I thought I heard my name, or the name of someone with the same name as mine. I was approaching the end of my internship year, and I thought I heard Doris-Doris say that I was a good man. I thought wrong.

"It's good to find a hard man," Jennifer told Doris in response, after Doris-Doris had finished her lunch and while Doris was eating Jennifer's lunch.

Doris-Doris laughed, and raised her voluptuously obese eyebrows up and down. "Your Eddie is a good catch, I think. A definite DILF. Solid, tall, smart as a whip, trustworthy," affirmed Doris-Doris. "I wouldn't trust him for a second."

Jennifer was taken aback by the trust issue, but surprisingly not by Doris-Doris's slang description that I was DILF, meaning roughly, 'a Doctor I Like to Fornicate with.' "What do you mean? Not trust Eddie?"

"Nah, Jen. You can trust Eddie. You just can't trust men."

"Eddie is a man."

"Yes, he is. Every casket has a silver lining."

"Is Eddie's silver lining that he's a man?"

"Nope, honey. Man's silver lining is that there is an Eddie. And, you're right sweetie. It *is* good to find a hard man."

I overheard all this because I was standing right in front of them and they couldn't have missed noticing me there. Maybe they did. I don't know. But they couldn't have.

"Oh, hi Eddie," said Jennifer at about the same moment that Doris-Doris said, "Oh, hey Dr. Marcus."

Okay, so they saw me now.

Doris-Doris added, angrily, "Dr. Marcus, you're late. You were supposed to be here at noon for our Ward Quality Improvement Meeting."

Blow had recommended me for the committee because I had behaved poorly in rounds one morning by suggesting that maybe JCAHO was right to demand that milk shouldn't be allowed to be in the refrigerators past dates.

"I'm sorry Doris. I got delayed. Pulled over by the cops on the way in."

Jennifer interjected with "For what?"

"For speeding in a No-Speeding Zone. I didn't see the sign." I really hadn't seen the sign.

"I hear that fines are doubled in No-Speeding Zones," Doris-Doris offered, to make me feel better by making me feel worse. The fine was $150.

"Seemingly. But I don't think I have to pay the fine."

"Why is that?" asked Jennifer, concerned not for me, but because we were soon going to not be married forever and therefore our finances were forever to be tightly linked henceforth.

"Because I don't feel like it." I smiled and walked away, toward the room in which the Quality Meeting had been. I grabbed two donuts and an orange from the massive pile of food that the caterers had not yet taken off the table (Quality Meeting participants are all well-fed, for why else would they come to the meeting?). Then I turned around and snagged a couple of those big cookies, too. I elevatored and marched down to the Emergency Room, where I found Officer MacFarlane, one of my many friends from my days working in the ER before medical school. I gave him the ticket, a donut, and a cookie. He made all three go away.

Chapter 34

The Idea that Won't Change the World

"Blow," said I, "I'm gonna start a union."

I was disgruntled and grunting, and Blow knew how to deal with me.

"What are you crapping about, Eddie?"

"I'm going to start a union of doctors, and we are going to go on strike."

"Ok, count me in."

I looked at Blow as he flipped though the pages of a patient's thick medical record, stuffed with papers that didn't exist because we were a green hospital and everything was electronic. That gave me an idea.

"Hold on a minute, Blow. I'll fill you in after I perform an official duty."

I rushed over to the computer terminal on Doris-Doris's desk, opened up my email account, and rapidly typed a message to the university community from Mark Edwards, Senior Director and Assistant to the Associate Dean of Environmental Conscientiousness.

> *"Recent empiric evidence that has been determined to be no longer debatable reveals that*

electronic medical record ("EMR") use consumes electricity at substantially greater rates than was previously assumed. The complexity of the process behind the scenes is not evident to most physicians. There are numerous whirling gadgets and blinking lights, each powered by dirty coal, the smoke and tar of which emanate directly into our working environment, endangering the health of both patients and staff, while substantially contributing to either global warming or climate change.

"Recognizing our duties to future generations, it is now time to act. Henceforth, electronic medical record use must be limited by means of a reasonable system of taxing and trading. As you know, all electronic medical record use is logged and documented automatically. This office always knows who is on the computers and why. This benign and excellent data collection system will be expanded to allow for charging the attending and the resident physicians for use of the system. Each doctor will be entitled to a certain number of minutes or hours of use each day, above which there will be salary deductions (taxes). It is allowable to trade for more EMR time with other doctors who are underutilizing their electronic medical record privileges. This office will determine the total number of hours allocated initially for each doctor. Recognizing the importance of free-market methodologies, this office encourages trade of EMR time among the physicians, within limitations of expected reasonable price controls, oversight, regulation, and fairness to all as determined unilaterally by

this office. This office must approve of all trades for money, and will take 10% of the trade value to assist with necessary bookkeeping. This policy has been approved by the relevant Quality Improvement Committee, the JCAHO oversight board, ACGME home office, the Center for Medicare and Medicaid Services (CMS), and other relevant supervisory agencies."

Blow looked at me inquisitively as I smiled and pressed "SEND" on my email. He shook his head in amusement, wondering what I was up to. I learned from the best. He would like it when he next checked his cyberspace inbox and found this message from Mark Edwards, Senior Director and Assistant to some Dean or other, mixed in among the multiple special deals on penis-enlargement systems that he could use in his own home and messages from the real Dean filled with propaganda about how wonderful our hospital is under his dictatorship. Doris-Doris came back from wherever she had been witnessing a nap, with a suspicious smile on her face, and shooed me away from her desk.

"What is this union crap, Eddie?" asked Blow.

"Well, I was thinking. Doctors are sheep, right?"

"Of course."

"They'll follow a goat in sheep's clothing?"

"They'll follow anybody who leads 'em. They always do. What's your new thought?"

"You think that they may follow the dictum of a *sheep* in *wolf's* clothing?"

Blow tilted his head. "You mean, like a union wolf?"

"Yes. I'm thinking Teamsters Union, The Longshoremen's union. Public Service Workers Union. Did you know that the public service workers get 140% the pay of private sector workers?"

Blow shrugged and said he had no idea of that.

"Well, they do. And they get 75% more in benefits than the private sector."

"Amazing."

"It's because they have a union."

"A union, yes," replied Blow, always wise. "But they also work for the elected officials, in their offices, cleaning their trash, keeping their phones operating, providing secretarial services. They're always in the presence of the officials who determine the contracts. So, it ain't just that they're unions, but they are unions with the politicians' ears."

"Whatever. Look, my point is that the unions get stuff out of the government that should be considered impossible. It's time to put that power to good use."

"Eddie, in Poland, the doctors went on strike because their wages were so poor. Heck, a pediatric surgeon gets paid less than an English translator over there. It's ridiculous. So they went on strike. The government-controlled newspapers made them out to be money-grubbing rich bitches and they got nothing and the population started hating doctors."

"We don't have government-controlled newspapers here, Blow. And if the teachers in the US can have unions, why can't the doctors?"

Blow gave me one of those expressions of complete and utter disgust at my naiveté. "Government doesn't control the media. But the media goes for every populist banter that comes across their desk."

"So they should love the unionization of doctors!"

"Yep, just like they would support the unionization of Wall Street Bankers, Congressman, or Country Club members. Sure they will."

"Okay, Blow. What if we do it with good intentions loudly

proclaimed. We don't want money. We want the patients to be healthier."

"Sure, Eddie. That'll be met with no profound cynicism at all," replied Blow with evident profound cynicism. "What do you want to accomplish with your union?"

"I want to strike."

"You want to strike to get what?"

"Nothing."

Blow looked at me with a bit more respect. "Okay, maybe I'm gonna bite."

"You already agreed to join the union."

"Yep, that was before I asked you your plan. Now that I know you don't have a plan, I'm much more interested."

I approached Blow more closely, so that I could appear conspiratorial to anyone who happened to be gazing in our direction. "Look, Blow, I want to strike against the insurance companies. I want to strike against JCAHO. I want to strike against ACGME. But I need an attending like you to do it with me."

Blow nodded his head and said, "I told you already. I'm in."

"So you like it?" I asked, hopefully.

"I like it. Let's work the details out. When are you off duty?"

"Right after my mandatory witnessed strategic nap. 7 PM."

"Good. Take a shower and then let's get some mandatory strategic scotch and set up the union."

Chapter 35

An Improvement Made Better

"What can I get you, gentlemen?" asked the pleasant young lady in overly tight black pants as she bent down to reveal all that she could reveal within the bounds of the established etiquette at the fine dining establishment known as the "Beef and Pork".

"What do you have in the way of Scotch?" asked Blow, not expecting any reasonable answer. He didn't get one.

"We have Irish Whiskey, Jack Daniels, Bourbon, and a few others."

I chimed in, "Well, I wouldn't mind trying some of that Irish Kentucky Jack Bourbon Scotch."

Blow stared me down, stood up, walked to the bar, and picked out the best Scotch that the establishment had from behind the bottles of cheaper amber liquids. "Two MacCallan twelves, straight, no ice. Make 'em doubles."

And so it began.

"The union shall be called the "International Organization for Defending Patients' Rights and Responsibilities," I said, with resounding confidence.

Blow responded, "It shall be called the Society for

Prevention of Cruelty to Patients."

"No, it shall be named the "Union of Concerned Physicians."

"Or the Physician Professionals Anti-Defamation League."

"Look, Blow, we need to have a name that has cool letters that spell a neat word."

He held up the shot glass that had just been delivered. "Cheers."

I thought cheerily... "Coalition for Health Economics, Education, and Rational Science. CHEERS." And tossed my double back in my throat.

Blow smiled, did likewise, and said, "Done."

With the warmth echoing around our throats, we contemplated the purpose of CHEERS in more detail.

"I understand you want to strike, Eddie. The bureaucracy of the strategic napping initiatives must be overwhelming you and the other residents. It must cut into your sleep and rest."

"It sure does, Blow. Look, I still have two hundred more video camera documentation systems to deliver to the hospital at enormous personal effort on the part of my Indo-Sino-Mexican undocumented non-employee of Haftado Something NanoGreen Resources, LLC. I'm understandably exhausted."

"So, you want to strike to stop the mandatory reporting requirements for your strategic naps? I assume you mean, *after* all the wards and departments have ordered their documentation video devices and have them fully installed?"

"Naw, I like the naps. But I do have the summer coming. It is supposed to be a hot one, so there is reasonable expectation of numerous orders for frigipproppers this season, or so I am led to understand by a source within the Office of Environmental Conscientiousness. I have to be prepared. But the timing of the strike is not to improve the investment return for Haftado Something NanoGreen Resources, LLC. But rather to accomplish great things for humanity."

"Okay. So what do you expect to accomplish by striking?"

"Nothing at all."

"Well, your expectations are in the right ballpark then. That's a good start."

Blow signaled the waitress over and ordered another round. Only singles this time, a sadness explained by Blow as follows: "We faculty members need to keep our faculties about us as we ponder the future impact we will have on the facility."

"Blow, I want to strike against health insurance and other bureaucratic piles of shit, like I said. But mostly health insurance."

"Tell me your carefully thought-out plan."

So I did. Blow knew the background, but you, my gentle ignorant and naïve reader with no clue, may have no clue. In case that happens to be the case, please allow myself to indulge myself by informing yourself about how the medical insurance system works to make everything so wonderful for us all in America. Health insurance is such a wonderful thing, please remember, that politicians keep mandating that we all pay our hard-earned money for it. We will all pay for it more and more and more, and reap all the benefits for which such a massively subsidized moral hazard may allow.

During World War 2, everyone was employed building things that would either blow other things up or be blown up themselves, and there was an ever enlarging demand for both of these classes of goods. With most able-bodied citizens employed in the process of blowing things up, building stuff to be blown up, or having been blown up themselves, unemployment became so low that it was hard for companies to hire the best workers. Not wanting to spend more money for salaries, companies successfully lobbied Congress for a special tax break for a new attractive benefit: health insurance. And that was the false step that started the disaster we have to contend with now. Health insurance at that time was an incredibly cheap way to attract good help, at that time costing much less than 1% of a salary, and suddenly tax deductible. Most companies and people took advantage of this tax-shelter, and the ranks of the insured swelled, for employers and employees all liked avoiding taxes, even while most kept voting for representatives who liked to raise taxes.

The employees loved it, because they didn't have to be worried about how much their health care would cost. They could get the best available care. As the system grew, it turned out that the $10 therapy would cost the insured person $10. And the $100 therapy would cost the insured person $10. And the $1000 therapy would cost the insured person $10. So it was obvious why, in no time, costs had risen 100-fold, because nobody wanted the cheap stuff when the expensive stuff cost them only $10.

And that is when insurance companies were first considered evil. For they had to control costs somehow, and thus became the bad guys and started saying no to the patients. The patients didn't like hearing 'no', so the insurance companies arranged to communicate directly with the doctors. The AMA quickly became a co-conspirator in setting price controls through government programs, and then those price controls were adopted by the private insurers as well. Everyone except the insurance clerks lost track of prices. Ask a doctor today how much your visit, your procedure, your lab test will cost, and that doctor won't have a clue. No clue at all. Just ask Professor Bastiat. But the insurance company or Medicare clerk won't pay for it if they determine it's too much money, or for any other reason or whim.

Insurance companies *want* it to be hard for doctors to be paid. They want doctors to not apply for payment, not deal with the ridiculously dense paperwork, not fight with insurance denials. They know the patients will get mad at the doctor if they get billed for anything for which their insurance won't pay. They know the doctors won't push the issue hard, for they're too busy. The doctors will take it in the shorts rather than anger their patients. Insurance companies laugh all the way to the bank, laughing at how stupid the patients and the doctors are to be involved in such an insane program. The doctors—not terribly interested in business or monetary profits—decide to emotionally isolate themselves from the disastrous process and sign over all the billing responsibilities to back-office coding specialists—people whose career it is to optimize the diagnostic and treatment codes that the doctor should be billing under, so as to maximize the pay to the doctor. These people don't create any value, or help health care happen. They just re-order codes on insurance company reimbursement paperwork. The doctors then, in order to defend their own self-esteem, actively pay no attention to how much things cost. Neither the insured patients nor the doctors end up caring how much services cost. It becomes obvious then why everything starts costing so much.

So the government decided to give more power and profits to the insurance companies by forcing everyone to buy their evil product. Makes sense, doesn't it? Health insurance itself is what has caused the health care prices to spiral out of control, and everyone hates health insurance companies, so everyone is forced by the government to buy their product based on some strange idea that increasing demand for a product will keep its prices lower, an idea that can only work in a totalitarian country that can't do math or has actively decided it wants to collapse. The only alternative presented was to make government run the whole program.

I told Blow my carefully thought out plan. "So, I want to strike by not communicating at all with insurance companies, not doing any paperwork for insurance companies, and not following rules that insurance companies make. And I include the government in that name 'insurance company' because the government is the biggest most powerful one."

"Sounds good. The university will get pissed."

"They need to get pissed."

"At you."

"Yep. So what. They need someone to stand up and tell them to grow a pair and start working for the docs."

"You're only an intern, Eddie. The administrators don't think they work for the faculty; they sure as hell don't think they work for you."

"Huh?"

"Eddie, when I got here, the faculty were the bosses, and the administration worked to support the medical faculty—the doctors. Now it's the reverse. Now the faculty work for the administration. The administration has all the trappings of being the bosses: bigger offices, nicer suits, the ability to send out broad mandates. Like your friend Mark Edwards."

"Well, I don't know about that stuff. But it fits with everything else in this upside-down-world." I pondered. "But that's why you have to lead this, Blow. People respect you."

"Most people think I am a muckraking jerk, actually."

"But they respect you."

"Only my good looks."

I smiled and said, "Okay, this is how I see this happening."

After a few minutes of discussion, we were laughing hard. But we were also ready to actually do this thing.

Chapter 36

The Memo

MEMO

From: Mark Edwards, Co-Associate Dean for Insurance Mandates

To: All members of the Medical Faculty.

Re: Third party payer relationships

Importance: HIGH

Background: The third-party payer system in the US has reversed the power structure of medical care, demoting the patient to a position of that of a serf. Uneducated and uncaring clerks at insurance companies and politicians and administrators within government bureaucracies now make *de facto* health care decisions for patients whom they have never met. The hatred of insurance companies runs deep in society, prices for insurance have risen far beyond the rate of consumer inflation, customer service is horrible. Yet our government now has mandated that everyone buy this poorly made product. The University has been placed in an untenable situation of having to compete with the local community hospitals for the dollars coming into clinical practice, and to do so we have repeatedly made decisions that destroyed our teaching and research missions. For routine disease management, we have not been able to successfully compete with the private hospitals, so we are left with many weaknesses and no strengths.

Key leadership of the University has decided that this university needs to start leading the fight against this failed system. This is not a political matter, but a rational economic matter. The University medical system cannot sustain this path.

We are calling on all faculty members to voluntarily join us in a head-on assault against third-party insurance companies. From this moment forward, the University shall approve of any effort to thwart third-party insurance intrusions into the care of our patients. We endorse physicians who choose to have no communication with third-party payers. We approve of departments making arrangements for direct patient billing, setting their own prices, and providing charitable services at their discretion. We disapprove of any bills being sent to insurance companies (including Medicare) except for charges incurred that benefit those companies or Medicare—specifically, we endorse and strongly encourage billing insurance companies and Medicare for pre-authorization requests and any other time spent by physicians or nurses on the phone with or otherwise corresponding with insurance companies.

By this memo, the Legal Department of the University is detailed to provide full support, including assisting with recovery of all monies owed by insurance companies and the government. This University cares not at all for the internal policies of the insurance companies or the government that they use to prohibit common sense actions. The legal resources of the University will be available to assist the medical departments in the process of developing their systems of common sense medical economics.

By this memo, it be understood that no longer will the

University tolerate the stupidity, inanity, and economic childishness that has dominated medical economics for forty years and has threatened so severely the future of health care in the nation. The University feels it is our obligation to fight for the health of our patients.

All faculty members are urged to communicate directly with Dr. Blow, who has been selected by the Board to serve as point man for this major and important transition to sanity.

Faculty members who do not wish to participate in this transition may continue to function as best as they can, although there are anticipated to be few resources available to assist them as they try to remain slaves to the current system, because we plan to transfer to other jobs the employees whose only current job it is to bill insurance companies. Faculty who wish to depart the university because of their satisfaction with the current system will be granted approval to leave, and assistance will be offered to speed their departure.

This memo serves as notification to all levels of the University administration to begin processes necessary to implement the above initiative. All necessary approvals of JCAHO, ACGME, HIPAA, and CMS have been obtained to begin this initiative with high priority.

Authorized by: Dr. Mark Edwards, MD, PhD, DDS, FAA, FCC
Co-Associate Dean for Insurance Mandates

Chapter 37

Response to the Memo

The messages to Dr. Blow began coming in as rapidly as expected. Some furious, some adulating, some concerned, some bewildered. Blow and I sifted through the responses to pick out the leaders of the new union. Within 24 hours, we had 100 physicians ready to join the good fight. Within 48 hours, we had 200. It took 48 hours for the head administrators to figure out what was going on, and by that time it was too late. They tried to extinguish the fire by sending out another memo saying that the previous memo was a hoax, but messages from all the real administrators always get deleted by the faculty who don't care what they ever say, so only a handful of sheep ever read the official negation of the hoax.

Blow got called to the Dean's office. Blow conjured up substantial fury that he would be pulled into such a hoax. He regaled the Dean with stories of his email being consumed, with threats against his person, insults against his integrity and morality as a physician for participating in a process to undermine the federal health care initiative, and more horrifically traumatizing attacks on his character. The Dean profusely apologized and immediately sent out a supportive email saying that Dr. Blow was not to be treated poorly. Nobody read the email, but Blow forwarded an edited version to the community of the faculty, to clear his name while implicating himself more fully by adding a section in which the Dean insisted that the fascist components among the sheep apologize to him, and naming some names. Blow got a special one-time bonus in his paycheck for the hardship.

The first meeting of CHEERS was to occur at a nearby restaurant. We expected at least fifty to show, but had over one hundred. I had made arrangements with a local brewery-restaurant to serve as hosts for this and future meetings, in exchange for 10% of the alcohol revenue, which would be paid to Haftado Something NanoGreen Resources, LLC, as a booking fee.

Although Blow was the face of CHEERS, I was the nuts and bolts. I was the operating guy. The enforcer. The whip. The man who makes it all happen. That is me. I felt like I did when I was the only one trying to solve the murders that were happening in the hospital. I was glad that others took that process on. I had written JCAHO telling them about the murders. That prompted a major ruckus at all levels of the hospital, generating a new Quality Team that incorporated many members of the staff as well as community members and the F.B.I. The Quality Team would solve the murders now, leaving me to this new venture in which I would lead the way to solving the health woes of America and the world.

"Ladies and Gentlemen," I began, after ringing a glass repeatedly to garner the attention deserved by someone of my stature. "I am Eddie Marcus. Dr. Blow and I welcome you to this first meeting of CHEERS."

There was unnecessary but enthusiastic applause that for a moment prevented me from espousing the importance of our work. So I cut short the story and went for the meat.

"You are all well aware that our patients are being screwed by this medical system. Our profession is being screwed. Our families are being screwed. Our nation is being screwed. Future generations are being screwed. And the government and other bureaucracies are the screwdriver and it keeps twisting harder and harder. I won't go into the problems, because you know them. I am instead going to forward a solution. And that solution is a strike. Not a strike against patients, but a strike against health insurance." There was welcome applause, loud and sustained.

"We cannot say how the email was generated that notoriously suggested that Dr. Blow was working with the administration of the hospital in an apparently unreal effort by the University to bring common sense into medical care again. However, we do know what the effects have been of this hoax, which is that we are all here in this room, discussing how to accomplish the purpose of that fanciful email. So let's do it!"

Applause, sustained glorious applause. These sheep seemed ready to fight. Of course, they would likely succumb to the treacherous mudslide of paperwork piles, inbox accumulations, and useless administrative hassles and lose track of the importance of the long-term picture, unless I did something special now.

"So, here is what we propose: We need to keep focused and not be distracted by the piles of drudgery that the administration is going to dump on us to distract us. So, the first part of the plan is to 1) stop doing useless administrative drudgery that is mandated by organizations with lots of letters in their names, like JCAHO and ACGME. I propose we automatically mark as junk any email that even mentions those sets of letters. Once the administrators learn that any email with those letters is considered junk mail, they may start to think." Sustained applause again ensued.

"Second. Immediately tell our departments that we will no longer use the AMA's CPT coding system for billing. We will no longer tolerate the inanity of price controls. We will bill by the hour for our time or in some other fashion as each of us determines is appropriate, and bill directly to the patients, never their insurance. And we will bill our patients at much lower rates instead of the outrageously high rates we bill to insurance companies just so that the insurance companies will pay us half of what we bill." There was a fair amount of hubbub mixed with ongoing applause.

"Third, we pressure the administration to work for us, instead of telling us what to do." Loud applause.

"Fourth, we must adamantly refuse to accept any administrator's statement that we are 'not allowed' to do something that makes sense to do." Applause.

"Fifth, we must insist that the administration not make any new contracts that bind the doctors to any rules that are outside of the bounds of these concepts. No more insurance company contracts of any kind. We must remind everyone that the patients hire the insurance companies, and there should be no contracts between insurance companies and the hospital or doctors, for such contracts clearly are conflicts-of-interest, and we all know how the university wants to avoid even the appearance of conflicts-of-interest. We must get the insurance companies out of the doctor-patient relationship." Applause.

"Sixth, we must be willing to accept some transient decline in our financial income as this shakes through. Sorry... but the faster we do it, the better all will be for our patients and all the children for generations to come. Haftado Something NanoGreen Resources, LLC has volunteered to make available to us short-term loans at interest rates lower than the Federal Reserve for anyone who needs food and beer money."

"Seventh, we must not fall back into being sheep. We must be willing to stay strong, united and firm in our commitments. To do this, we must talk about why we are doing what we are doing. The dark side will try to convince us that we are being selfish. We must counter that with rational honesty about how guilty we will feel if we *fail* to act now to save health care for our children from the evil influences of force and fraud. So we must all be armed. Which means we need to read, talk, debate, and discuss. I hereby promise you that any argument you may hear that supports the current system of ever-increasing collusion between government, corporations and powerful groups may be made to sound good on the surface, but will fail with deeper thought and when appropriately named. And that appropriate name for a system of collusion among government, corporations and powerful groups is 'Fascism'. Those who support this horrible system will not be convincible to change their ways. They just need to retire and die and stop voting and leave the country and get out of our way."

"Eight, we stop doing things that we are told to do that we know full-well are stupid. Dictums from above, dictums from on high, dictums backed by organizations with lots of initials in their names and encouraged by threats. If these dictums are stupid, we don't do them anymore. We all know how stupid the whole concept of frigiproppers and frig'o'graphs are. Many of us commented about the stupidity. But our departments and wards complied with that foolishness because we were ordered to do so by a seeming authority and it was backed by threats. The hospital is ordering them by the truckload. Don't abide by this anymore! And don't do all the other inane and outrageous and wasteful and stupid and counterproductive things that those from above, beside, or below us try to force us to do. Stop being sheep!"

"Nine, we must spread the word, both in our own hospital and throughout the community and area. We are not grubbing for money. We are getting patient freedom back and working to lower the cost of health care. That is the truth, and that is the message."

My points made, I opened up the floor to whoever wished to speak. There was no shortage of people who wished to show how smart they were by speaking. One has to deal with some of this always. I prefaced this conversation by saying, "Please do not use this as a gripe session. We all know most of the gripes. Gripe sessions are used by our enemies to burn off our fomenting energy. We want to build our energy, build our numbers, and build our confidence. So, no gripes. Just constructive and helpful discussion points, please."

But the first person to stand had a gripe about health insurance. Then the second did too. Blow looked at me with his mouth in a twist. Even sheep who are trying to not be sheep still have their same dysfunctional personality quirks as the sheep who have no clue they are sheep. Oh well. That's people. People are people. I reiterated my requests for no more griping.

"When do we start this process of our strike against the insurance industry?"

I replied, "Whenever you want to. This should be an individual matter. Sooner the better. Tomorrow is good."

"But our departments will trounce on us."

"What can they do? Many of you are tenured. Those of you who are cannot be fired readily. And if enough of us do it, it is unstoppable even if we were all fireable. And, enough of us will do it, as long as we spread the word, combat the admin forces that will fight against us, and do it, do it, do it."

And so it began. The culmination of my medical education was to tear the medical system apart to help it come back from the ashes, like a phoenix. Because what else comes back to life after being ashes?

Chapter 38

A Rumble

At first, I didn't hear very much. Then, over a few days, there began a dull throbbing noise at the university hospital. It was hard to hear it initially, but you could feel it. It seemed like the living portion of the hospital was breathing easier. The built up gripes and frustrations were now no longer building up pressure to make occasional loud noises like a freight train whistle, but were rather used to generate a head of steam to get the locomotive of medical freedom moving along the track to better health for the patients. The doctors were no longer pissy, but rather now being constructive. It was refreshing to see.

The missives initially came out weakly from the administrators. It seemed that a few doctors were not filing their insurance paperwork any more. The administrators wished to remind the faculty that they needed to bill insurance appropriately in order to maintain all the functions of the university hospital. It was a gentle first missive, underestimating what was happening.

The second missive clearly indicated concern on the part of the administration, the Dean and the CEO. It stated that all faculty were mandated to comply with all insurance documentation deemed necessary by the hospital. Apparently, the hospital was an entity that could think on its own, and was treated by the adminosphere as a personalized conscious being, kind of like the bad centralized computer in the Terminator movies, in I Robot, in Eye in the Sky, or the Senate in pre-empire Star Wars movies, or the Borg in Star Trek, and every other Sci-Fi movie's evil entity manifested by a non-feeling distant self-justifying collective intelligence that doesn't care a whit for the individual.

The third missive recognized the size of the growing tidal wave and called for a mandatory medical faculty meeting to be held on Tuesday.

At the meeting, the Dean stood up and began. "I will begin with a summary of recent events, so that we can all be on the same page. There has been some disgruntlement among several of the faculty at the University's policies regarding third party payer interactions. Some doctors are refusing to bill, and there is real impact on the bottom lines of the hospital and the departments. This needs to come to a rapid conclusion or else we will suffer unrecoverable financial losses."

He introduced the Chief Financial Officer, who presented revenue statistics and scarily red graphs hockey-sticking their way to unimaginable budget deficits faster than Al Gore was heating up the planet. The situation was dire.

The Dean then took the podium. "So, there is no choice in the matter. We cannot change the country. We are stuck with this health insurance system. I know some of you think it is evil, but it is what we have. We have to work with it. We have to abide by its rules, good or bad. So, please, let's get back to the process of taking care of the patients and not trying to deal with changing a world we cannot change."

There was a small chorus of voices in the back that sang in disharmonious voices the word "BAAAAAA."

I stood up. I wasn't faculty, but then most people didn't have a clue who I was. "Dean, there are physicians here who have opened their eyes to the failures we have been abiding, and decided to do something about it. You know these people are heroes. Can you lead them instead of trying to shut them down?"

Applause roared from over one-third of the hall, and then grew. The Dean finally realized that the problem required drastic action. Drastic dictatorial totalitarian action was needed. This meeting was a microcosm of the federal government.

"I see," the Dean raised his voice, louder and louder. "This is an attempt at revolution. Well, it will fail. Such efforts always do! There is no point, and I won't support it. So, either play ball the way you are told to play it, or get out! I will not accept this attempted power-grab. JCAHO will not tolerate it! I will hold each person accountable!"

"Good to know where you stand, sir," I shouted over the din. "Now we can marginalize you officially. Do I have agreement?"

Loud applause and shouts emerged from six people, then more and more. The hall became loud as the doctors realized that they really did have the power, if they chose to take it back from the administrators.

I worked my way up on stage and stood in front of the Dean. I had a megaphone with me as a planned necessary tool. The Dean had never imagined anything like this, and stood there dumbstruck. Through the megaphone, I called out to the supporters, "My colleagues, this is only the beginning. Now take back your hospital. This man works *for* us, not us for him." I pointed to the Dean. "Administration shall once again help the doctors, as opposed to being the enforcers of every evil unconscionable policy that comes down from above. We will not take this anymore. We will not take this anymore. We will not take this anymore. We will not take this anymore!" The chant rose deafeningly in the hall, feet were pounding, vibrating the ceiling until bits of plaster were falling off. Never before in the faculty hall had such a stir been raised. Those who had no passion for fixing the broken system—so many sheep—were astonished. They had had no idea that there would be such fervor. Neither had the Dean.

Blow motioned to me to speak again. I raised my hands to quiet people down. It took two full minutes, but then there was calm again. I said, "Ladies and Gentlemen, please note that you have just all quieted down because I, who has no credibility and no authority, asked you to be quiet. Please don't do that again. And likewise, do not let the forces of complacency and slavery and stupidity manage to quiet your tongues or calm your actions. This is the time to break the bonds that have enslaved us and our patients. Break them, I say. Ignore the billing codes, ignore the insurance companies, ignore the government rules, ignore the administration, ignore the accrediting organizations, ignore everyone who contributes nothing of value but likes to make rules. Ignore...And then let's rebuild with intelligence and common sense, keeping first and foremost in our minds our desire to help our patients to be healthy, not only those patients we have now, but also the patients of the future. It is our moral mandate. We must fight for them and with them. And their victory will be our victory. We need Freedom in Health Care, not forced health insurance. With freedom re-established, the rest will follow naturally."

Loud applause followed, and I left the stage. The faculty hall emptied and hope filled the air. I had every expectation that the horrible problem that is our health care system was now on the road to health.

But pretty much nothing different happened at the hospital. The fervor died down, the forces of fascism crept back into ascendency and the crisis was declared over as the sheep all crowded back in their pen, that pen which was being pushed inexorably closer to the edge of the cliff.

Oh well. Who is John Galt?

Chapter 39

Flown this Acid World

"Eddie, what's this about you quitting residency after you finish internship?" Blow sat down next to me, on the last hour of my last day of internship, with a clearly concerned expression on his face. Word had gotten out.

I was quiet for a minute before I asked him, "How can you work in this system, Blow?"

"I ignore it. I cheat it. I lie to myself about it. I make patients better despite it."

"But doesn't it rot your insides?"

"Like a melon on a garbage truck."

"And ulcers?"

He pulled his shirt out of his pants and showed me his protuberant belly. "Ulcer should be popping right through here any day now."

I nodded.

"But Eddie, you're a fantastic and fascinating doctor. You're smarter and quicker and better than anyone who has ever come through here."

"Thanks."

Blow stopped before trying to make me feel guilty. I

wasn't guilty.

"What are you going to do?" he asked me.

"Practice medicine."

"What?" I had Blow honestly confused.

"Sure. I am going to practice medicine."

"How. Without completing residency, how will you practice?"

"I only need to complete internship to get my medical license. Then I can practice."

"As a GP? Insufficiently trained?"

"I will be trained well enough for what I plan to do."

"Eddie, I said you are really good, but you don't know enough yet. You aren't good enough. You can't go out there and practice on your own yet. I never took you for a cocky narcissistic shit."

"I'm not, Blow." I was a little hurt.

"Then what makes you think you are ready to practice medicine on your own?"

"I'm only going to do things I know I can do."

"Like what? Stuff creeps up on you kid. In medicine, it is the stuff you don't realize that you don't know that is the most dangerous. And you are clearly at that point in training where you don't realize what you don't know."

"You're right. I know that." I said. He had a great point that he didn't yet know was entirely irrelevant.

"So, you are going to stay and continue your training then?" Blow couldn't believe, wouldn't believe, and shouldn't believe that he would win the argument so easily. Indeed he *didn't* believe that he could win the argument so easily. "No way I won that argument so easily, is there, Eddie?"

"No way, Blow," I affirmed. "I can't stay for more training, because so much of it is indoctrination, so much is a program to program me, beat me down, castrate me, brainwash me, make me part of the system. The system made me into an asshole, not just an assholist. I don't want to be an asshole."

"So what is your real plan, Eddie? Stop toying with me."

"It's your fault, Blow. I'm going to take care of children in Liberia. You trained me very well for that. I don't need two more years of training to teach me how to better do paperwork, or how to use EMRs, in order to take care of orphaned children in Africa, do I?"

"Eddie, that's great. I envy you. You will be getting about as far away from this system as you could possibly get." He patted me on the back. "But, you know you can't make money in Liberia. How are you going to make money to pay for your work there? You tossed a big monkey wrench in the Frigipropper and Frig'o'graph sales, didn't you?"

"Actually, the orders have kept coming in. The powers of stupidity rage on. But I'm going to work in the U.S. too. Here, in the United States I am going to correct a great ill, right a great wrong, solve a troublesome horror."

"Yes?" prodded Blow after I stopped providing my series of noble four-word propositions.

"I am going to write prescriptions for medications that patients have already been prescribed."

"What's that mean," said Blow, with no hint of a question.

"In each of my clinics, there are always about ten percent of people who come in solely for prescription refills for medications that they have been on for years. They know that they're going to continue the meds. They know that they are supposed to continue them. But the prescription has to be re-written every year. The clinic won't even let doctors know when patients need refills, and won't allow us to call in prescription refills to the pharmacy if the patient hasn't seen the doctor in over a year. So the patient makes an appointment, drives through traffic, parks at great expense, waits in the sitting room in the clinic for two hours after the scheduled appointment time, all to get refills on his antihistamine and cholesterol-lowering drug."

"Yep, that's right."

"Why?"

"Because there hasn't been anyone like you, Eddie, to stick your big nose into that foolishness." Blow got it.

"Right. So I get my medical license. Then I advertise on TV, radio, buses, billboards, wherever. *'Need a prescription for something that you have been on for years? Can't get in to see your doctor? Email Dr. Eddie Marcus, MD. Specializing in prescription writing for those who need prescriptions. Sorry, no narcotics.'* That's my plan."

Blow nodded and smiled.

I added. "Blow, in the rest of the world, medications can all be obtained over-the-counter. Anybody can buy what they want without going to a doctor. Pretty much only in America do people get forced to go to the doctor to get medications prescribed. Think how much that costs. In this internet age, the patients often know more than the doctors do."

"That's true. But what if a patient's medication should be changed?"

"They can go to the doctor to get that advice."

"But what if they don't go, because you are making it easy for them to refill prescriptions that they no longer should be taking?"

"Who is the best person to make that decision?"

"The patient, along with their doctor," prompted Blow.

"Sure. So they *should* go see their doctor, if there is a reasonable chance that their medication or dosage needs to be changed."

"Right. That's my point."

"But, Blow, should they be *forced* to go to their doctor to get his advice? And what if their medication should be changed in four months, not twelve months? Now they get to wait twelve months before being forced to see their doctor, when they should be forced to come in at four months? Is that what you are shooting for?"

Blow was stumped on that one.

"You win, Eddie. But sometimes they *should* go see their doctor."

"Right. Sometimes they *should* go see their doctor. But that should happen when the patient determines it is necessary, not when the bureaucratic rules regarding durations of prescriptions determines it is necessary. Sure, they need to seek advice from their doctor. But that's up to them. I can advise them to do that, and I *will* advise them to do it. But no force. No force."

"So, you are going to make it much easier for patients to get their prescriptions refilled."

"That's right. That will be my job. And they will pay me fifteen dollars per prescription of Zipidufin or Omegeraplast or Esgetbeteral or whatever other silly-named medication they are already taking."

"Why will they pay you, Eddie. Why not just call their own doctor?"

"Because their own doctor is using extortion to force them to come back, instead of persuasion. No visit, no life-saving medicine! Physicians won't call in prescriptions for long, without seeing the patient, because of liability concerns and a complete lack of income. Insurance companies don't pay for doctor's time calling in prescriptions to pharmacies. Nor for phone advice or pre-authorizations. You know that. They only pay when the doctor sees the patient. So, sooner or later, the patient always has to come into the clinic and wait two hours, all so that the big pharmaceutical companies can make a bigger profit."

"But doctors will start competing against you, won't they?"

"Nah. They're sheep. The doctors are so stuck in their asinine paradigms that they really sort of believe it is unethical to be paid by patients for work performed. They won't know how to compete. They're completely paralyzed."

"How about the AMA? The AMA will despise you."

"Yes, they will."

"More concerning," said Blow, "how about the Board of Medicine? They may not like that you don't have a doctor-patient relationship when you prescribe medications to people that you have never met."

"I expect you're right. I wonder if there is a Board-of-Medicine-Patient Relationship?" I wondered. "You know, I'll have a relationship with each patient at least as good as the doctor-computer relationship of the EMR. I will have the patients fill out a history form on-line and I will ask appropriate questions. If the fact that I haven't met the patient in person bothers the Board, well, I'll cross that bridge when I get there." But that *was* my biggest concern, and always had been. The State Board of Medicine could revoke my license at a whim, even though what I was proposing would help patients. The Board of Medicine was the old guard, older docs raised in the era of the Great Society, and they were mostly true believers that government should be in charge of your life.

But I really didn't care. By the time they got around to arresting me, the steamroller would have started steamrolling. I would take the Board of Medicine to court and start tearing down the walls of the inanity that is the medical system in this country. I would expose the AMA's collusion with the government, and the FDA's collusion with the pharmaceutical companies, and the insurance companies' collusions with all of the above. I would expose the corruption, the fascism, the childishness, the rent-seeking, the manipulations of the health insurance companies. I would put an end to those power hungry narcissists of government and medical associations and accrediting organizations, all of whom were going to try to prevent me from helping patients because I didn't do it the way they wanted me to.

"Blow, this has always been my plan B. If I couldn't tolerate the medical system, the way you have figured out how to tolerate it, then I was going to work around it. I have enough businesses running now that I'll have at least some income even when the Board of Medicine tells me its illegal to practice medicine." I slid a newspaper over to him, the back page of which was loudly advertising 'GayBuddies'. "With this, we're gonna make hundreds of money."

"Hundreds of money, huh? I am going to miss you, Eddie." Blow was very serious. "You are the only doctor who really has any sense here." That wasn't true. I didn't have any sense at all.

Blow was my friend and mentor. I felt like I was abandoning him.

"Eddie, you aren't abandoning me. You are going out into the world to do what I want you to do, what I trained you to do, but won't do myself. We need you out there, doing something to fix the world. My job is to stay here, and try to find a few more of you and make sure that you don't get stuck in a casket, castrated, and nullified by the system."

"That's great Blow. Thanks for doing it all."

"Thanks for making it all worthwhile." There were real tears in Blow's eyes, but I couldn't see them because my eyes were all watery and blurry for some reason.

I shook his hand and walked out the door of the Sheep's

Pen. As the door closed behind me, the stink of the place disappeared altogether.

I had a wonderful adventure ahead of me, being a doctor outside the system. But before I began my adventure, I would start living life. I would find a beach in which to bury my toes, toss stranded starfish back into the sea, and toss back a few beers while I was at it. And every night, alongside my girl, I would watch the sunset.

www.ReadJohnHunt.com

A note from John:

If you have enjoyed this book, please recommend it to your friends. Please share the link above on Facebook, or send an email around far and wide. Consider writing a review or comment on Amazon.

Profits from this novel support the highly efficient work of Trusted Angels Foundation in Liberia, West Africa (www.trustedangels.org), a serious organization which provides real and tangible help to honorable but struggling individuals in a loving and efficient manner, and with economic sensibility.

Thank you.

John

P.S.

Please feel free to visit www.readjohnhunt.com for commentary, blogs, semi-sequels, sequels, and to communicate with me.

Please 'Like' ReadJohnHunt on Facebook.

Don't miss my serial novel, *Higher Cause*, published by Laissez Faire Books (www.lfb.org).

Made in the USA
Charleston, SC
19 January 2015